Word Power

Thousands of essential words you are most likely to encounter

- Important words with usage, roots, phrases and practice exercises
- Useful for GRE, TOEFL, IELTS & other Competitive Exams

NITIN SHARMA

Publisher

UNICORN BOOKS

F-2/16, Ansari Road, Daryaganj, New Delhi-110002
☎ 011-23275434, 23262683, 23250704 • *Fax:* 011-23257790
E-mail: info@unicornbooks.in • *Website:* www.unicornbooks.in

Branch : Mumbai

23-25, Zaoba Wadi, Thakurdwar, Mumbai-401002
☎ 022-22010941, 022-22053387
E-mail: rapidex@bom5.vsnl.net.in

ISBN 978-81-7806-356-0

Edition: 2017

Param Offseters Okhla New Delhi-110020

Introduction

Dear reader, nobody can memorise the whole dictionary *(and obviously you don't need to!)*, but there are words you just can't afford to ignore. You encounter these words quite often, and unless you know their meanings and how to use them, you are at a disadvantage. Those who use these words leave a strong impression on others, are thought to be more intelligent, are often selected for higher positions, and get better grades in English.

There has always been a subtle difference between important words and difficult words. Not every word that is difficult is also important or impressive. This book is a pool of thousands of essential words you are bound to come across. These words have been chosen from various sources including general conversations, news papers, magazines, texts, English language movies, dictionaries etc. They are important for both spoken English and written English. Since a single word can have multiple meanings, only the relevant and most important meanings have been given. Once you are acquainted with these words, I'm sure you'll feel much empowered.

Let's work together to improve and enrich your word power. Remember, nothing comes without effort but anything is possible with effort.

-Nitin Sharma

[**Note:** Instead of using *'him/her'* or *'them'*, we have used the word *'him'*, and instead of using *'he/she'* or *'they'*, we have used *'he'*, solely for the sake of convenience.]

Contents

1

Word Roots

A

Acerb, Acri = bitter in taste

Exacerbate = to make something bitter.

* Relations between them got exacerbated.
* Acrid smell of fumes.
* Acrimonious argument

Acro = height

Acrobat = a person who displays physical feats on rope tied to the erect poles at both ends as in a circus.

Acronym = (nym= name) short name of something that is given by taking first or top letters of all the words mentioned in it. For example, UNESCO – acronym of United Nations Educational, Scientific, (and) Cultural Organization.

Other acronyms – AIDS, RADAR, etc.

Acrophobia = mortal fear of looking down from a height.

Acropolis = (polis = city) a fort, citadel, etc. situated at height, e.g., on a hill-top.

Acrostic = word formed by taking first letters of each sentence or word used for expressing an idea or slogon taken from top downwards.

For example,

Loyalty is a virtue.
Integrity is a way of life.
Courage is an innate quality.
And
Discipline is taught in army.
i.e., licad in army is needed.

Aero = air

Aeroplane, Aerodrome, Aerobics

Ambul = walk

Ambulance, Per-ambulator

Ami = friend

Amity = friendly relation between people.

Amiable = friendly person.

Amicable = friendly atmosphere in which talks are held or disputes are settled.

Anima = soul, alive state

Animate = to make something lively (Animation film).

Animus = hostile feeling against someone.

Animosity = Anim(us) + mosity

Un-animus (decision)

Aqua = water

Aquarium = aqua + arium = place to keep, so, it means a place (usually a tank made of glass) to keep fish in water.

Aquarius = zodiac sign which resembles water carrier pot.

Aquatic = living in water (as opposed to terrestrial (living on earth).

Aqueduct = passage constructed to allow water pass across

Aquifer = under ground source of water mass.

Archae = old, ancient, of past

Archaeology = study of ancient period.

Archaic = belonging to ancient period.

Archi = first, chief

Archive = place where first (original) documents are safely kept.

Architecture = archi + (tectus = construction) art of constructing a building first on paper as a drawing.

Arch-bishop = chief bishop.

Arch enemy = main enemy.

Aster, Astro = star

Asterisk = symbol of star, used in books.

Asteroid = star-like celestial body which moves around a planet in the sky.

Astrology = study of effects of heavenly stars on the life of human-beings.

Astronomy = (nomy = law) law of stars, planets, orbiting in their paths in the sky.

Audio = hearing

Audible = what can be heard.

Audience = people sitting together to hear someone's speech.

Audition = test of voice quality by hearing a song or dialogue of a singer or actor.

Auditorium = place where audience gathers to hear speech.

Auto = self

Autograph = (graph = writing) signature of a famous person given by himself to his admirer.

Automatic = (a machine) working by itself.

Automobile = (engine) which moves by itself.

Autocracy = (auto = self + cracy = rule, governance) system of governance by one person himself.

B

Belli = fight

Bellicose = (a person) who is inclined to pick up a fight with someone.

Belligerent = (a country) which adopts war-like posture against another country.

Biblio = book

Bible = book regarded as respected source of knowledge on a subject.

Bibliography = written list of books which have been consulted by an author in course of preparing manuscript.

Biblio mania = strong liking for reading books so, you can guess meanings of Bibliophile, Bibliomancy.

Bio = life, living-beings

Biology = science of living beings.

Bio-divesity = (diverse = variety) variety of living creatures including plants which exist in harmony in a place or ecosystem.

Biography = book written by someone on the life of a famous person.

Brevi (s) = brief, short

Brevi-loquent = (loquent = speaking) a person who speaks in a few words.

Brevity = state of being brief

(continued alphabetically)

C

Caco = bad,

Cacophony = harsh sound.

* Cacophony of city traffic.
* Air is filled with cacophony of hoots, cackles of birds.

Cacography = bad handwriting.

Calli = beautiful

Calligraphy = beautiful handwriting.

* Calligraphy of inscriptions on stone plaques in memorials are worth appreciating.

Callisthenic = (calli = beautiful, good + sthenos = strength) of beautiful body strength.

* Callisthenic exercises.

Calypso = covered, folded, concealed

Eucalyptus = a tree, the leaves of which are well folded.

Apocalypse = not concealed prophecy of oracle.

Candidus = shining brightly.

Candle = a stick of wax which burns with shining brightly.

Candid = what is brightly frank.

* His reply was candid.

Candour = quality of being candid.

* Candour of his speech impressed audience.

In-candescent (bulb) = electric bulb which glows brightly to give light.

Capit = head

Capitulate = to surrender, to lower one's head before someone.

De-capitate = to cut someone's head.

Per capita income = per head income.

Carni = flesh

Carnal (pleasure) = pleasure derived from sensual feelings of body made of flesh.

Carnage = large number of killings of persons (made of human flesh).

In-carnation = coming in the shape of human body (made of flesh) as by God.

* Christ birth was the incarnation of God.

Chiro = hand

Chiromancy = reading of lines on palm of hand to predict one's future, palmistry.

Chiropodist = a person who treats a patient's foot (podi, pedi) ailments with hands.

Chiropractor = a person who practises manipulation of nerves with his hands to restore to normal position - thus relieving patient's discomfort.

Macro chira = a person having large-size hands.

Chromo = colour

Mono-chromatic = having one colour.

* Monochromatic paintings.

Photochromatic = changing colour with lights (photo-) falling on.

* Photochromatic glass.

Chrono = time

Chronometer = instrument which measures time.

Chronology = arrangement of past events in order of time of occurrence.

Chronicle = record of past events in order of time of occurrence.

Chronic = existing for a longtime.

* Chronic disease.

Clemen = kind, merciful

Clemency = mercy shown by authority to enemy, offenders.

* Govt. granted clemency to rebels and released from jail.
* Clement judge was lenient in awarding punishment.

In-clement = not showing mercy.

* Inclement weather.

Clude = to close, shut

Include = to take inside and shut the doors.

* His name was included in the list.

Exclude = to keep out and shut the doors.

* His name was excluded from the list.

Occlude = (ob + clude) to shut passage so as to prevent escape or entry through.

* He occluded upper and lower teeth so to prevent feeding.

Pre-clude = (pre = before) to foreclose a chance of happening.

* Physical disability precluded his chance of becoming an athlete.

Cardio / Cordio = heart

Cardiac = related to heart.

* Cardiac problems.

Cardiology = science / knowledge of diseases related to heart.

Cordial = heart-felt.

* Cordial reception.
* Cordial relations.

Con-cord = harmonious relation which is joing heart to heart.

Dis-cord = loss of harmony.

Corn = horn

Unicorn = having one horn.

* Unicorn animal.

Cornet = shape of a horn given to a wafer for holding ice-cream.

Cornucopia = a horn having magical power to provide food, or anything desired in abundance.

Coron = crown

Coronation = ceremony of crowning new king.

Coronette = small crown.

Corpora = body

Corporal = related to body.

* Corporal punishment.

Corporeal = related to physical state of body as opposed to spiritual.

Corps = body of / group of troops.

Corpse = dead body.

Corpus = body of / amount of collected funds to be used for a purpose.

* Corpus of funds contributed by employees is used for pension after retirement.

Corrigare = to correct

Corrigendum = list of corrections - usually printed at the end of a book.

In-corrigible = what is beyond correction.

* Incorrigible habits.

Credi = belief of something being true.

* Credible statement.
* Incredible performance.

Crypto = hidden

Cryptic = hidden.

* Cryptic message / remark.

Cryptogram = coded writing - hidden in code language.

Apo-cryphal = of hidden source of origin.

* Apocryphal story - authorship of the story is hidden / not known.

Apocrypha = a book written by unknown author.

Culp = blame, accuse.

Culprit = a person who is blamed to be guilty.

Culpable = what is blame worthy.

* Culpable action.

Ex-culpate = to clear someone from blame, to declare not guilty.

* The inquiry exculpated him of all charges against him.

Cura = care

Curator = a person who is in-charge of taking care of museum, art-collection, wild-life park.

* He is the curator of museum.

Cure = to take care of ill person by treating him with medicines so that he becomes fit.

* Doctors prescribe medicines to cure an ill person.

Sine-cure = (sine = without) an employee who gets salary without care of doing work.

Cyno = dog

Cynophile = (philo = liking) a person who likes dogs.

Cynophobe = (phobo = dislike) a person who dislikes dogs.

Cynologist = a person who is expert in subject of dogs.

Cynic = a person who does not believe in selfless motive of anyone, just as a dog does not believe in an unknown person and starts barking.

D

Dactylo = finger

Hexadactylous = (a person) having six fingers.

* A hexadactylous person.

Dactylographer = a person who is expert in matching finger-print

Dei, Deo, Theo = God

Deity = representation of God.

* Worship deity in temples.

Deify = to treat a person as God.

* Devotees of a saint deify him.

Theocracy = govt. run by saints in the name of God.

Theist = a person who believes in existence of God.

(Opposite : Atheist)

Demo, Demi = people

Democracy = rule of people.

Demagogue = (dem (o) + agogue = leader) leader of the people.

Epidemic = (disease) which afflicts people in large number.

* Epidemic disease.

Endemic = (disease) which afflicts people living in a particular locality.

Pandemic = (disease) which afflicts people all over the world.

Dermato = Skin

Dermatologist = skin specialist doctor.

Leucoderma = (leuco = white) skin disease of white patches on skin.

Pachyderm = (animal) having thick skin.

* Elephant is a pachyderm.

Dox = belief, faith

Orthodox = (ortho = straight) people who have straight faith in the religion.

* Orthodox Hindus.

Paradox = a statement, opinion, situation which is contradictory to the commonly accepted belief.

Dextro, Dexter = right hand

Dextral = right-handed (opp : sinistral).

* Dextral person.

Dexterous = skilled (in using right hand).

* A dexterous person.

F

Fac, Fic = to do, to make

Factory = place where some product is made.

* Garment factory.

Factotum = (Fac = to do + totum = total) a person who does all kinds of work for someone.

* Factotum employed by the family does all kinds of odd jobs.

Factitious = what is artificial (made - non natural).

* Factitious laughter.
* Factitious flower.

Fiction = story which is made / created by imagination.

Fictitious = what is created - not real.

* Fictitious name of a person.

Fide = faith, trust

Confide = to put one's own trust in someone and share secrets with him.

* He confides in his friend - and no one else.

Confidence = trust

* The president has full confidance in his secretary.

Confidant = a person who enjoys confidence of someone.

* He is my confidant.

Fidelity = faithfulness, loyalty

* Fidelity to one's country.
* Wife's fidelity to her husband.

In-fidel = a person who is not faithful to one's own religion.

Diffident = (a person) lacking faith in one's ability.

* A diffident person.

Perfidy = breach of trust.

Filius = son or daughter.

Filicide = killing of one's own son or daughter.

Affiliate = (ad = to + filiate) to adopt as one's son.

* University affiliates colleges.

Flex = to fold, to bend

Flexible = which can be bent, not rigid.

* Flexible opinion.

Flex = to bend

* He flexed his arms to show museles.

Flexuous = full of many bends / turns.

* Flexuous course of a river.

Genuflect = (Genu = knee) to bend knees as in prayer or in submitting before someone.

* Genuflect before deity in prayer.

Flux = to flow

Influx = flow into a place.

* Influx of tourists to hill stations increases in summer season.

Effluent = (ex = out + fluent = what flows) stream of waste which is discharged.

* Effluent of factory waste.

Influent = what flows into something.

* Influent streams of tributaries fall into river.

Confluence = place where two rivers meet and further flow together.

* Sangam is the confluence of Ganga and Yamuna.

Fracto, Fragmentus, Frang **(ere)** = break

Fraction = a part broken from the whole.

Fragment = a broken part of wood, stone, glass.

* Fragments of glass are scattered all over the place.

Fracture = breaking of bone, etc.

* His bone has fractured.

Infraction = breach / breaking of rules.

* Infraction of traffic rules.

Infringement = breaking into others' rights, powers.

* Infringement of others' privacy.

Fragile = What is breakable due to being delicate.

* Glass is fragile material.

Frangible = what is breakable due to excess pressure or impact.

* Frangible toys.
* Our bones are frangible.

Frater = brother (soror = sister)

Fratricide = killing of one's brother.

Fraternal = of brother, brotherly

* Fraternal relations.

Fuge (re) = to flee, escape

Fugitive = a person who flees from police arrest.

Fugacious = fleeing / disappearing soon.

* Fugaicous public attention.

G

Gamos = marriage

Monogamy = system of marrying one woman at a time.

Bigamy & Polygamy = system of marrying two women / many women at a time.

Gene = to produce

Generator = machine that produces electricity.

Generation = entire mass of people who are produced by their ancestors.

* Present generation is having broad outlook.

Progeny = children produced by same parents.

* His progenies are brilliant.

Progenitor = parents who have produced progeny.

Pathogen = bacteria which produces disease.

Geo, Terra = earth, land

Geology = science of structures below the surface of the earth.

Geography = subject which deals with the marking of different structures on the surface of the earth.

Perigee = position of the planet in its orbit which is the nearest to the earth.

Territory = land within the boundary of a country.

* Indian Territory.

Terrain = tract of land with specified features.

* Hilly terrain.

Terrestrial = living on land as opposed to aquatic, or aerial, or arboreal (= living on water, air or trees).

Terrestrial living-being.

Geri, Gero, Geronto = aged, old person

Geriatric = related with aged person.

* Geriatric problems.

Gerontologist = doctor who treats aged persons' physical problems.

Gerontrocracy = govt. run by aged persons.

Gnos = know

A-gnostic = a person who does not know whether God exists or not.

Ignorant = (a person) who does not know about a subject.

* He is ignorant of what is happening in the world.

Ignore = to pretend as if one does not know.

* He ignored me when we met.

Ignoramus = a person who does not know.

Dia-gnose = to know the nature of ailments in a person's body.

* Doctor diagnosed his ailment as malaria.

Prognose / Prognosticate = (pro = beforehand) to know beforehand the course of progress of a disease.

Gregare = flock, herd

Gregarious = living in herd.

* Elephants are gregarious animal.

Aggregate = (ad + gregate) to flock together, to bring together.

Segregate = (se = apart) remove apart from flock.

* Infected person is segregated from others to avoid spreading of infection.

Gress = walk, go, step

Progress = (pro = forward) to go forward.

Retrogress = (Retro = backwards) to go in backward direction.

Ingress = to walk into a place.

* The low-lying areas were inundated due to ingress of floodwater.

Egress = (ex = out + gress) going out of a place.

Transgress = (trans = across) to go across the limit.

* Do not transgress your authority.

Gynaeco, Gyne, Gyny = woman, female.

Gynaecologist = doctor treating females disease.

Gynaecocracy = govt run by women.

Gyro = rotate

Gyrate = to move round & round, rotate.

H

Haemo = blood

Haemorrhage = excess bleeding.

Haemoglobin = red cells in blood.

Haemopoietic = what produces blood in body.

Hagio = saint

Hagiocracy = rule of saints.

Hagiolatry = (latry = worship) worship of saints.

Hagiography = biography of saint.

Halitus = breath

Halitosis = foul smell coming from one's breath.

Exhale = expel air through breath.

Inhale = draw air through breath.

Helix = spiral shape

Helical = of spiral shape.

Helicopter = flying machine having wings (opter) which move rotate in spiral motion.

Helio = sun

Haliolatry = worshipping sun.

Heliotrope = (plants) which turn. (tropo = turn) towards the sun.

Horo = hora, hour, time

Horology = skill of making watches.

Horoscope = zodiac signs of the hour of a person's birth.

Hydro = water

Hydrometer = meter to measure quantity of water in liquid.

Hydrogen = what produces water.

Hydro phobia = morbid fear of water.

I

Iatros = Physician

Iatrogenic = what is produced by wrong treatment by physician.

* Iatrogenic ailments.

Paed(i) - iatrician = Paediatrician, Physician who treats ailments of children (paedi = child).

Icono = image

Icon = image, picture, portrait of Gods, venerated personage.

Iconoclast = (clast = breaker) a person who breaks images, traditional beliefs of a religion.

Iconolatry = worshipping of icons.

J

Ject = throw

Inject = to throw medicine into body.

Project = to throw forward.

* Missile was projected towards target.
* Film is projected on the screen with the help of a projector.

Reject = to throw away a discarded.

* His proposal was rejected.

Conjecture = act of throwing a wild guess.

Judic = Judge

Judiciary = institution / court of judges.

Ad-judicate = to judge a case on a matter of dispute.

Judicious = who / what is justified.

* Judicious decision.

Jure(re) = swear

Abjure = to swear to desist from doing something bad.

* Abjure violence.
* Abjure cigarette smoking.

Perjure = to make false statement by swearing to speak truth in court.

* Perjury is punishable .

Conjure = to swear by the name of spirit while showing magic, or producing something by magic.

* Magician conjured a miracle.

L

Liga(re) = to tie, to bind

Ligament = fibrous tissue which binds bone joints together in proper place.

Ligature = act of tying up.

* Ligature of operated body-part is done with required skill.

Ob-ligate = to bind legally or morally.

* Clause of contracts obligates the parties to fulfil it.
* His help in time of need has obligated me to him.

Oblige = to bind someone morally.

* One is obliged to return loan taken from bank.

Levi(s) = to make lighter (so as to rise up / float in the air).

Alleviate = (ad = to + levi = make light) to make a suffering light so as to be bearable.

* Pain-killer medicines alleviate pain.

Levitate = to rise up in the air and float due to lightness.

Locu, Loquaci = speech

Locution = style of making speech.

* Impressive locution.

Loquacious = taking too much, talkative.

* A loquacious child.

Luci = bright, shining

Lucid = shining, clear in understanding

* Lucid speech.

Lucifer = (Luci = shining + fer = to carry) What carries shining light.

* Lucifer planets.

Lucent = shining

* Lucent stars in the sky.

M

Magna = large, great, big

Magnify = (magna + fic = to make) to make big in size of something.

* Microscope magnifies the size of an object.
* Do not magnify a problem.

magnate = a person who holds big influence in a specified field of activity (beware of word 'Magnet').

* He is a literary magnate.

Magnanimous = (magna + (a) nimus = soul) (a person) who has big soul i.e., who is large-hearted, compassionate towards others.

* A magnanimous person.

Magnificent = (magni = big + fic(ent) = to make) what is made big in attraction, splendour, extra-ordinary in beauty, superb.

* Magnificent buildings.
* Magnificent paintings.

Magniloquent = (magni + loqua = speak) (a person, a speech) who or which is great in style of speaking.

* A magniloquent person / speech.

Magnitude = state of / extent of

something which is big / large.

* Magnitude of loss / devastation.

Male = bad, evil, harmful (opposite : Bene-)

Words formed with it are :

Malefactor = one who does harm, evil act towards others.

* Malefactors must be punished.

Malevolent = (a person) who wishes (volen = to wish).

* He is malevolent towards successful persons.

Mal(e)feasance = evil action of a public official.

Mal(e)function = (of a machine) not working properly.

Mal(e)ice = evil feelings towards someone.

* He harbours malice against me.

Mal(e)ign = to defame someone by speaking evil things.

* He maligned his opponent.

Malignant = what is harmful.

Manu(s) = hand

Manual = what is done by hands.

* Manual operation of a machine. (which is not automatić)

Manufacture = (manucs = hand + fact = to make) to make / produce something by hands.

Manuscript = (script = written) written by hands.

* Manuscript of a book is handwritten copy of the author.

Manipulate = to manage something in desired direction by handling (working with hands) skillfully.

* Manipulate a person to do what is desired of him.

Manicure = (mani = hand + cura = care) taking care of hands' nails - shaping and polishing nails.

Mater = mother

Matricide = killing of mother.

Matriarch = (matri + arch (y) = rule) mother who rules over family.

Maternity = related to motherhood.

* Maternity ward in hospital.

Memora = memory

Memory = faculty of remembering.

Memoir = recording events of one's life.

* He wrote memoir.

Memorabilia = preserved matters which are associated with event / occasion worthy of remembering.

* His room is adorned with memorabilia of his childhood.

Memento = object which is associated with a particular event.

* This is the memento of his visit to England.

Memorial = a structure which is constructed in memory of a person or an event

* A memorial of Kargil War.
* A memorial of war heroes.

Mense = to measure

Immense = (in = not + mense) vast as being beyond measurement

* Immense grief.
* Immense vastness.

Mnesi, Menti = memory

A-mnesia = (a = not + Mnesi + ia = diseased condition) deseased condition of loss of memory.

* He is suffering from amnesia.

Amnesty = official grant of pardon of offense by forgetting acts of offence.

* Rebels were granted amnnesty by the govt.

Mirari = wonder

Miracle = an event which makes people wonder over.

* His survival in accident is a miracle.

Admire = (ad + mirari) to express wonder over praise worthy performance of someone.

* People admired his work.

Miso = hate

Miso-gamist = a person who hates to marry.

Misogynist = a person who hates women.

Mit = to send

Transmit = to send across to another place.

Remit = to send money by money order.

Mori = death

Memento mori = remember that everyone has to die one day.

Morgue = place where deadbody is kept before bodies are claimed by relatives.

Mortuary = place where deadbodies are kept before funeral.

Morph = shape

A-morphous = without shape.

Meta morphose - to change the shape of something.

N

Nat, naissi = birth

Re-naissance = re-birth, revival of dead art, culture, etc.

Nascent = beginning to take birth

* The disease is in nascent stage.

Pre-natal = period before child-birth.

* Pre-natal care of woman is must.

Native = related to one's birth.

* This town is my native place.

Innate = (in + nat) from the time of birth.

* Innate habits die hard.

Congenital (deformity) since one's birth.

Necro = dead,

Necrophagous = (a person / insect) which feeds on dead body / carrion.

* Necrophagous insect.

Necrophobia = abnormal fear of a dead body.

Nicto, Nycto, Nocto = night

Noctilucent = (nocti + luci) shinning brightly in night.

Nocturnal = active in night.

* malaria mosquito is nocturnal insect.

Nyctambulance = habit of walking in night during sleep.

Equinox = equal night (and day).

Nomen, Nomin = name

Nominate = select name of a person for something.

* He was nominated a member on the management board.

A-nonymous = (a = not) without mentioning name.

* Anomymous caller on phone.

Nomenclature = system of naming things.

Nominal = only for the sake of name - not of any value.
* He is nominal head of the committee.

Nomo = law, rule
A-nomy = state of no rule of law.
* State of anomy.
Isonomy = (iso = equal) state of equality of all in the eyes of law.

Noxi, Nocu(us) = harm
Noxious = harmful.
* Noxious fumes.
Innocuous = not harmful.
* Innocuous insect.

Nova = new
Novel = new
* A novel idea.
Novice = (a person) who is new and hence in-experienced in a work
* A novice worker.
Innovate = to introduce new system in existing one.

O

Ocul, Ophthalmos = eye
Ocular = related to eyes.
* ocular drops.
Occult = (ob = away + (o)cul) hidden from eyes.
* Occult objects.
Ophthalmologist = doctor of eye's disease.

Odont, denti = tooth
Odont(o) + algia = odontalgia = toothache.
Orthodontist = dentist who has specialisation in making in irregular line of teeth straight.
Denture = set of teeth.

Omni = all
Omnipotent = (omni + potent = powerful) all powerful.
* Omnipotent person.
Omniscient = (scient = knowing) knowing all things.
* God is omniscient.
Omniphagous = (phagy = eating) eating all things.
* Omniphagous insect.

Opto = vision
Optician = one who makes spectacles.
Optometrist = one who measures power of glasses for vision of eyes.

Ortho = straight
Orthodentist = see in odonto.
Orthodox = see in dox.
Orthopaedics = doctor who treats bone problems.

P

Paedi = child
Paediatrician = doctor of child diseases.

Pano = all
Pan(o) demic = (disease) affecting people (demo-) of all places.
Panacea = cure of all ills / diseases
Panopticon = a place of which all corners are visible from a central position.
Panorama = (pano + (ho)rama = view) all view.
* Panorama of recent history.
Pantheon = temple of all gods
Pandemonium = (pan = all + demon = evil spirit) a place of evil spirits where state of chaos exists.

* Pandemonium broke out in the meeting.

Patri = father

Patricide = killing of one's father.

Patriarchy = systen of family where father rules.

Patriot = a person who is devoted to his country i.e., fatherland.

Ex-patriate = a person who has gone out of own country (fatherland) to settle in other country.

Pedi = foot

Pedicare = care of feet, its nails etc.

Pedal = device in a machine to be moved by feet.

* Pedal of a bicycle.

Peddle = to sell goods by moving on feet from place to place.

Pedestal = the foot on which a structure is supported.

Pedestrian = person who moves on foot on roads.

Impediment = obstacle in moving forward / doing something by holding the feet to prevent movement.

* Stammering is an impediment in speaking.

Expedient = (action) which removes obstacles as if the feet are taken out of hold.

* Expedient action.

Expedite = to move one's feet speedily so as to hasten the progress.

* Expedite the work.

Pend(ere) = hang

Depend = to hang from someone / something for support.

* I depend on my friend for advice.

Compendium = hanging with, a list added to the end of a report or book.

Pendulum = hanging weight in a watch.

Pendant = small ornament which hangs from a necklace or chain.

Petri = stone

Petri-dish = dish made of stone.

Petrify = to make motionless like a stone due to sudden fear.

* Encounter with a snake on the road petrified him.

Pleni, Ple(re) = full, fill

Complete = full

* Complete success.

Deplete = to take out from filled stock.

* Excess removal of water depleted the stock in tank.

Replete = filled abundantly.

* His speech was replete with juicy anecdotes.

Replenish = to fill up a vacant, exhausted stock again.

* Replenish used-up stock.

Plenty = state of being full.

Plic, plex = fold, bend

Complicate = to fold together to make ensnared.

* Complicate a simple matter.

complex = state of complicated.

* A complex problem.

Duplicate = in two folds.

Prehendere = to catch, hold, group

Prehensile = (limb) which is used to catch/hold something.

* Elephant's trunk is a prehensile limb.

* Monkey tail is a prehensile limb.

Apprehend = ad + Prehend(ere), to catch hold of.

* Police apprehended the thief.

Apprehension = state of catching a feeling of something bad to happen in one's mind.

* He is disturbed due to apprehension about his safety.

Comprehend = to catch hold of something with one's mind i.e., to understand something.

* I could not comprehend what he said.

Reprehend = to hold someone responsible for wrongdoing.

Punct = dot, to dot with piercing.

Puncture = to pierce with a pointed stick so as to take out filled air.

* Puncture a cycle tube.

Punctate = to make dots of small holes on a reciept book so as to tear it off along the dotted line.

Punctilious = (a person) who takes care of doing work with accuracy to the dot of finer details.

* A punctilious worker.

Punctual = observing time of doing work to the exact point / dot.

* Be punctual in one's work.

Q

Quarant = set of forty.

Quarrantate = to arrange in a set of forty each.

Quarrantine = to isolate a patient afflicted with contagious disease from healthy perosns for a period of 40 days to avoid others getting infected.

Quater = set of four.

Quaternate = arrange in a set of 4 each.

Quater-century = 400 years.

R

Racin, Radic = root

De-racinate = to root out from native place.

* People were deracinated for building a dam.

Radical = of roots, fundamental.

* Radical change.

Eradicate = (ex = out + radic = root) to root out, remove from the roots.

* Eradicate superstitions from the people's mind.

* Malaria eradication drive.

Recti = correct, right

Rectify = to correct a defect.

* To rectify defects in machine.

Rectitude = right morality.

* Rectitude of motives.

Erect = be in upright position.

* He is sitting erect on chair.

Regi = king, rule of a king.

Regicide = killing of the king.

Regime = rule of a king or govt. of a political party.

* Congress regime.

Regimen = rule to be followed for regaining health, or recovery from illness.

* Follow the regimen of taking medicines and of regular exercise.

Rupt = split, burst

Rupture = to burst

* Blood vessel may rupture due to high blood pressure.

Erupt = to burst out

* Violence erupted in the town.

S

Sacra, Sancti = holy

Sacred = (something) treated as holy.

* Temples are sacred place.

Sacrament = holy ceremony.

Sacrifice = (sacra = holy + fic = to do / make) to make holy offer.

* He sacrificed his life in defending the country.

Sacrilege = (sacri = holy + lege(re) = to steal) to rob of holiness of something.

* To defile a holy place is an act of sacrilege.

Consecrate = to make something holy.

* Consecrate a place as abode of Gods.

De-secrate = to destroy the holiness of a place.

* Desecrate a holy place by defiling it.

Sanctify = to make sacred, to consecrate.

Sanctity = state of sacredness.

* Sanctity of democratic institutions must be protected.

Sanctum sanctorum = place which is the holiest.

* The room of the temple in which deities are placed in the temple's sanctum sanctorum.

Sangui = blood

Sanguinary = characterised by blood shed, blood thirsty.

* Sanguinary fight.
* Sanguinary vampire.

Sanguine = full of blood which is represented by cheerfulness.

* A man of sanguine disposition.

Sanguivorous = (insect) feeding on blood.

* Mosquito is sanguivorous insect.

Scribe(re) = write

Scribe = a person who writes in newspapers.

Scribble = to write on paper quickly and carelessly.

* He scribbled his message on a piece of paper.

Script = written matter / text.

* Film script.

Scripture = sacred written text.

Pre-scribe = to write the names of medicines and other instructions in advance to be followed by a patient.

Sect = cut

Sect = a religious faith which has been cut away from the main.

* Various sects have come in existence from Hindu religion.

Sectary = member / follower of a particular sect.

Bisect = cut a line in two parts.

Sine = without

Sinecure = without care to do anything.

* Sinecures in the offices enjoy perks without doing any work.

Sine die = (sine = without + die = date) without date.

* The parliament was adjourned sine die.

Sine qua non = without whom none other, i.e., indispensable

* His presence in the meeting is sine qua non.

Sinistro, sinister = left hand (opp of Dextro)

Sinistral = using left hand.

* A sinistral person.

Sinu(us) = curved, winding in left & right directions alternately.

Sinuate = move in sinuous path.

* The snake sinuated on the ground.

Sinuous = having many alternating curves.

* River flows in sinuous path.

In-sinuate = to insert / move into someone / something by winding or turning left and right alternately.

* Roots of a tree insinuate through crevices in the rocky ground.
* He insinuated derogatory remarks against me in his speech.

Somnus = sleep

Somnambulate = to walk in sleep.

Somniloquy = habit of speaking in sleep.

In-somnia = loss of sleep.

He is suffering from insomnia.

Soror = sister

Sororicide = killing of own sister.

Sorority = (on the pattern of fraternity) sisterhood.

Spect = to see, to observe.

Spectacle = an interesting event which is worth see-ing.

* Solar eclipse is a spectacle.
* Independence Day parade is a spectacle.

Spectacles = pair of eye glasses which helps one see objects clearly.

Spectacular = impressive to see.

* Spectacular performance.

Spectator= a person who sees a programme/ performance / action.

Specter = imaginary view of dreadful thing or event to happen.

* Specter of imminent disaster haunts the minds of people.

In-spect = to look into something to examine it.

* Inspect the file.

Expect = (Ex = out + (s)pect = to see) to look out in future to happen.

* He expected to succeed.
* He expected my support.

Intro-spect = to look within one's own self to examine one's own actions.

* He introspected over the reasons of his failures.

Retro-spect = (retro = backwards) to look back.

Speculate = to see the possibility of profits on staking money.

* He speculates in shares of companies in the share market.

Spira(re) = to breathe

Expire = to breathe out the life i.e. to die.

* The oldman expired today.
* The validity of licence has expired (i.e., its life has ended).

Inspire = In + spire, to breathe life into someone to do / to have something i.e., to fill one with feelings.

* His exhortation inspired people to act against justice.

Perspire = (per = through) to breathe i.e. to send air (or vapours, water in the form of sweating) through pores of body surface.

* He was perspiring profusely due to hot weather.

Aspire = (ad = to + spire = breathe) to breathe life into one's desire to achieve something.

* He aspires to become an engineer.

Conspire = (con = with) to breathe with one's desire to do some evil against someone.

* He conspired against me to defame me.

Transpire = trans = (from one to another place) to breathe out / emit news about what happened at a place / another place.

* Decisions taken in a meeting soon transpired in the open.

Surge(re), surrect = rise up.

Surge = rise up.

* There is a sudden surge in crimes in the town.

Insurgent = a rebel who rises up against established govt.

Resurgent = what rises up again (re = again) after becoming non-existent.

* Resurgent custom.

Resurrect = to rise up again from the grave.

* It is believed that Jesus Christ resurrected from the grave after he was crucified.

T

Tacitus = silent

Tacit = silent, done silently.

* He gave tacit support to indiscipline amongst partymen.

Taciturn = (a person) who is reluctant to speak, inclined to silence.

* A taciturn person.

Tact (us), Tangere = touch

Tact = a touch of skill to handle a difficult situation appropriately.

* He is a tactful person.

Tactics = a plan to handle a complex situation skillfully.

Tactile = having power to feel something by touching it.

* Our fingers are tactile limbs.

Tactual = able to be felt by touching it.

* Tactual test is sometimes more reliable than analytical test.

Tangible = able to be felt by touching because of being real- and not imaginary.

* Tangible threat.
* Tangible grief.

Taxi, taxo = to arrange

Taxonomy = (taxo + nomo = rule) rule of arrangement of organisms in order of species.

Taxidermy = (taxi = arrange + derma = skin) art of arranging the skin of dead animal in life - like shape by stuffing sawdust inside.

Epitaxy = arrangement of something in layer upon (epi-) layer.

Terra = earth
(see geo)

Thanato = death (also, see Mori)
Thanatophobia = abnormal fear of death.
Eu-thanasia = (eu- = well, good) act of giving a suffering person painless death.

Theo = god
(see Dei, Deo)

Toxi, Toxsico = poison
Toxemia = (tox(o) + (ha)emia = blood) blood poisoning.
Toxic = containing poison.
* Toxic food.

Tract = stretch, draw
Tractable = which can stretched.
Extract = to draw out something.
* Extract juice from lemon.
Retract = to draw back.
* The bird retracted its wings.
* He retracted his words given to me.
Contract = to draw together.
* He contracted his lips.
Protract = (pro = forward) to draw forward in duration, prolong for more time.
* His illness protracted for a month.
Distract = to draw attention away.
* Noise distracted his attention from his studies.
Attract = (ad = toward + tract) to draw attention towards something.

Trude(re) = to thrust, to push
Intrude = to thrust oneself into a place.
* He intruded into my office.
Protrude = to thrust forward.
* He protruded his head out of window.

U

Usuri = exorbitant rate of interest on lending.
Usury = practice of lending money on exorbitant rate of interests.
Usurer = one who practises usury.

Uxor = wife
Uxoricide = killing of one's wife.
Uxorious = liking one's wife excessively.
* A usorious husband.

V

Vert = to turn.
Vertigo = a condition of everything turning around before eyes of a person.
* He is affected with vertigo.
Avert = to turn aside.
* An accident was averted.
Vertiginous = turning, rotating.
* Vertiginous staircase.
Advert = (ad = towards + vert = turn) to turn one's attention towards someone or something.
* He adverted to me after finishing his work.
In-advertent = (a person) who is not attentive to something.
* He committed a mistake inadvertently.
Revert = to turn towards something again.
* Revert to the old habit.
Convert = to turn into something else.
* To convert water into steam.

Pervert = to turn away from right course.

* A morally pervert person.

Advertise = (ad = to + vert = turn) to give information through newspapers / T.V. about something to turn people's attention towards it.

Divert = to turn away from right path.

Versus = opposed to, different

Reverse = opposite in direction.

* Go in reverse direction.

Perverse = opposite to what is expected.

* Perverse mood.

Converse = opposite of something.

Versatile = of performances of a person or thing which are different in nature.

* A versatile musician / writer.

Diverse = different in direction / nature / quality.

* Diverse opinion.

Adverse = opposed to someone's good or something in effect.

* To make adverse remark against someone.

Averse = opposed to something in liking.

* He is averse to joing politics.

Verb(um) = word

Verbal = of words

* Verbal experssion.

* Verbal communications.

* Verbal agreement.

Verbatim = (to tell / repeat) word by word.

* Repeat his statement ad verbatim.

Verbose = full of words.

* Verbose speech.

Veri = true

Verify = (veri = true + fic = to do) to ascertain the truth of something.

* Verify the report.

Verisimilitude = (veri + similarity) the state/ condition of being similar to truth.

Veritable = to be in true sense.

* Veritable victory.

Vince(re) = to win, to overcome

convince = to win over someone's, opinion by arguments.

* To convince someone about the need of helping poor people.

In-vincible = not be able to win. Who can't be won.

* Invincible enemy.

Vise, vid(ere) = look, see

Visage = face of a person which is seen.

Visible = able to be seen.

* He is not visible from here.

Vision = eye sight, faculty to see.

* His vision has become weak.

Visionary = a person who has the capability of looking into future - what will happen in future.

* He is a visionary.

Visit = go to see someone.

* He visited his family.

Visor = transparent glass in front of face of a helmet through which driver can see ahead.

Vista = a view visible through a narrow opening.

* A vista of surroundings.

Visual = of seeing.

* Visual effect.

Visualize = to see in imagination, form mental image.

* One can visualize the consequence of rash action.

Providence = (pro = forward, ahead + videre = look) foreseeing care of God.

* He survived accident by the grace of providence.

Provident = looking forward in future, having foresight of the future needs.

* Provident fund.

Improvise = (Im = not + pro + vise = look) to make something without prior looking for preparation.

* He improvised a poem on the spot.

Viva, Vita = life

Vivacious = lively, full of life.

* A vivacious person.

Viva voce = (voce = voice), living voice, oral interview of examinee.

Vivid = lively in appearance.

* Vivid paintings.

Vital = essential for life.

* Vital needs.

Vitamin = nutrients essential for life.

Vocab, Vocare = to call, speak

Advocate = to speak in favour of.

* Advocate freedom of women folk from social thrall.

Vocabulary = stock of words needed for speaking.

Vociferous = (voci = speak + fer(ous) = to carry) with loud speech.

* Vociferous portest of crowd.

Invoke = invocate, to call for help.

* To invoke God for mercy.

Provoke = to call forth a particular feeling in someone by inciting or instigating or stimulating.

* To provoke laughter / anger in someone.

Revoke = (re = back, again) to call back an order, law, etc. as by authority, govt.

* Govt. revoked ordinance.

Volen = wish, will

Volition = will

* He helped us on his own volition.

Bene-volent = (bene = good), (a person) who wishes good for someone.

* A benevolent person. (opp. Malevolent)

X

Xeno = foreign

Xenocide = killing of foreigners.

Xenophile = a person who loves / likes foreigners.

Xero = dry

Xerography = dry writing i.e., copying a document in xerox machine.

Xeroderma = dryness of skin.

Xerophthalmia = dryness of eyes.

Xerophyte = (phyto = tree, plant) plant which thrives in dry place / desert.

Exercise on Word Root (Chapter -1)

Write down the root words involved in the formation of the following words :

1. Extract juice of lemon
2. Revive
3. Expedient
4. Chiropractic
5. Paediatrician
6. Leucemia
7. Hydrophobia
8. Specter
9. Expire
10. Taciturn
11. Tactful
12. Distract
13. Uxorious
14. Provoke
15. Intrude
16. Incinerate
17. Insinuate
18. Eradicate
19. Erect
20. Purctual
21. Replenish
22. Apprehend
23. Depend
24. Innovate
25. Native
26. Miracle
27. Manicure
28. Magnate
29. Perjury
30. Helicopter
31. Exhale
32. Transgress
33. Segregate
34. Ignore
35. Territory
36. Progeny
37. Fugitive
38. Fragment
39. Flexible
40. Confident
41. Fiction
42. Ambidextrous
43. Panacea
44. Cynophobia
45. Curator
46. Coronation
47. Chronic
48. Carnage
49. Belligerent
50. Archive

Answers

(1) Tractus (2) Vivere (3) Pedi (4) Chiro (5) Paedi (6) Leuco + Haemi (7) Hydro + Phobia (8) Spect (9) Spir (10) Tacit (11) Tactere (12) Tractus (13) Uxor (14) Vocare (15) Tradere (16) Ciner (17) Sinuere (18) Radi (19) Rectus (20) Punct (21) Plenum (22) Prehendere (23) Penderu (24) Nova (25) Nat (26) Mirari (27) mani(us) (28) Magna (29) Jurere (30) Helic + opter (31) Halitus (32) Gress (33) Gregare (34) Gnos (35) Terra (36) Gene (37) Fugere (38) Fractus (39) Flexere (40) Fide (41) Fic / Fact (42) Dextro (43) Pan (44) Cyno (45) Cura (46) Coran (47) Chrono (48) Carni (49) Belli (50) Arch

❑❑❑

2

The Words You Must Know

A

Aback (be taken aback): to be shocked

I was taken aback by his rudeness.

Abandon: to leave

They abandoned the sinking ship.

An abandoned baby/houses

Abashed: embarrassed

She looked a little abashed there.

Abate: to reduce; to become less strong/intense

Finally the rain abated and we moved forward.

Abbreviate: to shorten by omitting some letters

Air conditioner is abbreviated as AC.

Abdicate: to relinquish (to abandon a throne or a position)

The old king abdicated the throne for his favourite son.

Abduct: to kidnap

The child was abducted from his school.

Aberrant/aberration: deviating from what is normal

Aberrant behaviour.

A mental aberration caused me to forget the appointment with my dentist.

Abeyance: suspension (a temporary one)

A business deal held in abeyance due to a minor disagreement.

Abhor: to hate; to detest

He abhors violence in any form.

Abide (by something): to act according to rules or laws

I'm a law abiding citizen.

They must abide by the director's decision.

Abject: to the maximum degree; extreme

Abject poverty.

A state of abject hopelessness among people living in a war-torn country.

Ablaze: burning strongly

The whole factory was ablazed within minutes.

Eyes ablaze with anger.

Abode: a place where one lives; home

I welcome you to my humble abode.

Abominate: to hate very much

She abominates the very idea of keeping a dog. She'll never accept it.

Abolish: to end a system or a law

The capital punishment should be abolished as soon as possible, he said.

Abort: to end something before it completes

Abort a pregnancy.

The project was aborted abruptly.

About-turn: a complete change

The company did an about-turn when it faced public anger.

Abrasive: rude; harsh

His manners are quite abrasive. How can she live with him?

Abreast (keep abreast of something): to have the latest information and knowledge of something

You must keep abreast of the latest developments in this matter if you want to succeed.

Abridged: made short by removing some part, words etc.

I have read an abridged edition of 'Pride and Prejudice'.

Abrogate: to officially end a law or agreement.

The old law was abrogated and a new law was passed soon after.

Abruptly: suddenly and unexpectedly

The meeting ended abruptly.

An abrupt change in the plan due to unforeseen circumstances.

Abscond: to escape and go away to avoid something unpleasant (such as a punishment or arrest)

The servant absconded with all the jewellery.

Absent-minded: one who doesn't pay attention to what is happening because he is thinking about something else; preoccupied

An absent-minded student who doesn't pay attention to what is being taught in the class.

Absolute: complete

The ruling party won absolute majority in the elections.

Absolve: to declare somebody 'not guilty'

He was absolved of all charges in the court of law.

Absorb: to understand and remember

I could not absorb all the info they provided.

Abstain: to avoid doing something one likes

If you want to live a healthy life, you must abstain from alcohol and smoking.

Abstract: existing as an idea but not a material reality

An abstract discussion not based on facts and figures but on general ideas.

Absurd: silly; stupid

What an absurd argument!

Don't be absurd! Why would she hate you?

Abundant: more than enough

There's abundant evidence to prove him guilty.

Abuse: to treat somebody cruelly, or to say rude and offensive things to someone

Child abuse is a menace to our society.

Your abusive behaviour will not be tolerated anymore.

Abysmal: very bad

Those poor workers still work in abysmal conditions.

Accede: to agree to a demand or request

Boss will never accede to your request.

Accelerate: to make something happen quicker and faster

Some concrete steps are necessary to accelerate the process of development of the nation.

Acceptable: satisfactory

I don't think their terms and conditions are acceptable.

Accessible: easy to approach; that can be obtained

The village is not accessible by railway.

An accessible chairman

Acclaim: to praise

The movie was widely acclaimed by the viewers.

Acclimatise: to get used to new conditions; to adjust

I need more time to acclimatise to this horrible weather.

Accommodate: to provide space for someone/something

This room can accommodate three more people.

Accompany: to go with somebody/something

She accompanies him everywhere.

This book is accompanied by a CD.

Accomplish: to achieve

Getting your book published is a great accomplishment.

He is an accomplished (very good) lawyer.

Accordance (in accordance with something): obeying a rule, law etc.

The latest move of the company is not in accordance with the law.

Accountable: responsible and answerable

Stop bothering me. I'm not accountable to you.

Accredited: recognized; given credit for something

An accredited college/ university

Accrue: to increase/accumulate at regular intervals over a period of time

When you put your money in a saving account, interest accrues on it at a fixed rate.

Accumulate: to collect over a period of time

The nation has accumulated a lot of debt over the years.

Accurate: exact

Scientists need to be accurate in their calculations.

Accusation: an allegation that someone is guilty of something

The accusations against the leader are all false. He has done nothing immoral or unlawful.

Accustomed: familiar

Soon they got accustomed to his peculiar ways.

Ace: a person very skilled at something

He is a flying ace. He shot six enemy aircrafts in the battle.

Acerbic: critical; bitter

He is known for his acerbic way of writing.

Ache: pain

I suffer from backache quite often.

Achievement: something done successfully

Her career is full of achievements. I think she deserves the job.

Achilles heel: a weakness

Her inconsistency has becomes achilles heel for the entire group.

Acid test: a tough and conclusive test of something

His first speech will be an acid test of his communication skills.

Acknowledge: to recognise or accept something

We acknowledge your contribution in the success of this project.

Acquainted: familiar with something or someone

I'm only acquainted with her. I don't know her very well.

Acquiesce: to accept unwillingly

Finally, she acquiesced to his demands and agreed to sell the old house.

Acquire: to get

The management intends to acquire two small firms in England.

Acquit: to declare 'not guilty'

He was found innocent and was acquitted of all the charges.

Acronym: an abbreviation created using the first letters in the name

'CAT' is an acronym for Common Admission Test.

Across: from one side to the other

They want to build a bridge across the river.

Action-packed: full of action

An action packed film.

Acumen: the ability to judge a situation and make rational decisions

MBA entrance tests are designed to test management acumen of the applicants, said the director.

Acute: severe

An acute pain in her right shoulder made her cry.

Ad hoc: created for a particular purpose, not planned beforehand

An ad hoc committee was formed to investigate the matter.

Adamant: unwilling to change or reconsider a decision

He's adamant that he won't go on the tour, no matter how important it is.

Adapt: to change to suit new conditions

I have adapted myself to city life.

Addict: one who cannot stop doing or taking something

The number of drug addicts has been going down steadily.

He is addicted to work.

Additive (food): something added to enhance the taste of food

Not all additives are good for health.

Address (to address): to speak to someone

He addressed a large crowd before leaving the country.

Adept: skilful at something

He is adept at getting the job done in any situation, that's why we need him.

Adequate: sufficient; enough

Get in! There is adequate room for all.

The information we have is not adequate to reach a conclusion.

Adhere: to stick

He will adhere to his moral principles in every situation.

Adieu (also Adios): Goodbye

Adieu, my love!

Adjacent: next

They are in the adjacent room.

Adjoining: next to and touching the thing being discussed

She has been studying in the adjoining room since the morning.

Adjourn: to suspend; to stop for a while

The parliament has been adjourned for half an hour.

Adjudicate: to judge and to make a decision in a matter

It's a bilateral issue and we need no adjudication in this matter.

Administer: to manage or direct; to give

The doctor administered him a combination of medicines.

Minimum dose of the medicine was administered to the patient.

Admire: to respect

I admire his courage.

Admirer: one who respects or is attracted to someone

That actress has many secret admirers.

Admit: to accept a truth; to confess

Admit that you hate your job.

He admitted his crime in police custody.

Admonish: to reprimand; to warn

He was admonished for being so careless while operating heavy machinery.

Ad nauseam : for a long time; without stopping

He always talks ad nauseam about cricket, and it all sounds very boring.

Adolescent: a young person moving towards adulthood

Adolescents have their own problems which they don't like to talk about.

Adopt: to begin to use something

The company adopted a policy of 'no exchange, no return'.

Adore: to love

I adore my children very much.

Adrift: loose; floating

An adrift, abandoned ship (a ship on its own, not controlled by any person)

An adrift, careless young man (one who has not set his goals in life)

Adroit: very skilful, even in stressful situation

He is adroit at handling irate callers.

Adulterate: to add something cheap to something

Adulterated milk causes various health problems.

Advance: to move forward

The advancing enemy forces were engaged by our army.

Advent: the arrival of a new invention, technology etc.

The advent of Polio medicine has saved millions of people.

Adversary: enemy

I make a very good friend and a formidable even dangerous adversary.

Adversity: a bad situation; a hard time

One must not lose hope in adversity.

Advise: to give somebody an advice

He advised me not to accept more responsibility than I can handle.

Advocate: to speak in favour of something

No peace-lover can advocate domestic violence.

Aegis: support or protection of something

Under the aegis of government, they can safely take a few financial risks.

Aesthetic: associated with understanding and appreciation of beauty

Artefacts have aesthetic values that few can understand.

Affectionate: loving

Kid's mother gave him an affectionate smile before leaving.

Affiliated: connected with a larger organisation

This school is affiliated to CBSE.

Affinity: similarity and liking

He has a natural affinity for hot weather.

Affirmative: that shows agreement; positive

Her response was affirmative.

Affliction: something one suffers from; pain

Face your afflictions with courage and determination.

Affluent: rich

She has affluent relatives who spend lavishly.

Aflame: burning

The building was aflame when the fire brigade reached.

Afloat: floating on a liquid

The log of wood was afloat in the lake.

The investors' money keeps his business afloat in difficult times.

Aforementioned: mentioned earlier

Aforementioned tactics have all failed in achieving the target.

Aftermath: the time following a bad incident; after effect

Aftermath of the war was even worse; atomic radiations caused cancer in many.

Aftershock: the shocks following an earthquake

Aftershocks are often less intense than the quake.

Afterthought: a thought that comes at a later time; something added later

As an afterthought, the pillars supporting the metro station were strengthened.

Agape: with one's mouth wide open due to surprise

Children watched their first horror film, their mouths agape in terror.

Ageing: the process of getting old with time

Scientists have been trying to find a cure for ageing since ages.

Ageless: that looks younger than one's age

Everyone aspires to have an ageless body.

Agenda: a list of targets to be achieved

The party's political agenda was quite impractical, so people rejected it.

Aggrandizement: to increase in power and stature; to exaggerate

A politician who prefers self-aggrandizement over public service loses public support sooner or later.

Aggravate: to make something worse

I tried a home remedy for my toothache but it aggravated it instead of reducing it.

Aggregate: total

His aggregate marks in Chemistry, Botany and Zoology were four hundred and thirty out of six hundred.

Aggression: threatening behaviour

'Any sort of physical or mental aggression is absolutely unacceptable.'

Aggrieved: Sad and angry because one has been treated unfairly

He felt aggrieved because he thought his mother always favoured his brother.

Aghast: shocked

He looked aghast at the decision given by the jury.

Agile: able to move quickly

A gymnast needs an agile body.

Agitate: to bother someone and make them nervous

The kids were agitating the animals in the cage.

Ago: in the past

A long time ago there was a brave king.

Agony: suffering and pain

The government must understand the agony of war victims.

Agoraphobia: fear of open spaces or public places

She suffers from agoraphobia and doesn't go to the market.

Aground: touching the ground at some point

The ship was aground and couldn't move from there.

Ailment: illness

It's a minor ailment and doesn't even require treatment. It will go away with time.

Aimless: without a purpose

Wandering aimlessly is sheer wastage of time.

Airfare: charges of a plane ticket

Airfares have gone down because of intense competition among airlines.

Airlift: to lift people trapped in a flood, sea etc. by aircrafts

Many people were airlifted from the flooded region but not everyone could be saved.

Airtight: tightly closed and not allowing air to pass through

Walnuts are usually packed in airtight packs.

Aisle: a space between rows of seats or shelves

Food grains can be found in the third aisle from the entrance.

Ajar: slightly open

The door was ajar and the thief got in.

aka: also known as

Rocky Balboa aka 'the Italian Stallion' was played by Sylvester Stallone.

Akin: similar

This animal is more akin to a sheep than a goat.

Ala carte: choices of dishes from various lists of a menu (not a fixed meal)

We always eat ala carte, as we don't like buffets.

Alarming: causing anxiety and worry

Suicide incidents among children are increasing at an alarming rate.

Alas: an expression of disappointment and unhappiness

I had expected a large crowd but, alas, there were hardly ten people to hear me!

Albeit: although

The hotel room was very cosy, albeit a little smaller.

Alibi: a proof that a person is not guilty of a crime because he was not present at the site when the crime took place

He has a strong alibi, officer. He wasn't in the country when the whole incident took place. You can check his passport.

Alienate: to lose support of people and make them dislike you

He has no friends because his arrogance alienates everyone who tries to befriend him.

Alight: burning

Many shops were still alight when police arrived at the scene of riots.

Align: to put in a straight line, especially for a better coordination

Our car tyres need to be aligned.

Alike: similar

The twins are so much alike that you can't tell one from another.

Alimony: A regular amount of money that a person needs to pay to their partner after divorce

The court ordered alimony of Rs 15000 to be paid to wife every month.

Allay: to make a fear, worry etc. less intense

He did every possible thing to allay the customer's fear of a possible fraud.

Allege: to accuse someone of committing something wrong

She alleged that he had ruined her life.

Allegiance: support and loyalty

I'm sure his allegiance lies with the rival firm, but I have no proof.

Alleviate: to make something less severe

Doctor gave pain-killers to alleviate the pain of accident victim.

Alley: a path with buildings or trees on both sides

That alley is so narrow that hardly two people can pass through at a time.

Allocate: to provide a share of something to someone

More funds need to be allocated to the space research program.

Allot: to give

The quarters were allotted according to the ranks of the officers.

Allowance: money paid regularly to a person for his needs

I think the company should increase the travel allowances this year.

Ally: a supporter

France was an ally of Britain in the World War II.

All-rounder: one who has multiple skills

The new wicket keeper is an all-rounder. He is very good at batting too!

Alluring: exciting; appealing

A second trip to the same place is never as alluring as the first one.

Alma Mater: a college, university or institute where one had studied

He doesn't talk about his alma mater.

Almighty: God

Almighty saved us that day.

Alongside: next to; together with someone or something

He stood alongside his teacher.

Aloof: one who is not friendly or sociable

Being aloof is not an option here, buddy.

Alopecia: loss of hair

Alopecia is common these days.

Aloud: loud enough to be heard by people around

The judge read his decision aloud.

Alpha male: the dominating male of a group

That silverback gorilla is the alpha male in this group.

Also-ran: one who tried but didn't do well and failed

All the also-rans were given consolation prizes.

Alteration: a change made to something to make it fit for a purpose

The trousers have been sent for alterations.

Altercation: a loud argument

Both the neighbours were engaged in an altercation over a bucket of water!

Alternate: every second; happening one after another

Good and bad days often alternate with each other.

Altitude: height above sea level

Oxygen becomes scarce (very less) at very high altitudes.

Altogether: in total

We spent five thousand rupees altogether.

Altruist: one who is willing to help others, even at one's own cost; one who donates a lot

Alumnus (plural alumni): one who completed his education in a college and left

He is a Harvard alumnus.

Amalgam: a combination

She is a unique amalgam of beauty and wisdom, so everyone likes her.

Amass: accumulate; to gather a large amount of something over the time

He has amassed a great wealth, so he has no financial worries now.

Amateur: one who does something for pleasure, not for a living

Only amateur boxers can participate in this tournament.

Amateurish: showing no skills or maturity

Such an amateurish behaviour will put you in trouble some day.

Amaze: to surprise greatly

He amazed everyone with his refined manners.

Ambidextrous: one who can use both hands equally well

Being ambidextrous is an asset.

Ambience: the characteristics and atmosphere a certain place has

Metros and towns have different ambiences.

Ambiguous: having two or more meanings

Ambiguous talks of politician confused the listeners.

Ambit: limit/range of something

There was a long debate whether the state police should come within the ambit of the central government.

Ambitious: having a strong desire to achieve something, especially money and power

He is very ambitious and will leave no stone unturned to become what he wants to.

Ambivalent: having two contradictory feelings at the same time

My ambivalent feelings towards them won't let me decide the right course of action.

Amble: to walk slowly and in a relaxed manner

We ambled along the river for minutes, but said nothing.

Ambush: a sudden attack

Five policemen were killed in terrorists' ambush.

Ameliorate: to improve

These steps are absolutely essential to ameliorate the condition of poor people in the city.

Amenable: one who can be influenced by an idea

Surprisingly, we found him quite amenable to our suggestions.

Amendment: a change made to a written document

In the twenty-fifth amendment to the constitution, some old laws were abolished.

Amenity: a facility that people need or desire

Basic amenities like hospital, school and market are within a kilometre from the house.

Amiable: friendly

An amiable person can always make new friends anywhere.

Amid/Amidst: in the middle of something

There were some friends amidst the crowd of haters.

Amiss: something wrong

The situation wasn't perfect; something was amiss.

Amity: friendship

UN tries to promote an environment of amity between the member states.

Amok: out of control

The prisoners ran amok in all directions as soon as the wall of the prison crumbled due to the earthquake.

Amoral: having no moral principles

Amoral individuals are often rejected by the societies they live in.

Amorous: showing sexual desires

She abhors his amorous gestures, but he doesn't understand.

Amortize: to pay a debt in small instalments

Amortize is an easy way to clear the hefty loans.

Amphibious: active on both land and water

Hovercraft is an amphibious vehicle. It can run on both land and water.

Amphitheatre: a circular arena where contests take place

The gladiators used to fight in the amphitheatres of Rome in ancient times.

Ample: more than enough

He was given ample

opportunity but he couldn't prove himself.

Amplify: to make something, especially a sound, louder

Amplified sounds reached miles from where the New Year party took place.

Amulet: an ornament one wears to keep evil spirits away

He wore a thick black amulet round his neck.

Amuse: to entertain

The clown failed to amuse the crowd.

Anachronism: something old and out of time

That hundred year old building looks anachronism when compared to the skyscrapers around it.

Anaesthetist: a doctor who gives anaesthetics (medicine that makes people unable to feel pain; often used during operations)

Dr. V. K. Singh is an anaethitist in this hospital.

Analogy: a comparison between two or more things, often to show how similar they are

An analogy between brain and CPU.

Analysis: detailed study and examination of something, done in order to understand it

The news reader's analysis of exit poll results was quite flawed.

Anarchy: a state of having no government

A state of anarchy prevailed when the military regime arrested the elected PM.

Ancestor: a person who lived long ago before one and is related to one

This tradition was started by our ancestors centuries ago.

Anecdote: a short story told to amuse people

The former soldier told anecdotes about his missions.

Anguish: great suffering

Riots cause unbearable anguish to the victims.

Animosity: anger and strong dislike

There has been a feeling of animosity between the two states since the war took place.

Annexe: to take something; to add something to something

The military regime annexed the agricultural land for the army's use.

Annihilate: to defeat badly; to destroy

The general believes in complete annihilation of the enemy.

Annoy: to make a person angry; to irritate

His amateurish behaviour often annoys his parents.

Annuity: a sum paid to someone every year

The policyholders will receive an annuity of Rs 2 lakh every year.

Anomaly: something different from what is usual

There are anomalies in the report and they are being studied by the experts.

Anonymous person: someone who keeps his name a secret or is not known for some reason

The author wishes to remain anonymous.

Many anonymous works have added significantly to the world of literature.

Antagonist: a rival; a person who dislikes something and opposes it

Many antagonists have stood in opposition to the new policy.

Antecedent: something that existed before and caused something later

Leonardo da Vinci's model of an aircraft is seen as antecedent to the modern helicopter.

Antediluvian: very old fashioned; out of date

His antediluvian hair-style makes people laugh at him, but he doesn't give a damn.

Anthropology: study of human beings (from ancient times to the modern times)

The recent excavations brought out some anthropological treasures.

Anticipate: to expect that something will happen in the future

He anticipated great success but didn't get any.

Anticlimax: an experience which is less exciting than it was expected to be

The final episode of the series was an anticlimax because it was far inferior to what was expected.

Anti-depressant: any drug used to treat depression

The use of anti-depressants is quite common in modern societies.

Antidote: something that reduces the effect of something harmful

An antidote to cobra venom is available in hospitals.

Yoga is an antidote to stress.

Antipathy: a strong dislike

A feeling of antipathy remained after the war between the two neighbours was over.

Antique: something that carries historical value and is rare to find

An antique clock

She has a valuable collection of antiques.

Antisocial: not respecting the norms of society; harmful to the society

Antisocial elements are a danger to our peaceful society, said the speaker.

Anxious: very much worried

My parents are quite anxious about my future, though I can't understand why!

Antithesis: opposite

They are twins, but their behaviours are antithesis of each other's.

Anyhow: anyway

Anyhow, they managed to reach in time.

Apart: separated by a certain distance

The two vehicles were parked metres apart from each other.

Apathy: a lack of interest and concern

Government's apathy towards the condition of poor lost them the election.

Ape: a big animal of monkey family (Chimpanzee, gorilla etc.)

Apes are distant relatives of human beings.

Apex: the top point

At the apex of her acting career she gave seven blockbusters in a row.

Aphrodisiac: any of the drugs that are believed to cause sexual desire

Many harmful substances are sold as aphrodisiacs.

Apiece: each

The umbrellas cost us Rs 150 apiece.

Apocalypse: a great destruction

An apocalyptic end of the world

Apolitical: not associated with politics

An apolitical step has been taken in public interest by the leaders of the nation.

Apologetic: sorry for something

She seemed apologetic for breaking the school rules, and promised not to do that again in future.

Appalling: shocking; very bad

The sanitary conditions in some famous hospitals are appalling.

Apparel: clothes

Fashion apparels are sold in the Sunday sales.

Apparatus: a set of equipment

Laboratory apparatus must be cleaned after the use.

Apparently: seemingly but not surely

Apparently, it's the end of his career.

Appealing: attractive

The impressive use of colours in the picture makes it appealing to the buyers.

Appease: to try to please someone annoyed by offering an advantage

The policy of appeasement may not always be in the best interest of the nation.

Appellation: a title or a name given to a person or place

'The Pink City' is an appellation.

Appetite: a desire to eat

I have a great appetite; I can eat as much as I like.

The smell of the food was quite appetising.

Applaud: to clap hands to show appreciation

Everyone in the hall applauded as soon as he entered.

Appraise: to examine

The great artist appraised the works of his juniors.

Appreciate: to recognise the value of something

We appreciate your concerns, but we are helpless in this matter. You must follow the rules.

Apprehension: a worry that something bad will happen

Despite his apprehensions he pretended to be calm and composed.

Apprentice: one who works for a skilled person to learn his skills

The trader has found a new apprentice just as smart as himself.

Apprise: to tell

He had been apprised of the growing concern among the locals, but he did nothing.

Approachable: one who can be reached easily

Unlike the former one, the new manager is friendly and approachable.

Appropriate: (1) suitable

I'll transfer your call to the appropriate department.

(2) to take something for personal use without owner's permission

He appropriated a million dollars from client's account and then tried to escape, but was caught.

Approve: to give permission; to agree

Our proposal was approved by the senior management within hours.

Approximate: close but not accurate

He owes me approximately 10000 rupees.

Apt: right for a situation; fitting

Writer's remarks are apt.

Aptitude: a natural or developed ability for something

The tests that measure business aptitude are often flawed.

Aquatic: related to water; living in water

Aquatic animals have been badly affected by the oil spill.

Arbitrate: to act as a judge in an argument

A former judge was appointed by the government to arbitrate in the companies' dispute.

Arcade: a covered area with many shops, offices, corridors etc.

Central shopping arcade is the centre of business in the city.

Archaeology: the study of ancient buildings, cultures, things etc. for historical purpose

He is best in archaeology.

Arch-rival: the worst/main rival or enemy

Many people believe that Pakistan is India's arch-rival in cricket.

Architect: a person who designs buildings

He is a perfect architect.

Archive: a collection of records of something

A family archive

Mr. Rohit has an archive of Indian film industry.

Ardent: keen; having strong feelings about something

She is an ardent supporter of child welfare.

Arduous: very difficult to do

The last match of the championships proved to be an arduous one to win, but he won.

Arguably: perhaps; possibly

He is arguably the best cook in the world.

Argumentative: one who tends or likes to argue

An argumentative society

Don't be so argumentative! Just listen.

Arid: dry

Nothing grows on this arid land.

Aristocrat: a person of high rank in the society

Aristocrats are often associated with lavish lifestyles.

Armageddon: a tremendous destruction

The movie is based on an Armageddon.

Armed: having weapons

An armed robber entered the store and demanded all the money from the clerk.

Aroma: a pleasant smell

Aroma of spices is a characteristic of Indian food.

Arouse: to cause a certain feeling

The movie 'Jurassic Park' successfully aroused people's interest in dinosaurs.

Array: a group of things arranged in an attractive manner

An array of sweets from all over the world was displayed at the show sweet.

Arrogant: very proud

An arrogant person can't have too many friends.

Arson: to set fire to someone's property

Arson is a very serious crime.

Artefact (or Artifact): a man-made object of historical value

The sword of Tipu Sultan is a very valuable artefact, so the government is trying to buy it back.

Articulate: able to express one's thoughts clearly

He articulated his feelings very well and was able to win her love.

Artless: honest, not deceptive

His artless manner won many hearts.

Ascend: to rise in position

If you want to ascend to a higher position, you'll have to keep the bosses pleased.

Ascertain: to make certain

I wanted to ascertain that I was talking to the right person, so I asked her name again.

Ascetic: one who avoids pleasures and believes in living a simple life

His ascetic lifestyle was just a disguise to cover his crimes.

Ascribe: to give credit of something to the thing that caused it

He ascribed his failure in sports to his unhealthy eating habits.

Ashamed: feeling shame about something

You must not be ashamed of your small mistakes.

Ashore: to the shore (from the sea)

As soon as he saw a shark, he quickly swam ashore.

Asinine: very stupid

"What an asinine blunder we made!" he said.

Askew: not level

That wall clock is slightly askew.

An askew picture frame

Aspect: a feature of a thing or a problem

The worst aspect of this Math problem is that it needs the knowledge of formulas I don't know!

Another aspect of someone's life

Aspirant: one who seriously wants to get something

The lists of MBA aspirants are getting longer every year.

Assailant: an attacker

How many assailants committed the crime?

Assassinate: to murder, especially an influential person

The terrorists planned to assassinate the U.S. president.

Assault: an attack

Assault on parliament is an assault on the democracy itself.

Assent: to agree

They wanted to marry but their parents didn't assent, so they resorted to court marriage.

Assertive: one who acts confidently and firmly but not rudely

You must be assertive if you want to get your point accepted in the meeting.

Assess: to measure/estimate the ability, value etc.

They assessed our performance in the contest.

Asset: something valuable

Hardworking employees are an asset to our company.

Assiduous: having qualities such as carefulness, diligence etc.

You need to be assiduous to succeed in this field.

Assign: to give a work to someone

I was assigned the task of publicising the company in the local market.

Assimilate: to absorb; to take in

It is hard to assimilate new knowledge quickly.

The organisation wishes to assimilate new talent.

Assist: to help

Will you please assist me in locating this book in the library?

Associate: (i) a friend or a partner

Meet my new business associate, Karan.

(ii) to connect

His fever was associated with a bigger problem.

Assorted: various things mixed together

At the dinner, he was provided a dish of assorted vegetables and rice.

Assuage: to weaken an unpleasant feeling

Relatives tried hard to assuage her pain of loss of her father but to no use. She kept crying.

Assume: to accept something as truth without bothering about a proof

We assume that you did it only by mistake, still you must pay for her losses.

Our assumptions were all wrong.

Astonishing: amazing; surprising

It's astonishing that he beat the world champion in the first round!

Astounding: shocking; surprising

She gained an astounding victory of 6-0 over her professional opponent.

Astray: deviated from the correct path

The satellite went astray and fell into the Pacific Ocean.

Astride: with one leg on each side

He sat astride the horse, very tense and not moving a foot.

Astronomical: great; very big

His astronomical success made him arrogant and careless.

Astute: smart; able to take advantage of a situation

An astute politician like him made such a blunder! What a pity!

Asylum: protection given to someone in a foreign country; safe heaven

The president escaped with his family and sought political asylum in London.

Atheist: one who doesn't believe in God

She is very religious but her husband is an atheist.

Athletic: healthy and strong

He has an athletic body.

Atone: to make amends for a sin or wrongdoing

This is no way to atone!

His action caused many people to lose their jobs, and now he wants to get them their jobs back as an act of atonement.

Atrocious: extremely bad; terrible

What an atrocious movie! I've already got a headache.

Attainable: something that can be achieved

It is hard but not impossible. It is attainable.

Attempt: to try

I attempted the exam twice but failed both the times.

Attentive: one who is paying attention

Be attentive in the class!

Attenuate: to reduce something's effect; to weaken; to calm

Ozone layer attenuates the ultraviolet rays of sun.

Attribute (attribute something to something): to state something as a cause of something

She attributed her success to her husband's cooperation and help.

Attrition: gradual reduction in strength

Employee attrition rate is quite high in BPOs.

Auction: to sell goods publically using the process of bidding

The little antique box was auctioned for five thousand bucks.

Audacity: bravery and boldness

His audacity impressed people very much and he was elected the new President of the nation.

Augment: to add something to something else; to increase

In this case, alternative therapy augmented the effect of his medicine and helped him recover faster.

Aura: The feeling one gets around a place or person

She has an aura of saintliness.

Auspicious: showing signs of a promising future

An auspicious start to the journey

Authentic: real and true

He possesser an authentic vintage car.

Authorise: to give official permission and rights

The commissioner authorised the police action on the suspects.

Autobiography: a person's account of his own life

I have been reading Nelson Mandela's autobiography these days.

Automate: to make a process automatic with the help of machines

An automated car factory is much more efficient than a traditional one.

Autonomous: having power to make its own decisions

Nepal is an autonomous state with additional rights.

Auxiliary: something supporting something more important; assisting

After the bomb blasts, auxiliary nursing staff was put on stand-by, just in case they were needed.

Avail: use

He did his best to persuade the chief to consider his plan, but to no avail.

Avarice: greed

His avarice is well-known in the city.

Avenge: to harm somebody because they harmed one earlier

The hero of the movie vowed to avenge the death of his father.

Aver: to announce loudly; to assert

I wish to aver that we'll win the match.

Averse: opposed to something

He is a risk-averse person.

Avert: to avoid

The authorities tried to avert any conflict with the government.

Avid: eager; enthusiastic

She is an avid reader. She reads day and night.

Avow: to admit; to declare

He avowed she had broken his heart.

Await: to wait for something

Results are awaited, he wrote in the admission form.

Aware: having knowledge of something

Are you aware of the ground reality? I think you're not.

Awe-inspiring: causing respect; splendid

An awe-inspiring view of the sea from a hotel room

Awesome: wonderful; causing admiration and respect

What an awesome sight!

Awful: very unpleasant

Oh, this is an awful place! Let's get away from here.

Awhile: just for a short time

I watched TV for awhile, then went out for shopping.

Awkward: hard to deal with; uncomfortable

It was an awkward moment when I forgot my lines.

Awry: not as intended

The things went awry for police when people broke the barriers.

B

Babble: to talk quickly and not clearly about something

He babbles all the time about a cricket match he saw last week.

Babysitter: one who takes care of children when the parents are out

She's an awful babysitter. The kid's rolling in the mud and she's busy on her mobile!

Bachelor: a man who has never married

He is a happy bachelor and doesn't intend to marry.

Backbiting: saying unpleasant and defaming things about someone in his absence

I hate backbiting and those who indulge in it.

Backbone: the most important part of something

The Flagship program of the institute is its backbone.

Backfire: to have opposite results

He wanted to please the boss but the trick backfired and now the boss wants to throw him out.

Backlash: an anger among people about a change

The authorities weren't expecting a backlash in this matter.

Backlog: the things which a person had to do earlier and is forced to do now

He is struggling under a huge backlog because he doesn't work on time.

Backstabber: one who says harmful things about a person in his absence

I thought he was a friend but he proved to be a backstabber.

Backtrack: to reverse one's action or opinion

After a lot of criticism the government backtracked on the issue.

Backup: something that can be used in case of emergency; support

I always copy my computer files in a separate hard disk as a backup.

Backwater: a part of river where water is very calm

Backwaters of Kerala are famous throughout the Indian subcontinent.

Bad blood: a strong feeling of hatred among two people

We have no bad blood between us, we're just competitors.

Bad-tempered: one who can be easily made angry

He is a bad-tempered guy. You'd better keep away from him.

Baffle: to confuse very much

The reasons he gave for the failure of this project are not only baffling but also ridiculous.

Bail: the money that an accused needs to pay to the court to stay out of jail until his trial

He paid Rs 25000 as bail and was released temporarily, but soon he was arrested for committing another crime.

Bait: something used to lure an animal in a trap

The fish didn't take the bait.

The police used a fake Facebook profile as bait and trapped the thief.

Balderdash: nonsense

Whatever he just said is nothing but balderdash.

Baloney: nonsense

Baloney!, he shouted.

Bamboozle: to trick someone

He was bamboozled by a thug who acted a fortune teller.

Banal: boring and unoriginal

His writing style is banal and uninteresting.

Bananas (to go bananas): to get very excited or angry

When he came to know he had failed yet again, he went bananas.

Bandwagon: something successful and trendy which everyone wants to do

When organised retail became successful, many companies jumped on the bandwagon and opened their own retail stores.

Bane: something that causes trouble

Some people still believe technology is a bane to the society!

Bang: to hit something

She accidentally banged her knee on the bed and cried afterwards.

Banish: to get rid of something

While meditating, you must banish all the negativity from your mind.

Bankrupt: unable to pay one's debt

The company went bankrupt three years ago and the investors lost their money.

Banshee: a female spirit

She likes to read banshee stories.

Banter: to exchange teasing remarks in a humorous way

Children stood there, bantering each other.

Bar: to prevent someone from doing something

He was barred from the board exams because he was caught cheating.

Barbaric: cruel

His barbaric behaviour made him a villain in the society.

Barbeque (BBQ): a meal cooked on a special metal appliance which is often used when cooking outside the house

Barbed: having sharp metallic thorns

Army secured the border with barbed wire.

Bare: uncovered or without clothes

A bare sword

He was barefoot in the hot summer noon.

Barely: hardly; only just

The food is barely enough for four of us, let alone inviting the guests.

Bargain: to negotiate to get the price of an item down

We bargained hard and got twenty per cent off on the written price.

Barkeeper: one who serves drinks at a bar

Rathore is a barkeeper, but his act has puzzled me.

Barren land: land unable to produce plants

Barren land of the desert is not suitable for agriculture.

Barter: to exchange goods for other goods, not for money

They bartered rice for wheat.

Baseless: not based on facts; unfounded

It's a baseless allegation, your honour! he said.

Bash: to criticize severely; to strike hard

They started a website to bash their political rivals.

Bashful: shy

She has always been so bashful.

Bask: to enjoy the warmth of sun while resting

Basking in winter sun is a great pleasure.

Bathe: to take a bath

He bathed in scented water.

Batter: to hit someone repeatedly

The body was found severely battered and covered in blood.

Beacon: a light on top of something, acting as a warning signal

The court ordered MLAs to take red beacons off their vehicles.

Beam: to give a broad smile

He beamed at her but she didn't respond.

Bearable: something that can be tolerated

A bearable winter

Bearer: one who carries something

The palanquin bearers were very tired.

Beast (not the animal): a very cruel, brutal person

So unkind to his own children! That man is a beast, I tell you.

Beautify: to make something more beautiful

The government has a plan to beautify the city.

Beckon: to tell someone to come near or to do something by head or hand gesture

He beckoned to the waiter to come and take the order.

Bedlam: a noisy environment; chaos

It was all bedlam and confusion in there.

Bedridden: confined to bed because of illness

After the accident he remained bedridden for three months.

Bedside: beside a bed

There's a book on the bedside table.

Befall: happen to someone (something bad)

Tragedy after tragedy befell them, making their lives miserable.

Befit: suit

The treatment he got befits him, she said apathetically.

Beforehand: before something happens

I knew beforehand that she was bluffing.

Befriend: to become friends with someone

He befriended the wrong guy and got into trouble.

Befuddled: confused; puzzled

He was so befuddled he couldn't understand the simplest question.

Beguile: to attract in order to deceive

The exteriors of the house beguiled him and he ignored its major faults completely.

Behead: to cut someone's head off

The dictator ordered beheading of all the elected leaders.

Behemoth: very large and powerful

An aviation behemoth

Belated: something coming later than the appropriate time

A belated wish

Belated happy birthday!

Belie: to reveal one's lies; to contradict

The terror on his face belied his apparent composure.

Belittle: to make someone look less important

They used lies to belittle the popular leader but failed.

Belligerent: willing to start a conflict

She was in a belligerent mood so I thought it better not to discuss the point with her.

Bellow: to shout loudly

Stop it!, he bellowed at his children.

The buffalo bellowed and we knew it was time to feed her.

Belongings: whatever a person carries with him

"Customers must take care of their belongings." the notice read.

Beloved: much-loved

"Beloved daughter, you need to be more careful about your health", wrote the mother.

Bemused: a bit confused

She looked bemused at his odd behaviour.

Benchmark: a standard against which quality of similar things can be measured

This book has set a benchmark for the other books in this category.

Beneath: under

Soon we were to know what secret lied beneath the hollow ground of the basement.

Benefactor: one who gives money to help someone

He never came to know who his benefactor was.

Beneficent: one who loves to help people

A beneficent man who gave away all his wealth to help the needy ones.

Beneficiary: one who receives money as a result of something that happened

Police suspected that the beneficiaries of the will had a hand in old man's murder.

Benevolent: kind

Fortunately, his neighbour is a benevolent man who always helps him.

Benign: not fatal

A benign tumour doesn't cause cancer.

Berate: to talk to someone in an angry manner

Boss berated me for his fault! It's not fair.

Berserk: out of control

She went berserk when she came to know of his deception.

Beseech: to beg

I beseech you, tell them the truth!

Besiege: to surround a place with the help of armed forces

The fort was besieged and the water supply was blocked.

Bespectacled: wearing glasses

A bespectacled boy was seen talking to the robbers.

Bespoke: specially made; not readymade

A bespoke study table

Bestow: to honour someone by giving them something; to confer

An honorary doctorate was bestowed upon the president.

Betray: to deceive own country, king etc. by helping the enemy by giving them secret info

He betrayed his own father, the king, to get his crown.

The political history of the state is full of betrayals.

Betterment: improvement

We have taken concrete steps for the betterment of the people, said the politician.

Better half: spouse

My better half is angry with me, said John.

Beware: be careful about

'Beware of the dogs.'

Bewilder: to confuse

The explanation he gave only bewildered me more.

Bewitch: to attract someone so much as if one has done magic on him

Her natural beauty bewitched the visitor.

Biannual: happening twice a year

The biannual competition is about to begin.

Biased: favouring someone against someone else; partial

The judges were biased towards them, so we lost the dance round.

Bibliophile: one who loves or collects books

The rich man is also a known bibliophile.

Bicker: to argue on unimportant matters

They kept bickering about who should have won the cup in 1975.

Bid: offer to buy an object being auctioned

Her bid was twenty thousand rupees.

He bid a very high price for that ugly statue.

Biennial: every second year

A biennial sports event.

Bifocal glasses: glasses that can be used to see the near as well as distant things

Bifurcate: to divide into two parts

A sign board was placed where the road bifurcates.

Big brother: one who has complete power over people and shows it often

You must be aware of the rules made by the big brother- the central government.

Bigamy: being married to two people at the same time

Bigamy is against the law.

Big day (the big day): the day one marries

I'm sure you're waiting for the big day, buddy!

Big mouth (have a big mouth): talk too much and tell secrets

He has a big mouth. He tells defence secrets in bars.

Bilateral: between two groups or countries

Bilateral relations of the US and Russia have improved in the last few years.

Bimbo: a beautiful young lady who is not very intelligent

She called her a bimbo in a fit of anger.

Bilingual: one who knows two languages

Being a bilingual has many advantages.

Binding agreement: an agreement enforced by law

They couldn't break the deal because of a binding agreement.

Biodegradable: something that is environment friendly because it decays naturally

The CM laid an emphasis on the use of biodegradable products.

Biography: The life story of a person written by someone else

His biographies are available in the market.

Birthright: a right that a person enjoys from his birth

Freedom is my birthright, and I will have it, said the revolutionary.

Bisect: to divide into two equal parts

The river almost bisects the state.

Biting (weather): extremely cold

He bought an ice cream in this biting weather.

Bitter (experience) : a very bad experience, thinking about which makes one angry

Being thrown out of the club was a bitter experience for him.

Bizarre: strange

His tastes are so bizarre.

They issued a bizarre statement, without thinking.

Blabber: to talk too much

She went on blabbering about her shopping while we were trying to focus on studies.

Blacken: to make something black or become black

The ends of the new tube light are blackening already!

Blacklist: to add an organisation to the list of banned organisations

As soon as the scam came out, the government blacklisted the company.

Blackmail: to try to get something from a person by threatening them to tell a secret of theirs to other people

Theyused edited photos to blackmail their partners.

Blackout: a time when all the lights are kept off

Blackout was enforced during the time of enemy air-raids.

Blah: a word used to show that someone's talk or speech is boring and meaningless

I've heard his 'blah blah blah' before.

Blame: to hold someone responsible for something

He blames me for his failure.

Blame game: when people blame each other instead of finding a solution

The authorities are busy in a blame game on the issue of traffic jams in the city.

Blasphemy: something that is understood to be an insult to God

Blasphemy laws are very strict in some countries.

Blatant: not concealed; obvious and deliberate

Her blatant lies annoyed the teacher and she was punished.

Blaze: to burn strongly

His eyes blazed with anger as he thought about the injustice done to him.

Bleak: hopeless, or with little hope

Despite bleak chances of victory, they fought on courageously.

Blemish: an ugly mark

The whole incident is a blemish on the nation's reputation.

Blend: a combination of different things

The new DC is a unique blend of courage and intelligence.

Blindfold: to cover someone's eyes

They blindfolded him and took him to a strange place.

Blink: to close and open eyes quickly

Why is she blinking so much? Any problem with her eyes?

Bliss: perfect joy and happiness

Dancing takes her to eternal bliss and she forgets all her problems.

Blistering hot: extremely hot

He went out in blistering hot weather. No wonder he fell ill.

Blithering idiot: very stupid person

Arguing with boss on the first day of job! He's a blithering idiot.

Blockade: the action of sealing off a place to prevent anyone from going in and out

Police blockaded the area in order to catch the absconding criminals.

Blockbuster: a hit film or book

His third film was a blockbuster and made him a star.

Blonde: a woman with yellowish or golden hair

Blood-curdling: causing terror

Some parts of the movie were blood-curdling. I had to close my eyes.

Bloodshed: violence in which people are killed

The UN must intervene to stop this bloodshed.

Bloodthirsty: one who loves killing

A bloodthirsty ruler liked to see gladiators killing each other

Bloom: the period when a flower opens

It's the season of bloom. Let's go to Mughal Gardens!

Blooper: a little mistake, often funny, made by a news anchor

Come on, they won't fire her for a blooper!

Bluff: to deceive someone by convincing them of something that isn't true

When she said she had three aces, I knew she was bluffing because I had two.

Blunder: a big mistake that could have been prevented

Attacking two enemies at the same time proved to be a blunder for the aggressor.

Blunt: not sharp

A blunt arrow

A blunt attack

Blurred: not clear; difficult to see and understand

A blurred picture.

Blush: to feel so much embarrassed or shy that one's face goes red

When he asked her to marry, she blushed.

Boast: to proudly tell someone about something one has done or achieved

He never fails to boast about his accomplishments.

Bob: to move up and down quickly

The rubber ball fell into the water and bobbed up and down on the waves.

Boggle: to confuse

It was a mind-boggling site and we couldn't understand how it was even possible!

Bogus: fake or false; fraud

A fake doctor with a bogus MBBS degree was caught last week.

Boisterous: noisy and full of energy

A boisterous celebration of a child's birth

Bolster: to support something to make it strong; to reinforce

Some bright students also failed the test. I think they need to bolster their confidence.

Bombard: to drop bombs at a place

The enemy bombers bombarded the city and ruined it completely.

Bombastic: pompous; one who uses difficult words in speech to make himself sound more intelligent

A bombastic speaker often loses public attention.

Bona fide: real (not fake)

You need to obtain bona fide certificate from your school in order to get admission in a college.

Bonanza: something good in a large quantity (especially wealth, profits etc.); a prize

The apparel store has announced its summer bonanza promotion. It promises quality and more style.

Bonfire: a fire usually created in the open, for pleasure or for burning waste material

They sat around the garden bonfire, listening to his stories.

Bonsai: a small, decorative tree

I want that bonsai for the drawing room.

Bon voyage! : Happy and safe journey!

Bony: very thin

A poor, bony little girl was sleeping on a footpath.

Boo: an expression of dislike and disagreement

The match was so boring that the viewers started to boo at the players.

Bookworm: a person who reads all the time

He is a bookworm and reads all sorts of books.

Boom: a period of rapid growth

An economic boom is much needed at this point of time.

Boomerang: to hit back

Our plan to please mother boomeranged when she got angrier.

Boorish: rude; ill-mannered

He is a boorish man who has made more enemies than friends.

Boost: to increase

His recent victories have boosted his confidence.

Booty: stolen money; loot

The thieves got into a quarrel over the division of booty.

Booze: wine; alcohol

Boss (verb): to order someone all the time

You are not his junior. Don't let him boss you around.

Bother: to disturb and annoy someone

Children, stop bothering me!

Bothersome: something that bothers

A bothersome kid who wouldn't let me work!

Bottleneck: a hurdle that stops progress; a narrow part of a path

This pass often proves to be a bottleneck for the climbers.

Lack of funds is another bottleneck.

Bound: certain

He gossiped away all his time. His failure was bound to happen.

Boundless: limitless; infinite

This kid seems to have boundless energy.

Bounty: reward money

He has a bounty of Rs 50000 on his head.

Bout: a short period of something, especially illness

A bout of cough cannot stop me from going out and doing my duty, he said.

Boycott: to stay away in order to show one's anger

They called for a boycott of goods from the rival nation.

We have decided to boycott the chairman's conference.

Brag: to boast about something

He never stops bragging about his muscle power.

Brainchild: an idea or plan

The whole idea was my brainchild but he took the credit for it.

Brain drain: a condition in which educated and talented people leave own country to work in another country for better opportunities or more money

The nation needs to find a way to stop brain drain.

Brainwash: to set a thought in someone's mind by repeatedly telling it to him

Innocent young men are taken away and brainwashed by the terrorists.

Brainy: smart and intelligent

A brainy kid
He is short but brainy.

Brandish: to wave something in the air to threaten someone

He was arrested for brandishing his gun to threaten the constable.

Brat: a spoiled child

You little brat! Why don't you leave me in peace?

Bravado: unnecessary show-off of one's courage

This stupid act of bravado in front of the enemy could cost you your life.

Brawl: a loud quarrel or fight

A brawl has no use. You should use peaceful ways to solve a matter, said the old man.

Brazen: shameless and bold

A brazen act of vandalism shook the city.

Breadwinner: the family member who earns

He is the only breadwinner in his family.

Break-in: an incident of entering a building illegally

The thief broke in and took whatever he liked.

Breaking point: a point when a person loses control over himself or over a situation

He beat his wife again and it was the breaking point of their marriage.

Breakthrough: an incident of finding an answer to a long time problem; an important discovery

Discovery of 'the God particle' is considered to be a major breakthrough in the field of science.

Breathtaking: very exciting; remarkable

A breathtaking view of Grand Canyon from the sky

Brevity: briefness; shortness

Brevity is the speciality of his writing (He uses few words to say more).

Brew: (1) to make beer (2) to add hot water to coffee or tea leaves to prepare the drink

Bribe: to pay someone illegally to get a favour

They wanted to bribe the policeman to let them escape but he was honest.

Bridal: related to a girl who is about to be married

They specialise in bridal makeup.

Brigand: an armed robber, especially in the countryside

A brigand who terrorises the entire state is no ordinary criminal, said the chief.

Brilliant: very good

He is a brilliant tennis player.

Brim: The edge of a glass, any other container or a hat

The cup was full to the brim.

The brim of the magician's hat is sharp enough to cut a banana into two.

Brink: the point beyond which a change occurs

We are to the brink of war with our neighbour.

Brisk: energetic and quick

A brisk walk is good for health.

Broach: to mention; to begin to discuss a subject

Finally, he stood up and broached the matter of her indecent behaviour with the manager.

Brood: group or family of young birds born at the same time

Brook (brook no insult): to accept or tolerate no insult

I can brook no insult. I'm going to take the matter to the court.

Browse: to just go through a book or a website without reading everything

He is browsing the internet.

Bruise: an injury in which there is discoloration but not bleeding

Her bruised body told the story of her sufferings.

Brunch: a meal between breakfast and lunch

I'm having a brunch. Would you like to join?

Brunette: a white girl who has dark hair

Brutal: cruel and unkind

The brutal force of the storm threw our boat on the rocks.

Buckle: to bend; to collapse

He buckled under the pressure of his parents' great expectations and married soon, though he didn't want to.

Budding: beginning to develop

A budding actor/author

Budge: move

We tried to explain everything to him but he wouldn't budge from his decision.

Buff: someone who is very interested in something

A shopping/cricket buff

Hari is habitual of a shopping buff.

Bug: any small device used to hear people's conversation secretly

The minister's office had been bugged and he had no hint.

Build-up: a gradual increase; accumulation

Build-up of germs in the gums and teeth causes mouth problems.

Bulge: a curve protruding out of something

His biceps bulged out as soon as he flexed his arms.

Bulky: occupying a lot of space

We don't need all those bulky items on the picnic.

Bulldoze: to force someone; to bully

They bulldozed the passengers to hand over their valuables.

Bullish (share market): a market in which share prices are rising

To invest in bullish is not risky if economy is growing.

Bullshit: complete nonsense

That's bullshit! I wasn't even there!

Bully: to threaten someone weaker

Those senior students were bullying a fourth grade kid.

Bum: a person's bottom

Bump: to hit or collide with something

He bumped into the old man's wheelchair and apologised instantly.

Bumpy: rough, not smooth

That bumpy ride broke my back!

Bunch: a group

A bunch of hooligans broke into my office and destroyed everything.

Buoy: a float, used as a marker in water or used to save a drowning person

A life buoy was thrown from the boat to save his life.

Burdensome: difficult

What a burdensome job to do!

Burgeoning: growing

A burgeoning market provides a lot of opportunity for business.

Burnish: to polish a metal by rubbing it

An old but burnished silver coin looks like a new one.

Burrow: to dig a hole in ground

Rats burrow holes in the ground.

Bury: to put dead body (or something else) in the ground

He was buried with all due respect.

Bushy: having thick hair

Bushy tail of the fox

Busk: to sing or to play music to collect donations from passer-bys

The poor flutist busked to participate in a contest abroad.

Bust: to unfold a criminal organisation and arrest the criminals

The drug racket was busted and four people were arrested.

Butchery: killing people cruelly; massacre

The dictator is dead but his butchery cannot be forgotten.

Buttress: to support

In the end, his research buttressed my opinion.

Buzz: to make a continuous low sound (just as a bee does)

The transmitter buzzed strangely.

The bumblebee buzzed its wings.

The new flexible mobile is the buzz of the market.

Bypass: to go around something without touching it

We didn't want to get stuck in the traffic jam so we bypassed the city by taking a side road.

Bystander: a person who stands near and watches something happen but doesn't participate in it

The injured man was crying for help but the bystanders did nothing.

C

Cackle: to laugh loudly and shrilly

After that the villain cackled and took another glass of wine.

Cacophony: an unpleasant mix of many loud sounds

I abominate the cacophony of honking vehicles.

Cadge: to get something for free by asking for it from others

Cadging a lift in a stranger's car is always risky.

Cadre: a group of people trained for a particular purpose

A new political party has no cadre in any part of the country.

Cajole: to persuade somebody to do something through sweet talks

He cajoled me into going to watch that boring movie I had seen already!

Cakewalk: very easy task

Passing qualifying exam was a cake walk, but cracking the entrance test won't be.

Calamity: a destructive incident or event; disaster

Wild fire was declared a national calamity.

Calibre: ability and talent

She has calibre but she lacks ambition.

Callous: careless about others; not having sympathy for others' pains

How callous! Her baby is crying and she doesn't even look at him.

Camouflage: a disguise

Chameleon has a very effective defence system- a camouflage. It takes the colour of the surface it sits on.

Canard: a false report

The opposition alleged that the report government presented in the parliament was a canard.

Candidate: a person who contends

The party has decided to change all their candidates and give election ticket to new faces.

Candour: the ability to tell the truth , especially when others don't expect one to do it; frankness

The leader's candour impressed the interviewer.

Cannibalism: the phenomenon of eating other individuals of own type

Cannibalism is found to happen in some animal species.

Canvass: to gather support

The organisation has been trying to canvass support for the great cause of stopping child abuse.

Capacious: having a lot of space

The new car is quite capacious and can accommodate all of us.

Capital punishment: death penalty

Many countries have abolished the capital punishment.

Capitulate: to accept something unwillingly; to surrender to others' wishes

At last, he capitulated to his seniors' demands and left for the tour, leaving his ailing wife alone.

Capricious: fanciful; changing behaviour suddenly

Have you ever met such a capricious child before? I haven't.

Capsize: to turn a boat upside down in water

The tsunami waves were powerful enough to capsize the ship.

Captivate: to hold; to catch (especially someone's attention)

She wore a captivating dress.

Captive: a prisoner

The captives were kept in temporary prisons.

Carcinogen: a substance that causes cancer

Many experts believe that tobacco is a carcinogen.

Cardinal: main; basic

A cardinal sin that cannot be forgiven

Career woman: a woman who puts career before family

She is by all means a career woman.

Carefree: free of any worries

Your carefree attitude will get you nowhere, said his father.

Cardiologist: a heart specialist

Caress: to touch someone affectionately

The mother caressed baby's cheek.

Cargo: goods carried in a plane, ship etc.

A cargo ship sunk near the bay, but the crew was rescued.

Carnage: cruel killing of many people

The whole scene of carnage was heartbreaking.

Carnival: an event of celebration

Carnivals of Brazil are world-famous.

Carnivore: an animal that eats other animals

Lion is a carnivore.

Cartel: a group of organisations in the same field; an association

A drug cartel

Carve: To cut and shape (usually stone or wood)

He carved a beautiful rose in the rock using his tools.

Cascade: a little waterfall

That lovely cascade was the main attraction of his garden.

Cash flow: Flow of money in and out of a business

With such a handsome cash flow available, they can trade in whatever they like.

Casket: coffin

Castaway: a person who escaped from a sinking ship or boat and managed to reach an island, and is now away from the society

Castigate: to criticise severely

Boss castigated him for his laziness.

Casting couch: an arrangement by which a person is compelled to have sex with an influential person in order to get a role in a film

Casting couch is an unethical practice and our film industry must get rid of it.

Castration: the process of removing testicles of an individual or animal

Chemical castration has been suggested as a punishment against rape.

Casual: not very important or serious

His attitude is too casual. He'll never become a doctor.

Casual clothes (not formal)

Casualty: a person who either died or got injured in a war or a campaign

The casualties were quite high in the battle that took place last year.

Catalyst: a person or event that causes rapid change

The new banking policy has proved to be the catalyst of boom in the economy.

Catastrophe: a great destruction; disaster

The oil spill in the sea led to a catastrophe; thousands of sea birds died within hours.

Catchy: captivating; easy to remember

A catchy phrase is important for a product's advertisement.

Categorise: to put things into different categories

The books are categorised into different genres, such as fantasy, sci-fi, classics etc.

Cater: to provide

They catered to the demands of employees and made necessary changes in the policy.

They are food caterers.

Causative: being the cause of something

Human error is one of the major causative factors of plane crashes.

Caustic: unkind; cruel

Her caustic remarks were most unwelcome.

Cavalcade: a group of cars, horses etc. that accompany an important person

The president's cavalcade was interrupted by a strange jeep.

Cavalry: a military unit consisting of tanks and armoured vehicles or horses and camels

Cease: to come to an end

The protests ceased as soon as government accepted the demands of the protestors.

Cede: to unwillingly give one's position to someone else

The ruler ceded the throne to his son, as he feared a revolt if he didn't.

Celestial: related to the sky or the universe; not of our world

The celestial beauty of the universe is unimaginable.

Celibate: a person who does not indulge in sex and doesn't marry

He has been a celibate ever since I've known him.

Cemetery: a place where dead bodies are buried; graveyard

Censor: to remove objectionable parts from films, books etc.

Many parts of this film have been censored.

Censor Board of India didn't approve the film.

Centenarian: a person who has crossed hundred years of age

The number of centenarians in the country is on rise.

Cerebral: related to mental abilities

A cerebral book compels the reader to think seriously about a subject.

Certify: to accept and declare something to be true; to verify

Who are you to certify anyone?

He is a certified financial advisor.

Cessation: Ending

The cessation of peace efforts in the region is most unfortunate.

Chagrin: disappointment

To my chagrin, my husband has never shown interest in the social gatherings.

Champ: Champion

Changeable: something that changes quite often

I won't dare go skiing in such a changeable weather.

Changeling: a baby that has been swapped/exchanged for another baby

A film based on a story of changelings

Chant: a word or phrase which people, especially those meditating, repeat over and over

The yogi was chanting loudly and he didn't pay attention to what was happening around him.

Chaos: a state of confusion, often mixed with anxiety

I had never been in such a chaos in all my life.

What a chaotic scene! People are running here and there; no one to take care of animals and babies.

Chap: man; guy

The old chap is always smoking.

Characteristic: a noticeable quality of a person or place

All the successful people share some characteristics, such as passion for their work, ambition and hard work.

Charade: a false and fruitless exercise

The screen-test is just a charade. Director has already chosen the next hero.

Chargeable: something that one has to pay taxes on

Income above Rs 200000 is chargeable in India.

Charisma: personal ability or power to influence others and get their admiration and respect; charm

The charisma of the new manager is such that no one comes late these days.

What a charismatic personality! I can't take my eyes off him.

Charity: giving money for the poor and needful people

Many film stars have been collecting for a charity of blind people.

Charlatan: a fraud; a fake (especially doctor)

Stop meeting that charlatan. Go to the hospital and see a real doctor.

Charm: quality of being attractive and appealing

She used her charm to get that promotion, he said, frustrated. I deserved it!

Charmless: an unpleasant, ill-mannered person

He is a charmless guy. No girl can like him, she added.

Charter: a document that formally states the rights of people or a group of people

A charter gives a department certain exclusive rights.

Chary: cautious and unwilling to do something because of risk

She is chary of investing in dotcom companies, but I want to do it.

Chase: to follow someone in order to catch them

The army chased the retreating terrorists but some of them managed to get away.

Chastise: to criticise someone severely; reprimand

The supreme court chastised the police for not acting on time.

Chatter: to keep talking informally about unimportant things

They keep chattering from dawn till dusk, wasting all the time they have.

Chauvinist: one who believes in superiority of own race or gender

He has been accused of being a male chauvinist.

Cheap: low in quality and price

My wife bought a lot of cheap items from the sale, but we don't really need them, he said.

Cheapskate: a person who hates to spend money

He is a cheapskate. He won't buy you a rose, let alone a bouquet, said her friend.

Cheat: to deceive

People cheat each other in relationships, and this causes the end of many marriages.

Checkmate: to defeat someone completely

His tactic checkmated the rival firm.

Checkmate! said the inspector and handcuffed the criminals.

Cheeky: a bit rude and funny at the same time

What a cheeky fellow! He really annoyed his dad.

Cheerful: happy

A cheerful kid hardly ever cries.

Chequered: having both successful and unsuccessful periods

The politician has a chequered career. He has won many elections and lost many.

Cherish: to preserve and care for

I cherish the sweet memories of my childhood.

Chic: stylish

The chic office of the fashion designer impressed her.

Chicanery: trickery; deceptive talks

The professional buyers didn't fall victim to the chicanery of the contractor.

Chick (highly informal or humorous): a beautiful young lady

Chickenfeed: a very small amount of money

This chickenfeed will not help the project in any manner, he said.

Chieftain: the leader of a tribe

The chieftain ordered his men to arrest every outsider.

Childish: manner or behaviour that is expected from a child and not from an adult

His childish attitude will get him into trouble one day, his father said to his mother.

Childlike: having qualities which a child has; naive

Her childlike innocence makes her more prone to deception.

Chill (weather): very cold

This chill is going to kill me, he said, shivering.

Chink: a crack or a small opening

There are chinks in the wall.

Chirp: high-pitch sounds made by birds

The sparrows were chirping on the tree.

Chit-chat: an informal conversation among friends

I still remember the chit-chat we used to do in the college canteen.

Chivalrous: honest, polite and dignified man, respectful towards women

She had never met a more chivalrous man in her entire life.

Choir: a group of singers

The choir sang a devotional song.

Choke: when a person stops breathing because of something blocking his wind pipe

He choked on a banana. He must not talk while eating.

Chomp: to chew food noisily

Don't chomp, kids! Eat properly.

Choosy: Very selective about things

This customer is very choosy about dresses. Show her the exclusive collection of our store.

Chore: a boring work one needs to do regularly

I'm wasting my life doing these chores, she said in a depressed manner.

Choreography: managing the dance moves for a scene in a film or a performance

She is the favourite choreographer of the Hollywood.

Chortle: to laugh noisily

The kid's father chortled at his innocent mistake.

Chorus: a group that sings together (often in the middle of a song)

The chorus performed badly otherwise the song could have been recorded.

Christmas eve: 24th December (a day before Christmas)

Chronic: something that has been there for a long time (especially a disease)

I have suffered from chronic headaches from last seven years.

Chronicle: written record of something that happened in the past

The historian is reading the chronicles of war.

Chubby: fat but in a pleasant manner

What a cute chubby kid!

Chuck: to throw something carelessly

Chuck the empty can in the dustbin over there, he said, not taking his eyes off TV.

Chuckle: to laugh, but in a quiet manner

The old man chuckled at the kid's joke.

Chug: the explosive sound that the engine of a vehicle makes when it is running slowly

The car chugged along the road and finally stopped.

Chum: a friend

Hello, chum! he said.

Chump: a stupid person

How dare he call me chump?

Chunk: a large piece of something

A chunk of cake isn't enough for me. I want more, she said.

Churlish: rude

Her churlish behaviour could annoy anyone.

Churn: to mix vigorously

Churning the milk using a hand-held mixer till the cream collects on the top

Cinder: a burned piece of coal

Don't step on the hot cinders!

Circulate: to move something, especially a liquid, inside something

Let the cool air in the car circulate for a while.

Circumstance: a notable factor in a situation

He was compelled to shoot under those circumstances.

Cite: to mention something to explain something else

Cite an example to explain your point.

Civilised: a society which has developed with time and has a culture, government and set of rules applicable on everyone

Anti-social elements are not welcome in a civilised society.

Clad: dressed; covered in something

A warrior clad in armour

Claimant: one who has claim over something

The claimants want to know if they will get their shares once the excavation is over.

Clairvoyant: one who claims to see what others can't; a psychic

Don't waste your money on such clairvoyants.

Clamber: to climb difficultly, using hands and feet

I can't believe how easily he clambered up the hill!

Clammy: sticky

A body clammy with sweat

Clamp: a device that holds two things together tightly

Clang: the sound of two metal objects hitting each other

The clang of a bell

Clarify: to make something clear

You need to clarify the butter to obtain ghee.

Clarify your point.

Clash: a fight

The groups clashed over the damn tennis ball.

Clasp: to hold something tightly with one's hand

The kid clasped his toy when his uncle demanded it.

Classy: fashionable and elegant

He wore a classy suit and looked quite good.

Clatter: the continuous sound made by objects hitting each other

The loud clatter was disturbing the class and the teacher went out to find where it came from.

Clause: a section of an agreement or legal document

Look at the clause 3-B. You must give a month's notice before vacating the house.

Claustrophobia: a fear of closed spaces

His claustrophobia is so intense that he wouldn't get an MRI done.

Cleanse: to clean thoroughly

Herbal water that cleans the internal systems of the body

Clearance: an official permission

You can export the goods once you get clearance from the authorities.

Cleave: to split

He cleaved his path through the plants.

Cleft: an opening, a hollow area, or a crack etc.

His chin has a cleft.

Clemency: kindness; mercy

He wrote to the president for clemency.

Clench: to tighten

He clenched his teeth in anger.

Cliff: a rocky area with at least one steep side

Cliff-hanger: a very exciting situation because the outcome is not predictable

That novel is full of cliff-hangers and I loved it.

Climax: the most exciting and often the final part

I didn't like the climax of the movie. It was too obvious.

Climber: an athlete who climbs mountains

Mr. Raman is a good climber.

Cling: to hold on to something tightly

He clung to his point despite all the opposition.

Cling to the rock! I'm coming, shouted the guide.

Clink: the sound made when two glasses hit each other lightly

They said Cheers! and clinked their glasses together.

Cloak: a cover

Under the cloak of darkness, he used to import illegal wine and drugs.

Clobber: to hit repeatedly

He clobbered the man with his fist.

Clogged: filled with something; blocked

When the arteries are clogged, the chances of a heart attack increase.

Close shave: just avoiding an unpleasant or dangerous situation

His car slipped on the road but didn't get uncontrolled. Yet it was a close shave!

Closet: a cupboard

Cloudy: with clouds

This cloudy weather is not good for flying.

Clueless: having no hint of something

The crime took place a month ago but the police are still clueless about who did it.

Clumsy: having an awkward manner or movement

He was scolded for mimicking her clumsy gait (walk).

Cluster: a group of people or similar things

A cluster of fans welcomes her wherever she goes.

Clutch: to hold something tightly

He clutched her letter to his heart and cried, remembering his dead lover.

Cluttered: untidy

Don't clutter every room! At least one of them should be tidy enough to welcome the guests, said the housewife.

Coagulate: to acquire a solid state from a liquid; to form a clot

The blood of the wounded man coagulated soon and the bleeding stopped.

Coalition: an alliance of political parties or various groups

A coalition government

Coalition forces

Coarse: not smooth or soft

His coarse voice is not pleasant to my ears, she said proudly.

Coax: to persuade someone gently

She coaxed the diplomat to tell her the state secret.

Cobbler: one who repairs shoes

Go to the cobbler and get the sole of this shoe fixed.

Cobweb: spider's net

Cocksure: excessively confident

He was cocksure about his victory. No wonder he lost.

Cocktail: an alcoholic drink prepared by mixing different drinks together

Codswallop: nonsense

Codswallop! None of them told the truth.

Coerce: to force someone to do something unpleasant

He was coerced by his father to choose the only career he didn't like.

Co-exist: exist together

Both countries can peacefully co-exist if the terrorism stops.

Cognitive: related to conscious mental processes

He can't hear properly. His cognitive hearing ability has been found to be affected by the accident.

Coherent: clear and easily understandable; logical

Her coherent speech was welcomed by the audience.

Coincidence: a chance occurrence of two events happening simultaneously

What a coincidence! I also got 50%!

Cold-blooded: extremely cruel

Only a person with no heart can commit such a cold-blooded murder.

Cold-hearted: one who doesn't feel others' pains

What else could you expect from such a cold-hearted man?

Collaborate: to work together for a common purpose

Many business leaders collaborated to unite the industry against the new tax.

Collapse: to fall down or to fail

He collapsed with a thud.

The economy collapsed as soon as the big scam was uncovered.

Collateral: a property against which a loan is given, and if the loan is not paid back, it becomes the lender's property

Her father pledged his farm as collateral to pay her medical school fees.

Collective: combined; of many people, groups etc.

Only our collective efforts can make this project successful.

Colossal: huge; very big

The colossal task of collecting donations for elections had been assigned to their group.

A colossal statue of a great leader

Combine: to join together

Many small companies combined together to form a business giant.

Comeback: to return; to regain something one had lost

His comeback as a world champion after five years was surprising.

Comfort zone: a situation in which a person remains comfortable in a familiar environment which is not challenging at all

If you want to make progress in life, you will have to leave your comfort zone and move ahead.

Comfy: comfortable

A comfy bed

Comical: funny and silly

She thinks she looked impressive, but in fact she looked comical.

Commemorate: to remember someone in a public ceremony

Before the function began, they commemorated their founders.

Commence: to begin

The meeting commenced as soon as the chairman arrived.

Commend: to praise someone

The brave kids who saved lives were commended in the Republic Day function.

Commensurate: comparable; suitable and appropriate

We have been overburdened with additional work. I hope we get commensurate bonus also.

Commission: to include or appoint officially

Two hundred new recruits were commissioned into the rapid action force this week.

The new aircraft carrier has been commissioned into the navy.

Commit: to do, especially something wrong

It was proved that he had committed the crime.

By deceiving your loyal wife, you have committed a sin.

Commitment: a promise and dedication

I won't let the enemy step on my soil. It's my commitment, said the commander.

Commodity: something that can be traded

Tea is one of the most valuable commodities of our country.

Communicable: something that can be transferred from one person to another; infectious

No sufficient steps were taken to prevent the spread of the communicable disease.

Communicative: willing to talk

She is very communicative and friendly, and that's the reason she has so many friends.

Commute: a regular journey between work and residence

Regular traffic jams make the commute very difficult. I'm thinking about renting a room near my office.

Companion: a friend or co-passenger

My companion in the railway coach was a strange man.

Books have always been my companions.

Comparatively: when compared to something else

Comparatively, group A is better than group B.

Compassion: ability to feel others' pains, and a willingness to help them

The Dalai Lama always emphasises the need for compassion.

Compatible: people or things that can live or work together easily

This software is not compatible with my PC.

They were not compatible with each other, yet they married.

Compelling: strong; convincing

There is compelling evidence to believe that the accused is innocent.

Compensate: to make up for a loss by giving something else

He dented my car and then offered me only 500 rupees to compensate.

Competent: one who can do something as good as expected; capable

Half of the items in the menu are not available. What a competent hotel!

He is competent enough to take care of his father's business.

Compile: to collect and arrange

Could you compile some articles on global warming for the presentation?

Her new album is a beautiful compilation of sweet melodies.

Complacent: satisfied, and not willing to try harder

His complacent attitude is what I like about him.

Complement: to make something better; to match

Choco cookies complement coffee quite well.

Complex: difficult to understand

Such a complex problem is hard to solve.

Compliance: agreeing to obey the rules etc.

The new constructions are in compliance with the specifications of seismic zones, so they are more resistant to earthquakes.

Complicated: difficult to understand or do

My brother draws complicated pictures for me.

Compliment: to say something nice to someone

She complimented me on my success.

Give her a nice compliment as soon as you meet her.

Compose: to create (music, literature etc.)

The music he composes is not only unique but also pleasant.

Composure: calmness

He maintained his composure throughout the interview.

Comprehend: to fully understand

We were able to comprehend his intentions and act accordingly.

Comprehensive: including everything on a subject

A comprehensive guide of Bio-chemistry

Comprise: to have as its parts

A toy comprised of many separable parts

Compromise: to agree to settle for less than the best

We must not compromise on food. We deserve the best.

They compromised, and settled the matter outside the court.

Compulsion: a strong desire that can't be controlled

Don't let any compulsion stop you from getting ahead in life.

Conceal: to hide something from someone

The truth couldn't be concealed for long.

Don't conceal your injury. Apply some antiseptic.

Concede: to admit something unwillingly

He conceded that he had not been studying hard.

Conceited: extremely proud of oneself

A conceited rich man who thinks he's above the law

Concentrate: to focus

If you won't concentrate on your studies, you'll fail again, said the boy's father.

Conceptual: based on principles and ideas

A conceptual mistake

Concerned:

(i) related

A letter addressed to anyone concerned

(ii) worried

A concerned person

Concerted: planned and coordinated

A concerted event

Concerted action to prevent the spread of wildfires

Conciliate: to end one's annoyance or disagreement with someone

It is hard to conciliate the opposition of the public and carry on with the effort.

Concise: using no unnecessary words; brief and clear

A concise answer is better than a long, unfocussed one, said the professor.

Conclusive: something that ends all doubts; decisive

A conclusive piece of evidence, sufficient to prove him guilty, was presented in the court.

Concord: a state of agreement and harmony between people and nations

While both the countries could live in concord, they kept fighting on minor issues.

Condemn: to criticise in strong words

The leader condemned the act of terrorism in the state.

Condensed: to reduce something and make it concentrated

Condensed milk is used in preparation of sweets.

Condolence: expression of sympathy on the occasion of someone's death

She wrote a letter of condolence to her friend.

Conducive: providing conditions helpful in development of something

The environment in our country is not conducive to the development of sports.

Confederation: an organization of people or groups

A confederation of various media companies

Confess: to admit one's wrongdoing

Now that I've confessed, I feel much better, said the guilty.

Confide: to tell a trustable person a secret

The chief confided his secretary with his passwor.

Confidential: secret; something that can't be revealed

A confidential report on army activities

A confidential bank document

Confine: to limit

Fire-fighters successfully confined the fire to a limited area.

Confiscate: to take away someone's possession for a limited time, as a way of punishment

The court ordered his passport to be confiscated until the case was over.

Conflict: a disagreement (sometimes an armed conflict)

The conflict between the family members worsened and they stopped talking to each other.

The conflict between the two countries developed into a war.

Conform: to behave as society expects one to behave

All the new army recruits were expected to conform, and that's what they did.

Confront: to face

They confronted each other twice during the tournament.

Avoid a direct confrontation with the boss.

Congenial: friendly

She found her new neighbourhood quite congenial.

Congested: blocked ; packed

I don't want to be in such a congested room.

Conglomerate: a big firm that owns many small firms

A well-known business conglomerate

Congregation: a gathering

A congregation of wolves around a rock

A congregation of people around a religious leader

Conjecture: to guess

They conjectured that the economy would get over the recession soon.

Conjure: to make something appear from the thin air, as if by a magic trick

Magician conjured a bird with a flick of his wand.

Suddenly he conjured out of the thick fog.

Connive: to plan dishonestly for one's advantaged

He connived with the company and provided them secret information, and was caught receiving a commission from them.

Conquer: to take control of a foreign country by force

Alexander the Great conquered many countries.

Conscience: something inside a person that judges his actions to be morally right or wrong

My conscience is clear, said the informer.

Conscious: awake; aware of something

He was conscious before he took the medicine.

Conscript: to force someone to join army

Many young men were conscripted during the world war.

Consensus: an agreement; a generally accepted opinion

There was a consensus among people that the new tax was unfair.

Consent: to agree to something

They all consented to go to France on a holiday.

Consequence: result of an action (often a negative one)

He was fully aware of the consequences of his action, yet he did it.

Consider: to take into account; to think about something

He didn't even consider their opinion before making the final decision.

Considerate: kind

How considerate of him to lend us his room for a night!

Consistent: not changing quickly; steady

Her performance has been consistent.

Consolation: something that makes a sad person feel a little better

The losers got consolation prizes.

Consolidate: to strengthen something by uniting its components

The consolidation of the IT industry is important, said the minister.

Conspiracy: a secret plan to do something bad

When the dictator came to know about conspiracy against him, he ordered the conspirators to be shot dead.

Constantly: all the time

He sings constantly when taking a bath.

Consternation: a feeling of dismay and anxiety

To my consternation, the chemist had left already.

Constraint: something that limits something

Despite all the financial constraints, he started his own business.

Constrict: to become narrow

The pipe constricted due to the vacuum.

Constructive: something positive and useful

Your constructive actions will get you ahead while your destructive acts will pull you back, the teacher said to the class.

Consume: to use or eat

The new software has consumed all the phone memory.

The consumption of fuel in the country has increased.

Contagious: something, usually a disease, that spreads by touching; infectious

A highly contagious unknown disease killed millions of people in the 19th century.

Contaminate: to make something impure by adding harmful substances

Contaminated water causes many health problems.

Contemplate: to consider something for a long time

He's contemplating doing a Ph.D. after M.Sc.

Contemporary: of the same time as something else, or of the present

Many contemporary authors have learned from his style of writing.

The Palace, whose remains can still be seen, was described in detail by the contemporary historians.

Contempt: disrespect; dislike

Contempt of court is a serious matter.

Contend: to compete

He is contending in the national archery championship.

Contention: disagreement

A contention that worsens the relations of two countries

Context: the situation in which the event being discussed takes place

Please consider the context in which he made that statement.

Contingency: something that can happen in future and block the progress of something

A contingency plan must always be kept in mind, just

in case the main plan seems to be failing.

Contortionist: a person who can twist and bend own body in a very unusual manner

I can't believe what that contortionist just did! He rotated his feet at an angle of 180 degrees!

Contraceptive: a pill taken to avoid getting pregnant

Contract: to become smaller

The sweater contracted after the first wash.

Contradict: to oppose

His point contradicts yours. Now it's up to the judges to decide who is right.

Contravene: to break a law or rule

None of your acts should contravene a law, said the lawyer.

Contrive: to arrange cleverly

Would it be possible for you to contrive a meeting with her? I really want to meet her.

Controversy: a disagreement that affects and interests many people

The whole controversy was politically motivated.

Conundrum: a difficult problem

This conundrum has puzzled many people.

Convalesce: to rest until one recovers after a health problem

The doctor advised her to convalesce for a month after her knee surgery.

Convene: to meet; to assemble

The heads of departments convened to discuss cooperation between various departments.

Convention: meeting

Geneva Convention

Converge: to meet at a point

Side road and main road converge after one kilometre.

Converse:

(i) the opposite

The converse is true.

(ii) to talk

We conversed for hours.

Convey: to tell; to express

I hope he conveyed my message to him.

Convict: the guilty

The convict was taken to another prison.

Convoluted: twisted; complicated

A convoluted paragraph that one can't understand

A convoluted path

Convoy: a group of vehicles, ships etc.

The convoy was attacked by enemy submarines.

Convulsion: an uncontrollable, jerky movement of muscles due to an illness

He was admitted in the hospital after a convulsion.

Cooperate: to help; to work together

They cooperated with each other.

He cooperated with police in the investigation.

Cope: to deal

It is hard to cope with high fever without medicine.

Copious: more than enough; abundant

She shopped copiously with my credit card.

Copycat: one who copies others' works

The director was called a copycat by movie critics, because many scenes in the movie were stolen from the foreign works.

Cordial: friendly

Cordial relations between the two neighbours

Core: the centre; the most important part of something

Earth's core is extremely hot, he said.

The core process must be carried out with caution.

Cornucopia: a large quantity of something

A cornucopia of books of all genres

Corpse: dead body

The corpses of the dead soldiers were all over the battlefield.

Correlation: connection; relation

There is a correlation between malnutrition and retarded physical and mental growth.

Corresponding: resulting from something

Depreciation of currency and corresponding price hike

Corroborate: to add evidence to a statement, theory etc.

The discovery of dual nature of light has corroborated his theories.

Corrode: to get damaged slowly by rain, wind, chemical process etc.

The mountains corroded over thousands of years.

Cosmic: of universe

Cosmic waves

Cosmopolitan: having things and experiences from various parts of the world

Singapore City is a cosmopolitan city.

Cost-effective: good value for a person's money

A cost-effective alternative to an expensive product

Cosy: comfortable

A cosy room with everything one needs

Couch potato: one who watches TV for many hours every day

He has become a couch potato since we have shifted here.

Countdown: counting backwards to zero

The countdown has begun. Exactly fifteen seconds later the satellite will be launched.

Counteract: to take an action opposite to another action

The gas had leaked out but the authorities counteracted quickly and neutralised it with another gas.

Counterbalance: to produce equal and opposite effect against another effect so that a state of balance is attained

Her low grades in science were counterbalanced by excellent grades in Math.

Counterpart: a person who has the same work as another person has, but at a different place

Coincidentally, they and their European counterparts were working on the same topic at the same time.

Countless: too many to be counted

At present, there are countless job opportunities in the country.

Countryside: rural area

Our countryside is so beautiful that I don't want to live in the city anymore.

Coup: taking over the government by force

The elected government of our neighbouring country was replaced by its army commander in a bloodless coup.

Courteous: polite; showing respect for others

His courteous manners impress everybody.

Court marshal: a trial in a military court

The captain was court marshalled for not being on duty when he was ordered to be.

Courtship: a period of romantic relationship before marriage

Not just human beings, but many animal species also exhibit courtship behaviour.

Cover-up: hiding a crime or wrongdoing from people

The government's cover-up of the scam was condemned by media.

Covet: to desire something that belongs to someone else very much

An Olympic medal is what every athlete covets for.

Cower: to move back and crouch in fear

He cowered in the corner, fearing his father's anger.

Crack: to find a solution to a difficult problem

We cracked the problem at last!

He cracked the entrance test in his second attempt.

Crackdown: dealing with something severely

The Prime Minister promised a crackdown on corruption.

Crackle: a sound of many short, sharp noises

The crackle of popcorn in the machine

Crackle made when a paper is crushed by hands

Crafty: dishonest and cleverly chosen

Her crafty language doesn't impress me.

Crap: very bad and useless

What a crap movie!

Crave: to desire something very much

He is not a bad person. He craves love!

Crawl: to walk slowly, usually on knees and hands

The baby crawled across the room and his parents watched him.

The project crawled to the end somehow.

Credential: qualification; skills

She doesn't have credentials required for this job.

Credible: trustable

Credible information

Creditworthy: a person who a bank can trust for the repayment of loan

Bank didn't find him creditworthy and refused a loan.

Credulous: one who easily believes others

My son is so credulous that he has been cheated many times.

Creep: to walk slowly and quietly, without attracting attention

The thief crept to our roof but was caught there.

Creepy: strange, and causing fear

A creepy story

A creepy voice

Crematorium: a place where dead bodies are burned

Crescent: a curved, half-moon like shape with two pointed ends

Mother Teresa Crescent road in Delhi

Crest: the highest point of a hill

We reached the crest with great difficulty.

Crew: a group of members employed on a ship, plane etc.

The entire crew was punished for showing negligence towards the passengers.

Crib: a small bed for a baby

Cross-examine: to ask questions to get information out

The lawyers cross-examined the witness.

Crossfire: bullets being fired from two or more directions

Many soldiers were caught in the crossfire and lost their lives.

Crucial: extremely important

Hard work is crucial to success.

Crude:

(1) not refined

Crude oil

(2) rude

Crude manners of a person

Cruise: a fast ship on which people enjoy holidays

We took a cruise to Canada.

Crumble: to break; to fall down

He crumbled under the pressure of vigorous investigation and told the police everything.

Crumpled: having many folds; wrinkled

A crumpled cloth that needs to be ironed

Crunchy: solid food that breaks with a cracking sound

I like crunchy chocolates.

Crush: a strong feeling of attraction and liking

He had a crush on her, but when she paid no attention, he moved on.

Crust: solid outer covering of something

There is molten chocolate inside the thin crust of the cookie.

Crux (the crux): the most important part

The crux of the matter is that we must reduce the amount of salt in the diet.

Cry-baby: one who cries and complains a lot

Don't be a cry-baby, man! You know you have to do it alone.

Cuddle: to put one's arms around someone or something and hold it close

The baby cuddled the teddy bear and fell asleep.

Cul-de-sac: a dead end; a road that leads nowhere

The house is located at the end of a cul-de-sac.

Culinary: related to cooking

Culminate (culminate in something): to end in something

Our holidays culminated in a disaster when our car broke down on the icy road and we got stuck for the night.

Culprit: one who has done something wrong

The culprit behind the riots was found and arrested soon.

Cult: a religious group with strange beliefs

Cumbersome: heavy and awkward

The cumbersome process of starting a business in India

Cumulative: increasing by more and more additions

Cumulative stresses may cause major health problems.

Cunning: tricky and clever

The cunning salesman sold us damaged goods!

Curative: able to cure a condition

Curative Herbal products

Curb: to limit

The central bank has now been taking steps to curb inflation.

Curdle: to get thick and develop lumps

The soup began to curdle after a while when we were boiling it.

Curious: eager to know something; interested

The new student is very curious, and it's good for him.

Curse: to say bad and rude words to someone when angry

He cursed the colony kids who broke his glass.

Curtail: to limit

We really need to curtail our expenditure if we want to save some money.

Cushy: quite easy

Well, it was a cushy task.

Custody: legal right to take care of a child who doesn't live with both of his parents or has no parents

The custody of the child was given to his grandmother.

Customise: to make or design according to the customer's specifications

A customised holiday tour is usually expensive.

A customised suit

Cutback: to reduce the use of something

I should cut back on my coffee. I've already had seven cups since the morning!

Cut-throat: fierce and often harmful

Cut-throat competition among various news channels to attract viewers

Cutting-edge: modern; latest

Our institute uses cutting-edge technology to teach students.

Cynical: one who believes others are selfish

Don't be cynical! You don't know her circumstances yet.

D

Dabble: to try something for a while

He dabbled in tennis at the age of sixteen; of course, he didn't know he would make it his profession.

Damn!: an expression of frustration and anger

Damn! I forgot to bring the passes.

Damp: slightly wet; moist

I can't wear these damp clothes! I should iron them first.

Dangle: to hang loosely

He dangled the keys on a nail on the wall.

Daredevil: one who takes unnecessary risks by doing dangerous things

He thinks he is a daredevil, but in fact he is just a fool performing those silly bike-stunts without prior training.

Daresay: to agree with someone

He's a damn idiot. I daresay he is.

Dash: to move hurriedly

He dashed to the counter and threw the stuff he had bought in front of the attendant.

Dashing: stylish and quite confident

A dashing young man

He made a dashing presentation.

Daunt: to worry and scare

They were daunted by the technology they had never seen in their life.

Dawn: the time just before the sunrise

The birds wake up well-before the dawn.

Daydream: to dream while awake

He thought he could pass the test without preparation. He was daydreaming, of course.

Dazzling: an extremely bright light that makes one unable to see for a while

A dazzling white light from the other vehicle forced me to slow down.

Deadlock: a point in an agreement which neither side is willing to compromise on

We hit a deadlock in negotiations when they refused to lower the price even a bit, and our management refused to buy at that price.

Deadly: something that can cause death

He delivered a deadly blow which made his opponent fall unconscious in the ring.

Deafening: very loud

They played music at a deafening sound.

Death-defying: extremely dangerous

His death-defying stunts are unbelievable.

Debacle: a complete failure; a disaster

No debacle can stop me, he said.

Debase: to degrade; to humiliate

Every crime against tourists debases the image of the nation.

Debatable: not necessarily true

Whether genetically modified foods are safe is a debatable subject.

Debonair: confident and good looking

He is a debonair and many girls want to marry him.

Debut: first public performance or exposure

His debut speech established him as a good speaker.

Her debut film was a flop, but she gave many hits afterwards.

Decaf: decaffeinated; something from which caffeine has been removed

A decaf coffee

Decapitate: to cut a person's head

The king ordered to decapitate him.

Decay: to get damaged slowly; to decompose

Decaying flowers must be replaced with the fresh ones, she ordered.

Deceased: dead

A deceased man

Deceit: deliberately hiding the truth; dishonesty

The deceit became known to the customers and soon he lost his business.

Decent: socially acceptable and appreciable

His decent manners made him a respected person.

Decentralise: to transfer power and control of a central authority to smaller divisions or units

Decentralisation has proved to be beneficial for the company, as now our junior managers can make informed decisions.

Decimate: to destroy; to kill in great numbers

The weaker civilisations were decimated by the stronger ones.

Decipher: to decode a hidden message or to read a bad handwriting

Finally the navy engineers deciphered the coded message intercepted from the enemy ship.

Decisive: critical; something that strongly affects the result

His amazing performance was a decisive factor in the team's victory.

Decline: to become less; to go down gradually

The currency declined in value constantly over a year.

The decline of the empire was due to the overconfidence of its rulers.

Decorum: controlled and polite behaviour

Decorum is an important part of a gentleman's personality.

Decoy: something used as a trap

They mercilessly used children as decoys to carry out illegal activities.

Decree: an order or statement that something must be done

The decree authorised the possession of non-residents' properties by the state.

Dedicated: one who gives time and energy to a task; devoted to a task

He is a dedicated student of arts.

Deduce: to reach an answer from the known information, facts etc.

The conclusion we deduced proved to be wrong.

De facto: in fact

The de facto terrorist commander was never caught, but all the members were.

Defame: to make somebody infamous; to damage one's reputation

The news article was clearly intended to defame him.

Default: non-payment of a debt, bill etc.

So many people defaulted on the bank loans that many banks filed for bankruptcy.

Defendant: one who is accused in the court of law

The defendant had no proof to prove his innocence.

Deference: respect and polite submission

They mistook his deference for his weakness.

Defy: to refuse to obey the authorities

In the movie 'Gladiator', a gladiator defies a king.

Deflate: to remove air from something

Kids deflated the tyres of the car.

Deform: to spoil the shape of something; distort

Police found that the face of the dead body was deformed in order to hide its true identity.

Deft: quick and skilled

Obviously, a deft hand has created this statue.

Degenerate: to reduce in quality

The machines degenerated to pieces of junk after the factory remained closed for years.

Degrade: to lower something's value and quality

Adulteration degrades the food items.

He has degraded himself through his actions.

Deity: a god; or God

Déjà vu: a feeling that what is happening now has already been experienced by one in the past

The strange feeling of déjà vu shocked her a bit.

Delegation: a group of individuals chosen to speak on behalf of a country or an organisation

The French delegation doesn't seem satisfied with the talks.

Deliberate: intentional

A deliberate attempt to hurt someone physically

Delicate: something that should be handled with care because it breaks easily

How shocking! Those delicate glass items were thrown here and there carelessly.

Delight: a feeling of great pleasure

I can do anything for customer's delight.

Delirium: a state of confusion or hallucination

He was still in a state of delirium when the Chairman made an unexpected visit.

Deluded: believing what cannot be true

He is deluded if he thinks he is going to get that promotion.

Demagogue: a politician who wins by addressing peoples' emotions and not by his work or policies

Demagogues are in power at present, he said.

Demarcation: a fixed boundary

The borders were clearly demarcated on the map in order to avoid any confusion.

Demeanour: the way one behaves

He had a calm demeanour all the time.

Demerit: disadvantage; fault

Merits and demerits of the theory were discussed.

Demise: death

Sudden demise of the leader put the country in a state of grief.

Demographics: the characteristics of people living in an area (age, income etc.)

The company studied the demographics of the region before entering it.

Demolish: to destroy

The illegal building was demolished under the supervision of police.

Demoralise: to bring someone's morale down

Lack of government's support demoralised the armed forces.

Demote: to lower one's position

All those responsible for the huge loss of revenue were demoted.

Demystify: to make something clear

He demystified the matter for us.

Denigrate: to state that something is bad; to criticise unfairly

I denigrate no one. I say what must be said, she said.

Deny: to refuse to accept; to reject

You can't deny the facts. You must accept them.

Depart: to leave

The bus arrived early but it departed at the set time.

Depict: to show something by describing it or through a picture

He depicted his village life in his book.

Depletion: reduction in quantity

Depletion of Ozone layer is a matter of concern.

Deplorable: bad; awful

I can't become his friend. His thoughts are deplorable.

Depreciate: to lose value

The machinery in a factory depreciates every year.

Deprive: to keep something away from someone

Don't deprive your children of love.

Derail: to get off track

The train derailed but no one was hurt.

Our plans derailed when we couldn't manage the funds required.

Deranged: unable to behave normally, usually because of a mental illness

She is a drug-addict. No wonder she is a bit deranged.

Deride: to laugh at somebody as if they are stupid; to ridicule

Instead of deriding others, he should learn to behave sensibly.

Derive: to get something from something else

He derives his wisdom from books.

Deriving a formula from given equations

Derogatory: disrespectful; insulting

The actress made a derogatory remark against the great man but apologised later.

Descend: to come down

Kids descended the jungle gym and went home.

Descendant: successor; one who comes after someone in the same family line

All the descendants of the great king proved to be unworthy.

Dermatologist: skin specialist

Deserted: abandoned

The old fort is now a deserted place where nobody ever comes.

Deserving: one who deserves something

Only a deserving candidate must get the job.

Desiccated: completely dried

Desiccated grapes form raisins.

Designation: title

What is your designation, sir? I'm General Manager.

Desirable: attractive and wanted

He is handsome, intelligent and rich, and obviously a desirable groom for many young ladies, said the old man.

Desolate: isolated and not attractive anymore

A desolate garden

Despair: a feeling of hopelessness

He thought of leaving the country in a state of despair.

Desperately: extremely

"I desperately want her love!" said the boy.

Despicable: bad and unpleasant; dreadful

He is not a despicable man, if you ask me.

Despise: to strongly dislike

He despises his cruel boss.

Dessert: sweet dish eaten at the end of a meal

It's dessert time!

Destabilise: to make something unstable

The PM accused that the opposition was trying to destabilise the government.

Destiny: fate

She is boss's daughter. Reaching the top post was her destiny, he said bitterly.

Detain: to confine; to stop the progress

The police detained the suspects for questioning.

Deteriorate: to become worse

The condition of that patient deteriorates every day.

Deterrent: something which prevents someone from taking an action

The nuclear weapons of both countries acted as deterrent against war.

Dethrone: to force a ruler to abandon his position

The king was dethroned by his own son.

Detrimental: damaging

Smoking is detrimental to everyone's health.

Devalue: to reduce the exchange rate of a currency

The nation devalued its currency to boost trade.

Devastating: causing destruction

His third consecutive failure was a devastating blow to his plans.

Deviant: not normal; unusual

Her behaviour was deviant all the time and she acted very oddly.

Devise: to think or invent a new system, plan etc.

He devised a technique to overcome the problem.

Devotion: loyalty and love

Her devotion for her family is admirable.

Devour: to eat completely

I saw a king cobra devour a small snake.

Dexterity: ability to do something quickly and well

He makes clay-pots with great dexterity.

Diabolical: shockingly bad

The patients were kept in a diabolical condition.

Diaspora: the spread of people of one country; dispersion

The Indian Diaspora can be seen in western countries.

Dichotomy: a difference between two opposite things; division

There is always a dichotomy

between my New Year resolutions and my actions.

Diddle: to get money from someone dishonestly; to cheat

That general store diddles the customers by providing them less than the promised quantity.

Diffident: not confident; shy

Such diffident manners will not do in an interview, said the coach.

Diffuse: to spread

Blue diffused in the water quickly.

Dignity: calm and respectable behaviour

She acted with dignity and got everyone's appreciation.

Digress: to divert from the main subject

He was talking about marketing but he digressed and started telling us his stories.

Diktat: an order that must be obeyed

The dictator issued a diktat that everyone must pay ten per cent of their incomes as security tax.

Dilemma: a difficult situation in which one of the two options (each with own merits and demerits) has to be chosen

It was an ethical dilemma whether he should compromise his values to save his job.

Diligent: careful and hardworking

We need diligent employees for this task.

Dim: not very bright

Dim light of torch wasn't adequate for us to work in the dark basement.

Dip: to immerse (put) something in a liquid for a short time

He dipped the biscuit in the tea and ate it.

Dire: very serious

There will be dire consequences of new FDI policy, warned a politician.

Disapprove: to not approve; to condemn

The plan was disapproved.

She strongly disapproves any sort of violence.

Disarmament: giving up weapons

Nuclear disarmament is a step towards a safer world, he opined.

Disarray: a state of confusion

We left the house in disarray as we hurried to the airport.

Discard: to get rid of something

They discarded the old, useless custom.

Discerning: showing good judgement about quality, fashion etc.

She is a discerning woman and never buys faulty goods.

Disciplinary: related to discipline and its enforcement

Disciplinary action will be taken against those found guilty of disrupting the class.

Disclose: to show what was hidden

He disclosed that there were disagreements among company directors.

Discord: a state of disagreement

There was discord among family members due to property matters.

Discourse: a speech or an article on a subject

A yoga discourse

Discrepancy: a difference between two things which should not be there

Investigation was ordered after a discrepancy was found in company accounts.

Discrete: separate; distinct

The mosquito repellent they make has a discrete identity and is more popular than their other products.

Discriminate (against): to treat somebody unfairly due to personal reasons (hatred towards a religion, race, colour etc.)

A good teacher does not discriminate against any student.

Disdain: to not respect someone

He looked at me with such a disdain, though I can't imagine a reason why!

Disinherit: to prevent one's son or daughter from getting any share in one's property

He disinherited his son from his estate.

Dismay: disappointment

A feeling of dismay filled every heart as we lost the match in the last over.

Disobey: to not follow an order

He disobeyed his boss and lost his job.

Disown: to announce publically that one has no relation with someone

John's father said he would disown him if he didn't mend his ways.

Disparity: inequality

Disparity between rich and poor is increasing.

Disparity between the first benchers and the last benchers

Dispatch: send

They dispatched the reserve unit to the battlefield.

Disperse: to spread

The wind dispersed the dry leaves he had collected in a corner.

Disposable: something that should be thrown away after first use

A disposable syringe must not be reused.

Disrupt: to disturb something going on normally

The meeting was disrupted by an unusual noise in the air duct.

Disregard: no respect for something

Some students have disregard for the school rules.

Disseminate: to spread

Dissociate: to separate

I dissociate myself with the whole episode.

Dissuade: to persuade not to do something

She dissuaded him from starting his own business.

Distinguished: well-known and admired

A distinguished author has been invited to the institute.

Distracted: not paying attention because one has worries in mind

I found him a bit distracted. He didn't say a word.

Distrust: to not trust

She distrusts every outsider.

Ditch: to get rid of

She ditched him as soon as she met the new boy.

Ditto: to agree with what has been said

I think the exam was tough. Ditto!

Diverge: to become separate

The main road diverges into east and west roads in the next village.

Diversify: to become varied

The company diversified into three new sectors.

Divest (business): to sell either a business or its part; to get rid of

The company was doing fine. Nobody knows why three company directors divested so suddenly.

Divine: Godly; so good that it looks not of this world

The food was divine, I must say.

Divisive: something that divides people

Divisive politics is not good for communal harmony.

Divulge: to reveal

She won't divulge the company partners' names and details.

Dizzy: a feeling that everything around one is turning around

He felt dizzy after two drinks.

Docile: easy to control; quiet

He is not as docile as he looks at the moment.

Doctrine: a set of beliefs

Buddhist doctrine

Dodge: to avoid being hit (mostly by bending to one side)

He dodged the stones hurled at him.

He dodged my question.

Dogged: very determined

He doggedly supported his viewpoint.

Dogma: a belief everyone is expected to accept without questioning

I don't follow any religious dogmas.

Dog-tired: extremely tired

We were dog-tired after a busy day.

Domain: area

Take your technical questions to him. It's his domain.

Domesticate: to make an animal accept human control; to tame

Some monks have successfully domesticated tigers!

Domineering: one who doesn't care about other people's feelings and tries to dominate them

He is a domineering man. No one would want to work under him.

Doodle: to draw pictures when one is bored

The teacher caught him doodling in the class.

Doom: destruction

Don't see doom everywhere. There are positive signs too!

Doping: to take performance-enhancing, banned drugs before a sports tournament

Five players were found guilty of doping and were expelled from the Olympics.

Dormant: present but hidden

His dormant energy needs to be awakened.

Double-cross: to deceive the one who has been a partner in a wrong-doing

He was sent by the smugglers to get the consignment of drugs, but he took it and disappeared. In other words, he double-crossed his own partners.

Double standard: two sets of rules for similar situations, especially to favour someone

Dad scolded me for taking his car out but appreciated my brother for his driving when he did the same! Aren't these double standards?

Double standards of China are quite obvious, said the expert.

Double-talk: a spoken sentence that has more than one meaning

Double-talks of politicians

Downcast: hopeless

He seems quite downcast to me.

Downfall: sudden loss of power; ruin

Downfall of Hitler is attributed to his wrong and inhuman policies.

Downgrade: to lower something's value or someone's rank

Addition of silver or other metals downgrades gold.

His ranking was downgraded after he lost his first match in the tournament.

Downhill: towards the bottom of the hill

We rode downhill at a great speed.

Down payment: an initial payment made at the time of buying something

I made a down payment of Rs 50000 when I bought the plot. I'll pay the rest in monthly instalments.

Downplay: to make something look less serious than it actually is

The entire crisis was downplayed by the board of directors.

Downright: total; absolute

It was downright dangerous to cross the river when it was overflowing.

Downsize: to remove some employees from the service in order to make the company smaller and save money

The management decided to downsize to cope with the recession.

Dowry: the goods and money given to the groom by the parents of bride

Dowry is not an ethical or legal practice.

Doze: to take a short sleep; to take a nap

He dozed in the class.

Drag: to pull something along the ground

He dragged the heavy table across the room.

Dramatic: sudden

A dramatic decrease in his appetite could be a matter of concern.

Drawback: disadvantage

Drawbacks of a theory

There is a drawback of this plan- it is not practical!

Dread: to feel frightened by something

She dreads rats!

Dreamlike: that doesn't look real

They met in dreamlike weather-bright sunshine and rain at the same time.

Drenched: completely wet

He was drenched in rain water when he entered the hall.

Dribble: to flow in drops or in a very thin stream

Water dribbled into a natural pond.

Drift: to move slowly (due to wind or water) without being controlled by anyone

The log of wood drifted on the surface of the lake.

Drip: to fall in small drops

Blood dripped into the bottle drop-by-drop.

Driven: determined to do something

The driven young man succeeded at last.

Drizzle: rain in the form of tiny drops

It drizzled very pleasantly and I went out to enjoy it.

Drool: saliva flowing from the mouth

The baby was drooling and his mom came with a hanky in her hand to clean his face.

Droop: to bend downwards and hang

His droopy eyes told us he was about to fall asleep.

Dropout: one who left his college or school before completing the course

A college dropout who became a great businessman

Drought: a time period of very little or no rain and very little or no water available to people

Drought killed thousands of animals and human beings.

Drowsy: feeling sleepy

He didn't sleep for two days. No wonder he was drowsy.

Dubious:

(i) not able to be trusted

He is a person of dubious nature. No one trusts him.

(ii) one who doubts something

She has been dubious about me since our marriage.

Dud: having no value; useless

His latest novel is a dud.

Duet: a song sung by two people

A lovely duet

Dumbfounded: shocked and unable to speak

She was dumbfounded by the shocking overnight change in his behaviour.

Dump: to throw away carelessly

He dumped the garbage bag into the dustbin.

Dupe: to trick someone into doing something

He duped me into telling lies to his parents and I didn't even realise he had mislead me!

Durable: that lasts for a long time

A durable chair that will serve the buyer for years

Dusk: the time after sunset but before dark

He works from dawn till dusk.

Dwell: to live at a place

They used to dwell in the forests and hunt animals.

Dynamic: full of energy

A dynamic kid

A dynamic lifestyle

Dynasty: a family that has ruled a place for many generations

Maurya dynasty ruled a large part of India for years.

E

Eager: keen and impatient; wanting to know or have something very much

He said he was eager to know my story.

Earnest: serious

She wanted to marry an earnest and handsome boy.

Earshot: as far as one can hear; hearing distance

Now he is out of earshot, let's do the talking.

Earthly: related to physical life; not heavenly

Earthly joys are important too.

Easy-going: one who takes thing easy and doesn't get worried easily

An easy-going person is usually stress-free.

I like his easy-going attitude.

Eavesdrop: to deliberately listen to someone's private conversation

Many people tell me she eavesdrops, and I think they're right.

Ebony: a dark coloured wood

Eccentric: unusual

His eccentric ways make him stand apart from others, but sometimes they make him look strange.

Echo: when a sound is heard repeatedly, mostly in large open spaces or big halls

I could hear the echo of my own voice coming from the other side of the valley.

Eclipse: to make another person or thing seem less important

Her dance performance eclipsed all other performances.

Ecstasy (drug): a drug that makes a person see and hear things which aren't there, and makes the person feel good

Stay away from ecstasies if you want to live longer, the doctor advised him.

Edge: advantage

Her swiftness gives her an edge over the competitors.

Edification: exercising one's mind by learning new things

The students are instructed to read magazines and surf informative websites for edification.

Eerie: frightening and strange

An eerie silence spread across the hall.

An eerie feeling of someone's presence in the house

Efface: to remove; to wipe out

Efface someone's memories of something

Effigy: a thing which is made to look like a person and represents that person

The crowd burned effigy of the tainted and convicted leader.

Effrontery: rudeness along with boldness

His effrontery annoyed many people, including his teachers.

Egalitarian: believing in equality of all people

An egalitarian thinker

Egocentric: a selfish person who doesn't care about others

I never met such an egocentric woman in my life!

Egotist: one who is fully absorbed in oneself

That actress is an egotist. Wait for half a decade or so, and then she'll get down to earth.

Elaborate: to explain in detail

Could you please elaborate your point?

Elapse: to pass; to go past

Years elapsed, and he lost the youth he was so proud of.

Elated: excited due to happiness; delighted

He was elated by the news that he had made it into the merit list.

Electrifying: something that excites a lot

An electrifying speech

Elegant: Gentle and graceful

What an elegant personI met today!"

An elegant way of living

Elementary: basic; fundamental

Before you go for higher studies, you must have sound elementary knowledge of the subject.

Elevate: to lift

His speech elevated our spirits.

The hoarding was elevated with the help of long ropes.

Elicit: to draw out; cause

The announcement of huge profits elicited the demand for bonus.

Eliminate: to remove completely

There are some loopholes that must be eliminated from the law.

Elite: the most powerful and high-ranked individuals of a society

There is a growing discontent among the elites of the state. They believe that the government is taxing them too much.

Elixir: a liquid with magical powers that can cure a condition

The new medicine is proving to be elixir for the epilepsy patients.

Elongate: to make longer and thinner

The kid elongated the elastic as much as he could.

Eloquent: that sends a strong message clearly

An eloquent speech

Elucidate: to make clear

They must elucidate what they meant by 'not good enough', said the merchant angrily.

Elude: to just escape from one's reach

A medical seat just eluded him!

Emanate: to spread out; to express one's feelings by the way one looks and acts

Warmth emanated from the bonfire, and we enjoyed the cold night.

Emasculate: to reduce the effectiveness of something

All efforts to emasculate the effect of auditors' negative report on government's expenditure failed.

Embargo: an order that stops something temporarily; ban

An embargo on import of sugar from the neighbouring country

Embark: to board a ship

They embarked the cruise for Mumbai at Singapore port.

Embarrass: to make one feel uncomfortable and nervous

He felt embarrassed by his son's behaviour at the party.

Embedded: fixed

The diamonds were embedded in the golden belt.

Embellish: to decorate; to improve the looks of something by adding something else

A crown embellished with jewels

Embolden: to make one feel brave

He was emboldened by his father's high social rank.

Embrace: to hold tightly into arms

The mother embraced her daughter as soon as she saw her after years.

King Ashoka embraced Buddhism.

Emend: to correct

The article was emended after public demand.

Emerge: to come out of something; to appear

He emerged from behind a huge rock.

He emerged a winner.

Eminent: well-known

An eminent painter

Empathise: to feel other person's pain

She empathised with me and it felt good.

Emphatic: forceful; confident and bold; insistent

Audience were emphatic that they wanted to hear his song again.

Empower: to give someone power and authority to act

Women empowerment is necessary for the nation's progress.

Emulate: to try to achieve something that other person has

Now that she has done it, her sisters are trying to emulate her success.

Enact: to perform

The play was enacted beautifully.

Enamoured: liking very much

He is enamoured with our natural lifestyle.

Enchanting: very pleasant

An enchanting, breath-taking scenery

Enclosed: covered; surrounded by something

The city was enclosed within high walls and couldn't be conquered easily.

Encompass: to include

This description encompasses all the details we need.

Encroach: to gradually occupy or take away something

Fertile land of the jungle has been encroached on by the ever-spreading desert.

Endanger: to put something in danger

Many lives were endangered due to the leakage of poisonous gas from the factory.

Endeavour: to try to do something (often challenging)

We endeavoured to climb the mountain in minimum time and set a record.

Endorse: to support or promote

The famous actor endorsed the new brand of soap.

Endow: to provide money for building or to an existing hospital, college, school etc.

The millionaire endowed many libraries to promote education.

Endure: to suffer but not give up

He endured through difficult times.

Enervating: taking away all one's energy

Biking in such a scorching heat is really enervating.

Enforce: to make people accept something; to make compulsory

The military regime enforced new, tougher laws upon people.

Engrave: to cut words or pictures in a hard surface

To engrave one's name on steel utensils

He engraved a heart on a tree.

Engulf: to swallow; to overcome

Royal Python engulfed entire rabbit as we were watching.

Bigger firms engulf smaller ones.

Enhance: to improve

I want to enhance the shape of my body by reducing fat.

Enigmatic: mysterious

An enigmatic caller gave him the warning that he must be more careful in future.

Enlist: to join the armed forces

Both the brothers enlisted when the war began.

Enmity: strong feeling of hatred; hostility

He seems to be holding enmity in his heart.

Enormous: very large; huge

He has got enormous muscles.

Enrich: to improve something by adding something valuable to it

This class had been enriched by the foreign students who took admission this year.

En route: on the way

We are en route to Las Vegas.

Enslave: to make someone a slave by force

Thousands of people were enslaved by the new ruler.

Ensure: to make sure

We must try hard to ensure the safety of tourists.

Entangle: to get caught in a net or a similar thing

The insect got entangled in a cobweb and could not get out.

Enthralling: having one's full attention

The movie was enthralling. I will watch it again.

Enthusiasm: a great interest in something, and willingness to participate in it

He has a lot of enthusiasm for dancing. He will become a great dancer, I'm sure.

Entitle: to give someone something as a right

He is entitled to have his own opinion.

Entrap: to trap someone in doing something they wouldn't want to do

He was entrapped by the conspirators.

Enumerate: to name things in an order

They enumerated the disadvantages of the new policy.

Envisage: to have a vision of future

He envisaged the formation of a great nation.

Envoy: a representative from another country

An envoy from Afghanistan

Envy: a feeling that you should have something what another person has

Envy is the cause of unhappiness.

He envies her success, no doubt.

Ephemeral: short lived

Some beautiful flowers are ephemeral.

Epidemic: the appearance and spread of a disease among a large number of people

Dengue epidemic has troubled the country for a long time.

Equanimity: self-control in a difficult situation

She behaved with equanimity despite all the provocation by the critics.

Equilibrium: a state of perfect balance

He is trying to establish equilibrium between his work and his social life.

Equivocal: not clear, and having two meanings

His equivocal talks only confused people.

Eradicate: to destroy something completely

We must eradicate the weed from the garden.

Erode: To wear away with time

The river water eroded a large part of agricultural land.

Erotic: related to sexual desire

An erotic novel

Erupt: to explode

The volcano erupted after ages, destroying a large part of the city.

Escalate: to rise; to make something more serious

The tension between the two countries escalated.

Escort: to go somewhere with someone

She escorted him to the party.

Essence: the most important part or quality of something

The essence of his speech was that there is no place for racism in the modern world.

Esteem: respect; reputation

His esteem in the society has gone up significantly after he won the election.

An esteemed (respected) organisation

Eternal: lasting forever

An eternal love story

Ethical: related to one's sense of right or wrong

The businessman's action is not against the law, but it is unethical.

Ethnic: belonging to a country or race

Various ethnic groups fought each other for dominance.

Euphoria: extreme happiness

His euphoria made him believe that he was born to always stand first in the class.

Euthanasia: mercy killing

Euthanasia should be practised only in the rarest cases.

Evacuate: to remove people from a place to move them to a safer place

Many border villages were evacuated before the war.

Evade: to escape or to avoid

He evaded all the tough questions the renowned journalist asked him.

People tend to evade taxes, said the minister.

Eventually: in the end

Eventually, he won the tough match.

Evict: to force someone to leave

The beggars were evicted from the region during the Olympic Games.

Evoke: to make one feel something (an emotion etc.)

The politician's indifference towards the accident evoked the anger of people.

Exacerbate: to make worse

His letter exacerbated the relations between them.

Exaggerate: to make something seem bigger or more important than it actually is

I think he exaggerated his son's minor success.

Exception: something which is unusual and accepted as it is

Everyone listens to that old man, but his own son is an exception.

Everyone found the test hard; Sid being an exception.

Exclaim: to cry out something in an emotional state

Don't you dare accuse your father for your fault! his mother exclaimed.

Excruciating: very sharp; tremendous

I suffered excruciating pain when I fell down from the roof and broke my leg.

Execution: death penalty being carried out

The revolutionary's execution caused anger among people and they stood up against the regime.

Exemplary: very good; good enough to be copied by others

His exemplary behaviour helped him become the class monitor.

Exempt: to give someone freedom to not perform his duty at a given moment

He was exempted from the election duty because his wife was severely ill.

Some NGOs enjoy tax exemptions.

Ex gratia: a payment which has been made to show good intentions but is not legally important

The company made an ex gratia payment to the employees who had got injured in a road accident while going on a company tour.

Exhilarating: something that makes one feel excited

An exhilarating opportunity to travel abroad knocked at his door and he grabbed it.

Exile: when a person is not allowed to live in his own country due to political reasons

Many Tibetan leaders were exiled to other countries during 50s.

Exonerate: to declare someone 'not guilty'

He was exonerated of all the charges against him.

Exotic: beautiful and not ordinary, and usually foreign

We have some exotic plants in our botanical garden, the teacher told the students.

Expectorant: a medicine for relieving cough

Doctor prescribed him expectorants and nothing else for the violent cough he suffered from.

Expel: to force out someone from an organisation (school, college, company etc.)

He was expelled from the college after he was found guilty of supplying drugs to some students.

Explicable: that can be explained

His absence from the party is explicable- he was hospitalised.

Explode: break up into small pieces with a blast

The bomb didn't cause much damage because it exploded when nobody was there.

Exploit: to take unfair advantage of somebody

The factory owner was punished when he was found guilty of exploiting the labourers by paying them too little.

Extempore: a speech or performance without prior preparation or practice

I did terribly bad. I wasn't ready for the extempore round.

Extensive: covering a long range

An extensive study of cultural relations between various nations.

Extinct: no longer existing or alive

Many animal species have become extinct because of illegal trade of animal skins.

Extort: to threaten someone to get something

The kidnapper extorted the captive to get all the info he wanted.

Extradition: to send someone to another country where they will be tried for a crime

The President signed extradition treaty with many countries during his last foreign visit.

Extrapolate: to guess the future results by extending the available information

We tried to extrapolate the future of our economy by studying the current growth trends.

Extravagant: one who spends too much

All his salary is not enough to support his extravagant lifestyle.

Extrinsic: from outside

The extrinsic factors that affect this chemical reactions are temperature, humidity etc.

Extrovert: one who likes to talk to others and to be with them

She was not an extrovert earlier, but now she is. I can't believe she has changed so much!

Exuberant: a person full of energy

She is as exuberant as a child.

Eyesore: an ugly sight

The dumping site in the middle of the city is a real eyesore.

F

Fabricate: to invent something in order to deceive others

It was found that the evidences produced in the court were fabricated.

Fabricated reasons

Fabulous: excellent

What a fabulous painting!

The job was done fabulously.

Facilitate: to make something possible

Our education system does not facilitate much innovation.

Faction: a smaller group within a large one

One faction of the tourists behaved quite strangely, and is now facing an investigation.

Factual: related to facts

He made a factual mistake during his interview.

You are factually wrong, Raja!

Faculty: the teachers in a department of a college or university

Our science faculty is not pleased with the college administration.

Fade: to become less intense or strong gradually

The colours of my imported shirt faded right after the first wash.

Faint: to become unconscious for a short time

He fainted after standing in the sun for three hours.

Faithful: loyal

He has been a faithful employee for five years. I think he deserves this promotion.

Fake: not real; bogus

The artefact stolen from the museum was a fake; the real piece was kept at a safer place.

Fallacious: untrue; deceptive

His reaction was based on fallacious information he had been given.

Fallible: who can make mistakes

Every human being is fallible.

Falter: to lose strength, direction and purpose, and stop

The negotiations faltered and the two rivals went to war once again.

Famine: a period when food is scarce and people and animals die of hunger

The famine of 60s claimed thousands of lives.

Famished: extremely hungry

It was heartbreaking to see so many famished children living in those slums.

Fanatic: one who has extreme admiration for something

He is a bike fanatic. He doesn't talk about anything else!

Fanciful: one who is not realistic

Creating a raft to cross the sea- another fanciful idea he has.

Fancy: to like and desire

She fancies him, doesn't she?

Fang: sharp tooth of a dog

Fantastic: extremely good

The food is fantastic and the decoration is great.

Farce: a comic, silly and meaningless show; a mockery

I didn't come here so far for this farce! he said angrily.

Far-fetc.hed: hard to believe

A far-fetc.hed story

Farther: beyond; far

The hotel is still farther.

Fascinate: to impress and interest someone

All her books fascinate me.

Fascist: one who allows no opposition

I find the newly elected leader a bit of a fascist.

Fashionista: one who writes about fashion

Fastidious: fussy; very careful about small details

Only a fastidious person must be given this crucial job, because we can afford no mistakes.

Fatal: that causes death

A fatal injury/blow/illness

Fateful: bad but important; crucial

The fateful day when his father divorced his mother changed his life.

Fathom: to discover the meaning of something not understood till the time

It is hard to fathom the mystery of Black Holes.

Fauna: all the animals of a region

faux pas: a social mistake; a blunder

It is a faux pas to mention his son's name before him. He hates him!

Favouritism: favouring one person or group out of many

Favouritism by sports coaches is bad for the nation's future.

Faze: to be surprised and worried

She was fazed to see a stranger in her house, but he turned out to be a cousin she had never met before.

Fearful: scared

Students are fearful about the results.

Fearsome: that causes fear

Tiger is a fearsome animal when seen outside the cage, said the forest officer.

Feasible: something that can be achieved

The sales target that management has set for us is simply not feasible.

Feast: a meal for many people

She invited us to her wedding feast.

Fecund: very productive

Fecund mind of an author

Feeble: very weak

His feeble feet couldn't take him home, so we had to help him.

Feedback: opinion provided by a customer to the company about their services, products etc.

The hotel manager requested customer feedback from everyone who spent time in the hotel.

Feign: to pretend to feel an emotion

She feigned happiness at his success while actually she envied him.

Feline: graceful like a cat

A feline walk on the ramp

Felony: a crime

Fem/feminine: typical of women

Wearing jewels is considered feminine in many cultures.

Femme fatale: a pretty woman who persuades people to take risky actions

Ferocious: violent; causing fear

Crocodiles are ferocious, but some people still catch and breed them.

Fertile: (i) land that can produce many crops (ii) a female that can give birth

Fertile land of the Northern planes

Fester (of a wound): to get infected and produce pus

Soon his wound festered and it had to be surgically treated.

Fetc.h: to go and get someone or something

Boss is not in his office. Please wait here. I'll go and fetc.h him.

Feud: a quarrel that has lasted for a very long time

The cause of murder was found to be a family feud.

Fiasco: complete and embarrassing failure of a plan

Our road trip was a fiasco. We'll never try another.

Fickle: one who changes opinion or behaviour very often

Aryan is a fickle character in the Novel.

Fictitious: not true, but invented

His fictitious claims did not stand for a moment in the court.

Fiddle: to act dishonestly to get something; to touch something

Fiddling with the confidential records cost him his job.

"Don't fiddle with your hanky all the time," said the kid's mom.

Fidelity: loyalty

Her fidelity to her boss is enviable.

Fidget: to keep making movements in an annoying manner

He kept fidgeting nervously during the interview.

Fiend: an evil person

His own friend called him a fiend!

Fierce: violent

A fierce attack on enemy units broke their morale.

Filch: to steal in small amounts , especially something of little value

Filthy: dirty

How can you stay in such a filthy room?

Finale: the final, end part of a contest

The finale is due on Tuesday.

Finalise: to make final decision about something

The dates of second year exams have not been finalised by the university yet.

Finesse: fine skill

Finesse in a piece of art

Finger bowl: a bowl of warm water brought by the waiter to the customer after the latter has finished his meal

Finicky: one who can't be pleased easily

A finicky customer has come. He didn't like a single shirt.

Firm: strong; not changeable

He took a firm stand on the issue.

A firm handshake

Fishy: dishonest

There is something fishy about his politeness.

Fizzle: to make a weak, fizzy sound

The fire became weak and fizzled out in the end.

Flab: a thick layer of fat on the body

He needs to reduce the flab around his waist.

Flaccid: weak and soft

Flaccid arms

Flagrant: obvious and usually bad; blatant

Flagrant crime/flattering

Flagship: the most important of all things in a group

This institute's flagship program is MBA in marketing.

Flare: to burn brightly for a while

The lamp flared before going off completely.

Flashback: a part of a story that shows past events

A large part of the movie is in flashbacks.

Flashpoint: a point where violence could start

Some places have been identified as possible nuclear flashpoints by international agencies.

Flatly: without any emotions

She flatly refused to take his advice.

Flatter: to praise someone in order to gain his favour

Why is he always trying to flatter the boss?

Flaunt: to show-off something one is proud of

He never misses an opportunity to flaunt his Swiss watch.

Flawless: without any mistake/fault

Of course, he won, but you cannot call it a flawless victory.

Flee: to run away from a danger

The Prime Minister had to flee with his family as soon as the military ruler displaced him.

Flick: a short, sudden movement

With a flick of his wand, the magician turned the egg into a bird.

Flickering (of a light): a light that is changing from bright to dim and dim to bright very often

The candle by the window was flickering due to the wind.

Flimsy: weak, and hard to believe

Her flimsy excuses will not do anymore.

Fling: to throw with force

How far can you fling a stone? the kid asked.

Flip: to turn something over quickly

He flipped the toast over in order to heat both the sides.

Flirt: to behave as if one loves someone, though not seriously

He flirts with every girl he meets.

Flock: to be and move together

As they say, the birds of same feather flock together.

Flog: to beat someone severely, especially with a hard object such as a stick, to punish them

Unfortunately, some teachers still flog children for their mistakes!

Flora: plants of a region

Flora of this state is quite diverse.

Florist: one who sells cut and decorated flowers and bouquets

Flourish: to grow and become successful

Their business flourished as soon as they cut down the prices of their services.

Flowery (language): using a lot of complicated words to impress people

His speech was so flowery that half of the audience couldn't understand his meaning.

Fluent: able to speak a language quickly yet clearly

He is now quite fluent at English.

Fluffy: soft, like wool

The kid wanted to buy a fluffy toy.

Flush: to go red in the face

When I asked her if she loved him, she flushed.

A flushed, angry face

Flutter: to make quick movements up and down or side to side

The bird fluttered its wings.

Foggy: with fog

Don't go out yet. It's too foggy.

Foil: to prevent something from happening

His plan of running away with investors' money was foiled by police.

Folk: people

That old folk tells magical tales to children.

Folk tales: traditional stories often told by people to their children

The children went to their grandparents to hear folk tales.

Folly: foolishness

It was an act of folly and not a wise decision, he said angrily.

Foment: to cause trouble to grow

Harsh steps taken by police against the demonstrators fomented the unrest.

Fondness: liking

His fondness for books is well-known.

Foodie: one who loves and takes interest in food

They found a foodie to host the show.

Foolhardy: brave but foolish

His foolhardy actions must be stopped, or he'll get injured one day.

Foolproof: something that can't fail

A foolproof plan to deal with poachers

Foothold: a strong, firm position

As soon as he got a foothold in the local electronics market, he went ahead to expand the business overseas.

Foray (into): to try an activity for a while

He forayed into writing but didn't get the success he wanted.

Forbearance: patience and self-control

Her forbearance is admirable.

Forbidden: not allowed

A forbidden place where no one must go (such as a forbidden forest)

Foreboding: a feeling that something bad is about to happen

All his foreboding about exams was due the lack of self-confidence.

Forecast: to predict what will happen in the future by studying present and past patterns and trends

Forecasting the company profits is a hard nut to crack.

Foreclosure: when a bank takes control of the property of a person who couldn't pay back the loan he took against it

Foremost: leading; before others

One of the foremost banks of Asia.

The foremost thing we must do is to limit the damage.

Foretell: to tell what will happen in future; to predict

Don't believe him. Nobody can foretell the future.

Foreseeable: that can be predicted

The demonstrations were foreseeable but the government took no steps to deal with them.

Forfeit: to lose a right because one has broken a rule or law

He forfeited his right to vote when it was discovered that he had provided false information about himself.

Forge: to make a fake, illegal copy

The documents he submitted were found to be forged.

Forgetful: one who forgets things quite often

He is so forgetful that he forgot his marriage anniversary. Now he is in trouble.

Forgo: to let something pleasant go

I was forced to forgo the chance to go to see a movie with her because my boss gave me additional work.

Forlorn: left alone and therefore sad

The old man felt forlorn, lying alone on his bed in his room.

Formidable: one who causes fear and respect

He could be a formidable enemy to have.

Forsake: to abandon someone when they are in need

She had forsaken her friend when he needed her the most. You can't rely on her.

Forthright: straightforward; frank

His forthright talks impressed the jury.

Fortitude: courage that lasted for a long time

The commander's fortitude was praised by the king himself.

Foul: unpleasant; bad

The foul smell of burning tyre forced us to leave quickly.

A foul plan to disturb peace

Fragile: something that breaks easily

A fragile dinner set

Frank: straightforward in talks, even if someone finds it uncomfortable

He answered every question frankly.

Frantic: worried and excited

A frantic search for a lost child

Fraudulent: illegal and fake

The documents he produced to claim the land were found to be fraudulent.

Freebie: something given free of cost

Many companies couple a freebie with an expensive product.

Freelance: one who provides his services to many companies and is not an employee of any one

A freelance editor who edits contents of various websites

Frenzy: uncontrolled behaviour

His computer game frenzy occupies most of his time.

Fret: to be worried about something

We fretted a lot over the surprise test, but it was quite easy.

Frightening: very scary

The scene of the murder was a frightening sight.

A frightening movie

Fringe benefits: extra benefits

The fringe benefits an employee gets include mobile and travel reimbursements.

Frisk: to search someone using hands in order to detect any hidden weapons

They were frisked at the airport.

Frivolous: light, and a bit silly

His frivolous remarks were not welcomed by most of the guests.

Frostbite: injury to the body caused by extremely cold temperature

Two of his fingers were severely injured by frostbite.

Frown: to show one's annoyance by bringing eyebrows close to each other

The kid frowned when his mother refused to take him to the city zoo.

Frugality: using own money very carefully

His frugality shouldn't be laughed at.

Fruitless: that doesn't yield result

It proved to be a fruitless exercise.

Frustrated: annoyed and angry because of failure

The frustrated guy told the kids to stay away from his house.

Are you frustrated because your project failed?

Fugitive: one who is hiding from police

The fugitive took shelter in an abandoned house.

Fumble: to do something nervously and in an awkward manner

Stop fumbling and use the bat properly. It's just a ball, not a grenade!

Fumigate: to use a potentially harmful chemical mixed with a gas to get a place cleared of something

They fumigated the room with a spray to get rid of mosquitoes.

Funky: fashionable

A funky man

Funky clothes

Furious: very angry

He is furious because he was not selected for the finals.

Furnished: with furniture

'A fully furnished flat is available on rent.'

Furore: an angry reaction of people

There was a furore over the additional tax.

Furthermore: in addition

He disobeyed his mom. Furthermore, he talked rudely!

Fussy: one who cannot be satisfied easily

A fussy customer who finds imperfection in everything

Futile: useless

He made futile effort to persuade his friend to study instead of wasting time.

Futuristic: as if from the future

The newly launched car is said to have a futuristic design.

Fuzzy: not clear

The image was so fuzzy that no one in it could be identified.

G

Gaga: a bit irrational and crazy; not having a clear mind

He went gaga as soon as he got the news that he had won the lottery.

Gainsay: to refuse to accept something as truth

The tough competition we are facing from other nations cannot be gainsaid.

Gala: a celebration with people's performances; a festival

A gala in which celebrities participated

Gallantry: bravery

This year's gallantry awards were announced today.

Gallop (of a horse): to run very fast

The horse galloped across the plain.

Gamut (the gamut): the entire range

A gamut of various types of salads

Gape: to stare at someone or something with one's mouth open

He gaped at his favourite star in amazement.

Garnish: to decorate food with edible items

He garnished the cake with cherry and cream.

Garrulous: one who talks very much

A garrulous girl who keeps talking about film stars

Gasp: to inhale quickly, usually because of surprise or fear

He gasped as if he had seen a ghost.

Gatecrash: to go somewhere uninvited

A gatecrasher was caught and taken out of the annual function.

Gaunt: very thin

A gaunt fellow

Gavel: a small, usually wooden, hammer which a judge uses to maintain order in the courtroom

Gay: homosexual

Being gay is legal in some countries and illegal in some others.

Gaze: to stare at something in admiration

She gazed at the diamond necklace for minutes.

Geek: boring and unaware of current fashion

Some geeks are now millionaires, he observed.

Generalise: to talk or write on a subject with a very basic knowledge and to think everyone or everything belonging to a group or place is similar; not treat something as specific

In a discussion, one should never generalise but be specific as much as possible.

Generic: not belonging to a company; basic

Generic drugs are cheaper but not always safe.

Generous: kind and willing to help others with money and matter

He is a very generous rich man. He donates money to many old-age homes.

Genetic: transferred through genes

A genetic disease

Genre: category or type of a book, film, or music

Which genre do you write in? I write fantasy.

Genuine: real; true

A genuine historical object

Genuinely worried (not just pretending to be worried)

Geriatrician: a doctor who is a specialist of old people's problems

Gesticulate: to express using gestures

He gesticulated frantically at his favourite team.

Ghastly: shocking and not good

Ghastly act of exploiting poor labourers

A ghastly, disturbing image

Ghoul: an evil spirit

She is reading a ghoul's story.

Gibberish: nonsense and meaningless

He was talking gibberish in his sleep.

Gifted: having exceptional skills and ability; very talented

He is a gifted flutist. Just come and hear when he plays.

Giggle: to laugh lightly in a way that seems silly

He was giggling at the funeral!

Gimmick: a publicity stunt, and not serious or valuable

Some slogans are mere political gimmick. They are miles away from truth.

Gingerly: cautiously

We should move gingerly as the road is very slippery, he said, referring to adverse market conditions.

Gist (the gist): the main idea of what one said or wrote

I'm giving you the gist of his presentation.

Git: a stupid, unpleasant person

What a git he is!

Giveaway: given free of cost

A massive giveaway by a company to promote their new product

Gladly: happily

I'll do it very gladly.

Glam: glamour/glamorous; quality of being attractive

All this glam of the party will not impress him. He would want to see something rare and special.

Glance: look to quickly at something for a short time

A glance at the room was good enough for my father to understand what was going on.

Glazing: smooth and shining

A glazing white tile

Gleam: to shine

The car was gleaming after he cleaned it. Of course he got a handsome tip.

Glee: happiness

You could see the glee of success on his face.

Glimmer: to shine, but not continuously; to twinkle

The glimmer of hope kept him going.

Glimpse: seeing something for a very short time

I only got a glimpse of him, because there was such a huge crowd around him.

Glitter: to reflect light in bright flashes

The metal glittered in the sunshine.

Gloomy: hopeless

I just don't know what to do in such a gloomy situation.

Glorify: to make something or someone look excellent and impressive

Glorifying violence in the films cannot be justified.

Glossy: smooth and a bit shiny

A glossy surface

A glossy paper

Glow: a continuous light

You should have seen the natural glow on her face.

Glutton: one who eats too much

Gnarled: twisted and with a rough surface

His gnarled hands tell us he is a very experienced craftsman.

Gnaw: to bite something continuously, gradually damaging it

The rats gnawed at our new carpet and damaged it.

Goad: to keep provoking/irritating someone or an animal till they do something

The mahout goaded the elephant and compelled it to enter the river.

Gobble: to eat very fast

He gobbled down corn flakes and left for his class.

Goblet: a cup-like vessel used for drinking

Godsend: something that happens unexpectedly exactly when it is needed

The new, comfy chair I got in my new cabin is a godsend because the old one was breaking my back.

Go-getter: a person who tries and eventually gets what he wants

The challenge is tough but she is a real go-getter. I think she'll be able to do it.

Golden jubilee: the 50th anniversary

Golden jubilee of one's marriage

Good for nothing: useless

He is so lazy that he's good for nothing, I tell you!

Goodwill: a friendliness towards something

It's the goodwill of loyal customers that kept the company going running during the recent financial crisis.

Goof: to make silly mistake

I goofed up when I accidentally told her my magic secrets.

Goon: a criminal who threatens or beats people

The politician was accused of sending his goons to the news channel's office.

Gory: involving bloodshed

A gory victory changed King Ashoka's heart.

Gossip: conversations made for fun and on light matters

Our friendly gossip went on till the evening.

Gourmet: an expert of good food

Grab: to hold something suddenly

He grabbed my hand and pulled me aside.

Graceful: stylish and elegant

Her graceful behaviour shows that she is well-educated.

Grad: graduate

Graffiti: drawing, words, pictures etc. drawn or painted on walls, usually for fun

Graffiti covers the walls of the local bus stand.

Grandeur: state of being very large, lovely and impressive

The grandeur of the royal dining hall was unforgettable.

Grandiloquent: something made to look impressive by making it complicated

A grandiloquent piece of writing

Grant: to give

He was granted a medical leave.

Grapple: to fight to get something

People grappled for the first show movie tickets.

Grasp: hold; grip

His grasp on the subject is very firm. No wonder he is called an expert.

Gratify: to satisfy a need

A large meal gratified his appetite.

Gratuity: money paid to someone for their service to their company or department

He got a handsome amount as gratuity when he retired.

Grave: very serious

It's a grave matter and she is taking it so lightly!

Gravel: a mix of many small stones (such as pebbles), often used in the gardens

Gravity: seriousness

He failed to understand the gravity of the matter. He could be arrested for what he had done.

Greedy: one who wants something much more than he needs

A greedy businessman who wants monopoly on the whole industry

Gregarious: one who likes to be with others; sociable

He is a gregarious person, but he is not in a happy mood today.

Grievance: a complaint mixed with dissatisfaction

The manager addressed customers' grievances.

Grim: hopeless

All the future prospects looked grim to him after his big failure.

Groan: the long sound one makes when in great pain

The patient kept groaning until he was given an injection of pain killer.

Groom: to prepare

The stadium was groomed for the ceremony.

They were groomed for the common entrance test by their coach.

Gross: total

Gross income

His gross income is beyond the income tax limit.

Grouchy: one who can be annoyed easily

Ground-breaking: new and big

A ground-breaking success/ discovery

Growl: an angry sound (for example, the one made by an angry dog about to attack)

We heard a growl from the bushes and instantly got away from there.

Gruesome: shocking and unpleasant

A gruesome account of how people were kept in the concentration camps

Grumble: to complain

You never get me anything I want, grumbled the kid.

Grumpy: one who can be annoyed easily

Children were teasing a grumpy kid.

Guffaw: to laugh very loudly

They guffawed when I told them how I had been fooled by a mean shopkeeper.

Guileless: honest

Her guileless confession and apology changed his heart.

Gullible: one who can be deceived easily because he believes what others say

Children are gullible and innocent, that's why parents need to teach them to stay away from strangers.

Gulp: to swallow something quickly

He gulped down every bit of cake so that others won't have it. How ridiculous!

Gush: to flow quickly

Blood gushed out of his injured arm, so he was rushed to the hospital.

Guts: courage; bravery

That new boy has got guts! He refused to be cowed down by the bully.

H

Habitable: where one can live

Comfortable? I don't find this room habitable!

Habitual: as a habit

A habitual liar who can't stop lying

Hail: small but solid balls of ice that sometimes fall along with rain

Hair-raising: very scary

The movie had some hair-raising scenes and she kept her eyes closed.

Half-measures: actions that achieve just a part of what they are meant for

The time for half-measures is over. We must declare a state of emergency.

Halt: to stop

We were halted at the police barricade and told to give a sample of our breaths in alcohol-detector (called 'breathalyser').

Hamper: to prevent something from happening; to slow down

Fundamentalism hampers the development of our country.

Handcuff: to put handcuffs on a person to arrest him

He was handcuffed and taken to jail.

Handful: a few

Just a handful of terrorists took hundreds of people hostages.

Handover: to give the control of something to someone

When you leave, please handover the keys at the reception.

Hands-on experience: practical experience

He says he has hands-on experience on computer.

Handy: easy to use

A handy device/software

Haphazardly: disorderly and in a hurry

He haphazardly came up with an emergency plan, which, of course, didn't work.

Hara-kiri: a way of committing suicide

The last decision the chairman took proved to be hara-kiri for the company.

Harass: to irritate and upset someone repeatedly and continuously

If you keep harassing your employees, you will be in trouble sooner or later.

Harbour: to keep; to give shelter to

He was harbouring negative feeling in his heart since years.

Hardcore: one who has strong belief in something

A hardcore criminal is often hard to reform, but there is still hope.

Hardy: strong

These boys think they are hardy, so they're planning to jump from the first floor.

Harmonious: peaceful and friendly, and pleasant

Harmonious relations between the neighbouring countries are vital for trade.

Harness: to control and use

Turbine is used to harness the power of flowing water to produce electricity.

Hassle: trouble; bother

I want to live a hassle-free life, but no! I've to do everything in the world!

Haste: hurry; speed

The decision was made in haste. No wonder it proved to be disastrous.

Haughty: considering oneself better than others; proud

His haughty manner is the cause of people's dislike for him.

Haul: to pull a heavy item, usually with great difficulty

They were unable to haul the heavy log along the ground, so they took the help of elephants.

Haunt: to scare and cause one to worry

His criminal past kept haunting him.

The images of the murder she had witnessed haunted her for a long time.

Havoc: total confusion

Our forces wreaked havoc in the enemy camp by catching them unaware.

Hazardous: very dangerous

Smoking is not only hazardous but undoubtedly injurious to health.

Hazy: not quite clear

A hazy scene comes in my dreams almost every night.

Headhunt: to find and employ people from other companies into own company, by offering them higher salary and other advantages

Headlong: straight and without thinking; reckless

Headlong rush for limited medical seats

Headstrong: very determined to do something, not considering other options

He is headstrong and wouldn't listen to anyone once he has made up his mind.

Hearsay: something only heard and not confirmed to be true

All the talk about PM's resignation is hearsay.

Heartthrob: a male celebrity who attracts many women

The new actor was presented as a heartthrob but he failed to become one.

Heave: to move a heavy object using one's strength

He heaved the sack to the store.

Heckle: to interrupt a speaker

Both party members heckled the leader of opposition rudely.

Hectic: very fast and almost always active

Such a hectic lifestyle is definitely not healthy.

Heinous: extremely bad and shocking; monstrous

I'm shocked! Can a human commit such a heinous crime?

Helter-skelter: in all directions, without thinking

As soon as the earthquake jolted the city, panicked people ran helter-skelter.

Herbivore: an animal that eats mainly plants

Many herbivores are found in this jungle.

Herculean: huge; very big

Am I the only one who can be trusted with such Herculean tasks? he asked angrily.

Hereditary: passed to the next generation through genes

Unfortunately, some diseases are hereditary in nature.

Heresy: an opinion against popular and accepted belief

No heresy in his house!

Hermit: one who prefers to live alone rather than with the society

Heroic: as expected from a hero

It was quite heroic of you to jump in the fire and save the kitten.

Hesitate: to be uncertain about doing something

The policeman hesitated in arresting the powerful criminal.

Heterosexual: one who is attracted to a person of opposite sex; not homosexual

Hibernate: to sleep

Some animals spend winter hibernated.

The computer is on hibernate mode.

Hiccup: a small trouble

We can easily bear such hiccups.

Hideous: very ugly

He whipped his own child! He is such a hideous creature.

Hideout: a place where a person hides

At last, police caught him from his hideout.

Hierarchy: a social system in which people (or animals) are categorised according to their importance and power

Eagle is at the top of birds' hierarchy.

High-profile: very famous

Many high-profile guests attended his party.

Hijack: to take control of a plane, ship etc. by force

The plane was hijacked and turned towards another country.

Hike: increase

Price hikes have made life difficult.

Hilarious: very funny

That comedy was hilarious. I'll watch it again.

Hilt: handle of a sword

Hindrance: something that makes progress difficult

Being illiterate is a hindrance that very few can overcome.

Historic: very important from historical point of view

Winning football world cup was a historic moment.

Hitch: a small difficulty

Such hitches are not unexpected.

Hocus-pocus: tricks used to deceive someone

All his hocus-pocus is useless here. We know what's going on.

Hoist: to lift something using ropes, pulleys etc.

National flag was hoisted on the occasion of Independence Day.

Holdings: something owned

He sold his holdings (shares) in the blue-chip company.

Holler: to shout

Stop hollering! He's coming down.

Holistic: treating a whole rather than its parts

Ayurveda uses a holistic approach towards the body, and

therefore Ayurvedic medicine believes in rooting out the problem.

Holocaust: tremendous destruction

Multiple holocausts took place during the great war.

Homage: deep respect

Everyone paid homage to the martyrs.

Homely: simple yet pleasant and comfortable

A homely shelter

Homesick: sad because of staying away from home for a long time

After having been abroad for three years, he was no longer homesick.

Homicide: murder

This cruel incident of homicide has shocked the city.

Honey trap: a great attraction

Great Barrier Reef, a honey trap in Australia, needs to be preserved.

Honk: to use horn of one's vehicle

Many cars were honking madly.

Honorary: given as an honour

An honorary degree does not require the recipient to complete a course from the institution.

Hoodlum: a violent criminal

Some hoodlums broke my car!

Hoodwink: to trick

They were hoodwinked into buying fake goods by a dishonest man.

Hooligan: a person who acts in a violent manner

Some hooligans tore the banners down.

Hop: to jump on one foot

He hopped across the room because one of his feet ached badly.

Horizontal: parallel to the ground

Horrendous: very unpleasant

Horrendous condition of his room keeps the guests away from it.

Horrifying: frightening

A horrifying accident took place on the national highway.

Horticulture: growing plants in a garden and studying them

Hospitable: one who welcomes and is friendly to guests

I didn't find our host very hospitable.

Hostage: a prisoner; a kidnapped person

Three hundred people were taken hostage by the terrorists.

Hostile: not friendly; like an enemy

He was quite hostile to us, though we never harmed him.

A hostile neighbour

Hotchpotch: a disorderly mixture

His homework was a hotchpotch of irrational points taken stolen from others' answers.

That collection is nothing but a hotchpotch of stolen goods.

Hotly: angrily

The neighbours are arguing hotly again.

House arrest: to confine someone to their house

The famous Burmese leader was kept under house arrest for years.

Hover: to stay in one place in the air

The helicopter hovered above the forest, trying to locate the landing site.

Howling success/victory: a big success/victory

Huddle: to move closer, forming a group

They huddled together due to extreme cold.

Huff: bad mood

He has quarrelled with his wife, that's why he is in a huff today.

Hulk:

(i) a big, awkward man

He is a real hulk.

(ii) a wrecked ship

Hullabaloo: loud noises, usually the ones made by an angry crowd

There was a hullabaloo after our team lost the match.

Humane: kind, as a human should be

Mother Teresa's humane nature was respected by everyone.

Humble: not proud

Please accept my humble apologies.

Humidity: water content of the air; moisture

Humidity is too high today.

Humility: quality of not being proud

Her humility is what makes her a favourite employee.

Humorous: something that makes one laugh

His humorous nature makes people want to be in his company.

Hunk: a large piece cut off from something larger

He put a hunk of cheese in his platter.

Hunky dory: a pleasant situation

Life is hunky-dory, now!

Hurdle: a problem

There are hurdles in the way but I think we will be able to overcome them.

Hurl: to throw

Someone hurled a stone at him but it didn't hit him.

Hurtle: to move in a fast, dangerous way

The car hurtled towards the railing.

Hush: to tell someone to stay quiet

Hush! Baby is sleeping.

Hustle: to push or pull someone to make them move quicker

The kid didn't want to walk as he was annoyed, but his father hustled him along.

Hydrophobia: a fear of water

Hygienic: clean and safe

Hygienic conditions in a hotel

Hype: too much discussion or advertisement of something in the media

So much hype was created around the movie but it disappointed the viewers.

Hypertension: high blood pressure

Hyperventilation: breathing too quickly

Hypocrisy: When one tells others to do or believe something he himself wouldn't do or believe; state of being two-faced

See the hypocrisy of that man! He teaches everyone the purity of heart while he himself is a criminal.

Hysterical:

(i) too excited, scared etc. to control once behaviour

Such a hysterical reaction to a normal situation is a matter of concern, he said.

(ii) very funny

His last comedy novel was hysterical. I just couldn't suppress my laughter.

I

Icebreaker: an activity that makes people who don't know each other open up with each other

An icebreaker activity.

Icon: a famous person who has become a symbol of something

He was projected as a youth icon by the party members.

Iconoclast: one who opposes a popular belief, especially a religious one

He wanted to become an iconoclast but he was arrested when he hurt people's sentiments.

Ideology: a set of ideas and beliefs

His ideology is socialistic.

Not everyone agrees with communist ideology.

Idiosyncrasy: an unusual habit of a person

Blinking every time he says something is his idiosyncrasy.

Idle: lazy and not willing to work; not at work

He is too idle to be given such an important task.

Idol: a very respected and admired person/ a statue of God

Soon the honest judge became an idol of justice.

Ignite: to set fire

A spark ignited the dry leaves and soon the fire spread throughout the forest.

Ill-advised: not well-thought or wise; misguided

That ill-advised solution proved to be temporary and complicated the problem in the long run.

Illegitimate: not legal

Many illegitimate universities are running from houses and shops.

Ill-fated: unlucky

An ill-fated journey in which many people lost their lives

Illicit: illegal or socially unacceptable

Child marriage is illicit.

Ill-informed: not having sufficient knowledge

He was ill-informed when he supported the act.

Ill-mannered: rude

What an ill-mannered young lady! We should talk to her parents.

Illogical: not supported by logic or simple thinking

His illogical assumptions are bound to prove wrong.

Ill-tempered: one who is annoyed easily

An ill-tempered old man

Illuminate: to light up

Instead of simply telling her to switch on the tube-light on, he said, Let the room be illuminated, my dear!

Illusion: a belief that is not real or true; a false impression

He was under the illusion that she loved him.

Imitate: to copy

He tried to imitate the superstar but couldn't do it well.

Imbibe: to drink; to absorb

The soil imbibed every drop of water.

Immaculate: absolutely clean; spotless

Well done! I have never seen such an immaculate room in my entire life.

Immense: very much

We suffered in the immense heat of the desert.

Immerse: to put something completely into a liquid; dip

Baby immersed my mobile phone into the water.

Immigrate: to come and live in another country

Thousands of people immigrate here every year as this is the land of opportunities.

Immune: not affected by something

He is immune to all the unfair criticism he receives.

Immutable: that can't be changed

No rule can be immutable, opined a student.

Impair: affect in a negative way; damage

His hearing ability has been impaired since the accident.

Impart: to tell; to give a knowledge or information

This is the place where the lord imparted the secret of happiness with the world.

Impassioned: full of emotions

His impassioned speech impressed no one. People are more concerned about facts.

Impeccable: flawless; with no faults

An impeccable dance performance

Impede: to slow down; to create hurdle in the way

He has never felt impeded by his physical disability.

Imperial: belonging to an empire

The imperial hall has been decorated once again.

Impertinent: impolite; rude

"You will have to get rid of your impertinent behaviour, boy!" warned the father of the boy.

Impervious: that doesn't allow liquid to pass through

The impervious foil covering the dry-fruits protected them when the box fell in the water.

Implicit: suggested, not told directly; understood

The implicit message was that we must leave as soon as we can.

Impolite: rude

Impose: to force

Why should they impose more and more taxes on the common man? he complained.

Impostor: a fake; one who pretends to be someone else

He is not the chief guest, he is just an impostor!

Impotence: lacking the ability to reproduce

Excessive smoking may lead to impotence, said the doctor.

Impoverished: very poor

They lived in an impoverished state for years.

Impregnable: impossible to penetrate or break into

"The new locker room is impregnable," they say.

Imprint: to leave a mark

Tender hearts of kids were imprinted with the violent incidents they had witnessed.

Improvise: to perform without preparation

He improvised a song beautifully.

Impulsive: acting without thinking, merely by impulse

His impulsive behaviour may put him in trouble.

Impunity: freedom from punishment

It looks like the rioters have all the impunity they need. Nobody has been able to stop them.

Inadvisable: something that should be avoided

'It is inadvisable to go out after the dark.'

Inane: silly and unimportant

Such inane matters should not disturb our plans.

Inapt: not suitable for an occasion; inappropriate

Inapt remark/behaviour

Inaugurate: to put into use officially

The minister inaugurated the new community hall.

Inborn: from birth

He had an inborn ability to twist his organs at odd angles.

Incarnation: appearance of God in a human form

Some frauds say they are incarnations of God.

Incessant: continuous, without halting

Incessant rains

Incinerate: to burn completely

The criminal tried to incinerate the body but he had to flee when police arrived.

Incipient: initial; just beginning to occur

The Prime Minister failed to understand incipient anger among voters and did not take required steps. As a result, he lost next election.

Inclined: willing to do or favour something

He is always inclined to help his friends.

Inclusive: that includes everything

It's five hundred bucks, inclusive of all taxes.

Incognito: without revealing one's identity; without being recognised

Incognito internet browsing

A donation made incognito

Inconsequential: not important at all

They waste all the time and energy discussing inconsequential matters.

Inconsolable: one who has very great sorrow or unhappiness

Incontrovertible: that cannot be doubted

It is an incontrovertible fact that penguins don't fly.

Incorrigible: one who cannot be changed (especially a bad person)

No criminal is incorrigible, said the lieutenant.

Incredible: that is very hard to believe

An incredible story

Incredible courage in the face of danger

Inculcate: to make a habit, idea, feeling etc. stronger by persistence

It is hard to inculcate the feelings of hope in a person who has lost so much in life, yet it is possible.

Inculcate good habits in your children.

Indecent: not moral and polite

His indecent behaviour got him thrown out of the club.

Indecisive: not able to cause a decision to be made

Their victory was indecisive.

An indecisive meeting.

Indefinite: without any set limits

They went on an indefinite strike after the dispute.

Indemnity: a promise of payment to be made against a possible loss or damage

Letter of indemnity issued by an investment company.

In-depth: deep and thorough

An in-depth study of the newly developed markets revealed interesting patterns of consumer behaviour.

Indestructible: that cannot be destroyed

An indestructible metal/object/spirit

Indicative: a sign of something

The opinion polls are indicative of public mood.

Indifferent: not interested in something

He is indifferent to others' pains.

Indigenous: occurring or created in own country

Indigenous technology

Indispensable: that is too good or important to lose

Human relationships are indispensable.

Individuality: one's uniqueness

He never lost his individuality in all those years.

Indomitable: that cannot be defeated or frightened

He is an indomitable person with a firm resolution.

Indomitable spirit

Induction: introducing someone in a new company, or something related to it

Their induction training went on for two weeks.

Indulge: to get involved in something

Your son has indulged himself in illegal activities and will be arrested soon, inspector told his father.

Industrious: hard working

He is an industrious worker, and very honest too.

Inedible: not suitable for eating

This pickle is inedible, complained the customer.

Inept: not skilled

An inept, inexperienced worker

Inevitable: that cannot be avoided

Our team is heading towards an inevitable defeat.

Infamous: famous for something bad

An infamous villain

Infant: a baby

Infatuation: a strong but temporary attraction; obsession

It wasn't love, it was infatuation.

Infer: to form an opinion from the available information

They inferred that he could not possibly attend the meeting but he showed up.

Inferior: low in quality; not as good as something else

Why would you buy an inferior product when a superior one is available at the same price?

Infested: covered with; full of

Our house was infested with cockroaches but we got rid of them.

Infiltrate: to get somewhere secretly

The terrorists infiltrated into our territory.

Inflamed: red and swollen

Inflamed gums are quite painful.

Inflatable: that should be filled with air before using

An inflatable boat/pillow

Inflict: to force something bad upon someone

The new bombs used in the war inflicted a lot of damage on the city.

Infuriate: to make one very angry

His extreme carelessness towards the baby infuriated his wife.

Inglorious: not respectable or honourable; disgraceful

An inglorious victory

Inherit: to receive something after someone's death

He inherited a bungalow from his dead uncle.

Inhibit: to stop someone from doing or saying something

The priest inhibited his children from enjoying worldly joys. He wanted them to live a simple life.

Initiative (to take initiative): to do something before others do it

The NGO took initiative to save poor people from cold.

You must take an initiative to solve this problem.

Injurious: very harmful

Chewing tobacco is injurious to health.

Injustice: wrong; absence of justice

No civilised society will tolerate injustice.

Innate: from the time of birth

An innate ability to memorise things easily

Innovative: using one's creativity or new ideas

The new design is very innovative.

Inorganic: not consisting of living matter

Inquisition: when one is asked multiple questions about something; enquiry

The inquisition took place in the nearest police station.

Inscrutable face: a face very difficult to understand because it has no emotions

Her inscrutable face was due to the tough training she had undergone.

Insinuate: to suggest that something unpleasant is true

He insinuated that she was about to go out of business.

Insipid: not strong; dull

Insipid spice (with no strong aroma or taste)

Insipid colour

Insolent: rude

That kid is so insolent he wouldn't listen to his own parents.

Insomnia: inability to sleep

He suffers from insomnia and takes sleeping pills regularly.

Instil: to set a feeling in someone's mind

They tried to instil hatred in his mind but didn't succeed.

Instinct: the way one naturally reacts to something; an inborn pattern of behaviour

My instincts tell me we should start running now!

Insurgent: one who opposes his own government's authority

The insurgents have destroyed the harmony of this region.

Intangible: something that exists but can't be seen, touched etc.

Insurance has intangible benefits.

Integrity: honesty and high moral values

She lacks integrity, that's why nobody wants her in their group.

Intelligible: that can be understood; clear

An intelligible article on global warming

Interact: to communicate with someone

It is important for the unity of society that people interact with each other.

Interfere: to involve oneself in others' matters

Please don't interfere in doctor's work.

Interim: temporary

He was released on interim bail.

Intermittent: with short intervals

Intermittent rain wouldn't let the clothes on the line dry up.

Interpret: to determine the meaning of something

I'm afraid I couldn't interpret him correctly.

Interrogate: to question

They interrogated him for hours before releasing him.

Intervene: to try to stop something bad from happening by getting involved in it

He intervened in the dispute and prevented two groups from attacking each other.

Intimate: a close one

Intimate relationship.

An intimate friend.

Intimidate: to threaten someone to get something

The goons intimidated him into giving up all the money in his pocket.

Intricate: having very small details, often difficult to understand

An intricate machine with thousands of parts

Intriguing: that raises interest

The battle of Waterloo has always been an intriguing subject for that history buff.

Introspection: to look at own beliefs, ideas etc. and to examine them

It's time for them do an introspection since they've lost the election.

Intruder: someone who is at a place where he is not welcomed because of his criminal intent

The intruders crossed the border and got into our territory.

Intuitions: a feeling of something

My decision of leaving the hotel was based on my intuitions.

Invade: to attack a country in order to occupy it

Germany invaded Poland and this incident paved the way for World War II.

Inverse: opposite

An inverse correlation between reading and ignorance

Invincible: that cannot be defeated

He thinks he is invincible but he's not.

Invoke: to use a power given by law

The special law was invoked to end the strike of doctors.

Involuntarily: unwillingly

The policeman involuntarily obeyed his senior and arrested the juvenile guy.

Irate: very angry

Whenever we need to handle an irate customer, we call her.

Irksome: annoying

Frequent irksome calls from marketing companies

Irony: incongruity; the opposite result (of what was expected)

See the irony! The medicine he took to save his life killed him.

Irrational: not based on reasoning

His irrational behaviour is not a matter of serious concern. It will change with time.

Irrefutable: that cannot be denied

Irrefutable evidence of his crime

Irrelevant: not important to the matter under consideration

His proposal is irrelevant. It won't help us.

Irresolute: not able to take action; indecisive

Being irresolute is not an option here, buddy! Take a stand.

Irreversible: that cannot be reversed

The whole process is irreversible.

Irritate: to annoy someone

Stop irritating her and go back to your work!

Isolated: away from others

An isolated person who longs for company of others

An isolated building away from the city

Itinerary: detailed route of one's journey

I've checked the itinerary and I'm quite satisfied.

J

Jackpot: a large reward

Alas! they won the jackpot.

Jargon: words and phrases which are used by a group (usually a professional one) and not easily understood by others

His speech, full of management jargon, only confused us.

Jealous: envious; sad because someone else has what one wishes to have

I'm not jealous of anyone, he declared.

Jeer: to shout disrespectful words at someone; to boo

Cheers and jeers are part of the show.

Jeopardy: danger

The magnificent structure is in jeopardy because of lack of funds.

Jerk: a sudden movement

He jerked me awake as I had fallen asleep in the class.

Jettison: to throw away; to get rid of something useless

Unnecessary goods were jettisoned from the boat.

Jibe: an insulting comment or remark

He paid no attention to the jibes and remained calm.

Jingle: a ringing sound

Coins jingled in his pocket as he walked.

Jingoism: extreme belief of being superior to other countries

There was a feeling of jingoism in the country craving war.

Jinx: a thing which is believed to bring bad luck; a curse

To him, his old car was a jinx and he wanted to get rid of it as soon as possible.

Jitters: feeling of nervousness

She felt jitters the day her marriage was to take place.

Jolly: cheerful

A jolly guy who makes everyone around him happy

Jolt: a shock

The jolts of earthquake were scary but they didn't cause much damage.

Jot: to write down quickly, usually as notes

He jotted down main points as the teacher continued.

Jovial: pleasant and friendly

He is jovial by nature, but sometimes he is not in a good mood.

Jubilant: very happy

My true friend was jubilant at my success.

Judicious: showing good judgement

Being judicious makes him a strong contender for this crucial position.

Jumble: an untidy mixture

His little daughter's room is a jumble of toys.

Jumpy: nervous

He felt jumpy before his interview.

Junk: useless things

Get rid of all this junk, will you?

Junkie: one who likes an activity so much that he does it all the time

He is a movie junkie. There is no film he hasn't seen.

Justified: having a good and acceptable reason

Her anger at her husband is entirely justified.

Juvenile: a young person; a non-adult

The juvenile criminal escaped the punishment.

K

Keen: very interested in doing something

She had always been keen to help her friends.

A keen writer/rider

Keynote: the most important

As the keynote speaker, the President, began his speech, everyone went quiet.

Kindergarten: a nursery school

Kingmaker: one who affects the election of a person for a very important position

He is not the king but the kingmaker. Without his support, no one can become the Prime Minister.

Kingpin: the most important person in an organisation

He is the kingpin of Eagle gang.

Kith and kin: family and relations; people nearest to one

Kleptomaniac: one who has a strong and often uncontrollable wish to steal (due to a mental illness)

He is a kleptomaniac, that's why nobody invites him to the parties.

Knack: talent and skill for doing something

He has a knack for acting but his son doesn't.

Knead: to prepare a mixture of dough (for making breads) by pressing it and adding water or some other liquid

I'm not going to knead, she said angrily.

Knee-jerk reaction: an uncontrolled and automatic response to something

I punched him and he howled in pain; a knee-jerk reaction.

Whenever he sees her, he goes and talks to her. It's almost like a knee-jerk reaction now.

Kneel: to put one's knees on the ground

Kneel before the king! the prisoner was ordered.

Knock-off: a cheap copy of a popular and high quality product

That's not a Rolex watch but a cheap knockoff.

Knowingly: intentionally; while aware of the results

He knowingly took the side road and now we are getting late.

Knowledgeable: knowing a lot about something; informed

My brother is quite knowledgeable about gardening, and I'm learning from him.

L

Laborious: time-consuming and effortful

It is a laborious but very important task.

Labyrinth: A confusing formation of various paths in which one could easily get lost

Why are you late? Because we had to pass through a labyrinth of streets to reach here.

Lacklustre: not showing much effort or energy

We didn't expect such a lacklustre performance from an energetic guy like him.

Laconic: using few words to say something; concise

He has a laconic personality and hardly ever says an extra word.

Lad: a boy

He is a cheerful lad.

Laden: carrying a load of something

The table is laden with files.

Laggard: one who is slower than others and therefore lags behind

A laggard customer who is last to try a new product

Lambast: to criticise someone severely

Media lambasted the inaction of the ministry.

Lament: to express sorrow; to mourn; to regret

We lamented the great man's death.

Lame: not satisfactory

He says he didn't go because he didn't have black shoes. What a lame excuse!

Lampoon: to criticise someone by making fun of them

The news paper article lampooned the incompetent education system.

Landfill: a place where garbage is dumped and buried

Landmark: an important stage in something's progress

A landmark decision by the court which will influence many similar cases

Landscape: a natural area, especially of a countryside; a scenery of countryside

I can see a hut in the landscape.

Languid: slow and lacking energy

He sounded languid and I knew something was wrong with him.

Lapse: a failure; a slip

A security lapse put the star's life in danger.

Largely: mainly; almost fully

The cake has largely been consumed. Only a small piece has been left for me.

Lash: to hit someone physically or verbally

The king ordered him to be lashed ten times.

The customer lashed out at the department for all the delay.

Lasting: that exists for a long time; durable

Our first meeting had left a lasting impression on me. I still remember it.

Latecomer: one who arrives late

From tomorrow onwards, latecomers will not be allowed in the class.

Latent: present but not active; hidden

Her latent talent will be wasted if she does not develop it and

use it.

Laudable: something that should be praised

She made a laudable presentation.

Laughing stock: someone who people laugh at because of his silly actions, though the person doesn't mean such actions

Since he has tried that new hairstyle, he has become the laughingstock of the college.

Laureate: a person very respected and honoured (awarded) in a field

Look! A Noble laureate lives in that house.

Lavish spender (a lavish spender) : one who spends too much

Both her sons are lavish spenders, but she isn't one.

Law-abiding: one who obeys the law

Most people are law-abiding, while for the rest we have punishments, said the commissioner.

Lawsuit: a case taken to the court of law

File a lawsuit against your wife if she misbehaves with you again, suggested his friend.

Lay-by: an area at the side of a road where vehicles can stop for a while

A new truck lay-by has been built near the square.

Layman: someone who doesn't have professional knowledge of a subject

In layman's terms, this car is safe to drive.

Layoff: when people are removed from their company positions temporarily, in order to save money

A huge layoff has been planned to survive the current recession.

Layout: the way the components of something are arranged

I think the building layout is outstanding.

Leaky: something from which a liquid or gas can leak out through holes

A leaky gas pipe is dangerous.

A leaky container can't hold water.

Lean:

(i) thin

A lean but strong person

Lean meat is healthier than the red meat, said the expert.

(ii) to bend

I had to lean against the wall for support.

Leap: to jump

The leopard leapt at the vehicle.

She leapt at the opportunity without thinking much.

Lease: to give on rent for a fixed period and at an agreed rate

She leased out her father's old house since she had no money left.

Least: minimum; slightest

Are you interested in it? Not the least.

The least we can do for her is to give her a job till she pays her loan back.

Leery (of someone): not trusting someone

He was leery of his nephew.

Legacy: inheritance; something valuable received after someone's death or from the history

He left his family a legacy of love and prosperity.

This destruction is a legacy of war.

Legendary: very famous and heroic

The legendary warrior jumped into the battlefield to confront the enemy.

The legendary story was written by an unknown author.

Legible: that can be read easily

Handwritings of doctors are legible only to the chemists.

Legit/legitimate: lawful

A legitimate business

Leisure: the time when one is only enjoying, and not doing the routine work

I read in the leisure.

Lenient: a bit moderate, not strict or severe

The criminal begged to the judge to be lenient in deciding the punishment.

Lesbian: a homosexual female

Lest: to prevent something from happening

Let's hide all this garbage lest mom see it.

Lethal: so dangerous that it may cause death

A lethal blow on the heart region killed him on the spot, said the reporter.

Lethargic: lacking energy

This lethargic attitude won't do in my class.

Levitate: to float in the air

The magician levitated in the air.

Liable: responsible for something in the eye of law

The law holds the driver of the vehicle liable for this accident.

Libel: an article containing bad and false things about someone, intended to defame that person

We publish criticism, not libel, said the editor of the magazine.

Liberal: open-minded; one who can accept others' beliefs if they look appropriate

It's good that he has a liberal mindset.

I want to live in a liberal society.

Liberate: to free

The UN forces helped liberate the occupied nation.

Lick: to move tongue on something

The child licked the ice-cream from all sides as it started to melt.

Lieu (in lieu of something): instead of something

To give additional benefits in lieu of cash

Life expectancy: as much as one is expected to live

The life expectancy of city people has gone down since the level of stress has gone up.

Lifelike: that appears to be real but isn't

A lifelike painting

Lifelong: as long as a person lives

A lifelong friendship

Lifespan: the time for which a person lives

In his lifespan, he took hundreds of big and small risks.

Likeable: that can be liked

A likeable young man

A likeable place

Likelihood: chances that something will happen

The likelihood of comet appearing in the sky is extremely thin, but it is possible.

Likewise: in the same way

Read the course books and likewise other important books.

Limbs: arms and legs

I have a strange sensation in my limbs.

Lineage: a list of people who were born in one's family before him

His royal lineage is very impressive, I must say.

Linger: to stay behind; to disappear after a long time

He died but his memories lingered on.

Lingua franca: a third language which two different groupsthat do not understand each other's language use

English became the lingua franca between the Spanish and the Brazilians.

Linguist: one who studies different languages

Liquidate: to sell the assets of a company that can't pay its debt

His entire business was liquidated but still it wasn't sufficient to pay his debt.

Literally: meaning what one says and nothing else

Literally speaking, he was involved in hundreds of scams.

Litigation: taking a case to the court

Litigation became necessary to solve the matter when no compromise was made.

Litter: garbage; waste

Please clean it properly, kids. There is so much litter on the floor in your room.

Lively: full of energy and enthusiasm

What a lively person she is! Always smiling and chuckling.

My grandpa is still very lively.

Livid: very angry

Father will go livid when he sees my report card.

Loathe: to hate very much

She doesn't dislike you, she loathes you.

Loathsome: something that can be hated

Locomotive: a train engine

Lodge (a complaint): to file a complaint officially

The house owner lodged a complaint with police that the tenant wasn't leaving despite repeated requests.

Lofty: pompous; proud

His lofty ideas are not practical at all.

Loiter: to move about without any purpose

Police caught the terrorist loitering in the Sunday market.

Lonesome: alone; lonely

Longevity: long life

The concept of longevity of ancient humans is still inexplicable.

Long-term: for a long time

Long-term side-effects of some medicines are yet to be understood.

Look-alike: having very similar appearance

We saw a Nelson Mandela look-alike today!

Loony: stupid; silly

"She is a bit loony, they say. I think they're lying."

Loophole: a flaw in a rule or law that can be exploited by clever people

There are many loopholes in our tax system.

Lopsided: having one side more open, higher, bigger etc. than the other side

His mysterious, lopsided smile

Lopsided spectacles.

Loquacious: a talkative person (who talks a lot)

He is too loquacious to begin a conversation with, she said jokingly.

Loudmouth: one who talks a lot and in a rude manner

The old cab driver was a loudmouth.

Lousy: bad; terrible

What a lousy movie it was! I won't go to a theatre again.

Loving: affectionate; one who loves someone and expresses it

My loving daughter, ...

Loving grandfather

Low-spirited: having little hope; depressed

She has been quite low-spirited since her defeat.

Lubricate: to oil a machine, tool etc.

The mechanic lubricated the scooter engine.

Lucrative (business): attractive to investors because it makes handsome money

As soon as the company went public, it became lucrative to everyone.

Ludicrous: something silly that can be laughed at

His idea is so ludicrous that everyone in the meeting laughed at it, yet he wants to go ahead with it.

Lukewarm: very slightly hot; a bit warm

Add some salt to lukewarm water.

Luminous: producing light or reflecting another light

A luminous heavenly body (star, sun etc.)

Lunatic: a silly person who behaves in a risky manner

I never met such a lunatic guy before.

Lunge: to rush at someone, especially to attack him

He lunged at the Prime Minister and tried to hit him but the guards caught him.

Lurk: move slowly and secretly

She saw some shadows lurking behind the trees, and screamed loudly.

Lush: with lots of plants and greenery

This lush green forest looks so beautiful!

Lustrous: shiny

Lustrous surface of some leaves

Luxurious: full of pleasures and comfort

His luxurious lifestyle doesn't let him work hard and move ahead in life.

M

Macho: forceful behaviour, often thought to be typical of men

He is trying to be macho by making that dangerous jump, but in fact they have tricked him into doing so.

Maddening: something that makes one very angry

This continuous humming sound is so maddening! Let's go and sit somewhere else.

Maelstrom: a chaotic situation of confusion and violence

Maelstrom of riots

Maestro: a famous and highly skilled master (especially of music)

He went to a famous violin maestro to learn some skills.

Magic wand: an easy and effortless solution, like magic

It's like he swished a magic wand and solved the problem!

He said he had no magic wand to change the state of the nation overnight.

Magnificent: impressive, lovely and admirable

His performance in the game was magnificent.

Magnify: to make something larger or look larger

His description has only magnified the problem.

Maim: to waste a part of someone's body by physically hurting them; to mutilate

The arm of the lion-attack victim was maimed.

Mainstream: confirming to the ideas accepted by most people

The terrorists were given a chance to give up their arms and join the mainstream.

Majestic: beautiful; magnificent

The majestic royal garden takes the visitor to another world.

Makeover: a treatment to make something or someone look more beautiful

The makeover of city before the games is a clever move.

Malady: a disease

Cancer has always been a dangerous malady, haunting human beings since ages.

Malaise: a bad, discomforting feeling of a disease or something being wrong

A feeling of malaise has forced her to stay in bed today.

A malaise crept in the hearts of people as the vicious storm worsened.

Malevolent: causing or wanting to cause harm to someone

His malevolent speech was intended to cause riots in the country.

Malfunction: to not work properly

The engine is malfunctioning again.

Malice: a wish to harm someone or everyone

If you want to enjoy the life peacefully, get rid of all the malice in your heart.

A malicious plan to hurt someone

Malign: to criticise someone unfairly

The remarks were intended to malign the famous leader's clean image.

Malignant: a disease that causes more complications and may lead to death

Malignant malaria caused many deaths in the past.

Malnourished: suffering from a lack of essential nutrients in the body

A malnourished kid's heartbreaking picture was published on the front page of the magazine.

Mammoth: very big; huge

Once again, a mammoth task has been assigned to me, he said bitterly.

Mandatory: made necessary by the law

'It is mandatory to register your vehicles at the time of buying'- was the notice issued by the government agencies.

Mangle: to deform something's shape by twisting or tearing it

The right leg of one of the soldiers was mangled by enemy fire.

Manhandle: to use physical force in a rough manner to push or handle somebody

The leader accused that he was manhandled by the police.

Maniac: one who has a lot of enthusiasm for something

He is a cricket maniac. He thinks nothing else.

Manifestation: appearance

Some people called him a manifestation of God, but of course they were terribly wrong.

Manifesto: a written document listing the policies and goals of an organisation, especially a political party

The ruling party declared its manifesto three months before the elections.

Manifold: of many different types; diverse

His manifold talents were never taken into consideration.

Manipulate: to change something unfairly for one's advantage

The minister was accused of manipulating the report to suit him.

Manly: typical of a man

A manly figure

Not caring about minor scratches while playing is understood to be a sign of manliness, he said.

Mannequin: a human-sized dummy used to display clothes in a shop

I want the same shirt the mannequin has on it.

Manoeuvre: a movement or action needing courage and skill

Timely manoeuvre by the commander got our forces a tactical position.

Mansion: a large house

His mansions in various cities are worth millions of pounds.

Manslaughter: killing of a person by someone who didn't intend to do it

He wasn't charged with murder but manslaughter.

Manually: by hand; not by machines

The device is manually operable.

Marginal: extremely small in quantity; not much important

This initial victory is only a marginal one.

Those poor people have been marginalised (not considered important).

Maritime: near or at the sea

The famous crocodile farm museum is a maritime tourist attraction.

Marsh: land near a water body (lake, sea etc.), which is always wet

A large population lives near the marshes.

Martial: related to war

Martial law (rule and law of army)

Martial arts

Marvel: to be surprised by something

We marvelled at the beauty of their Japanese garden.

Mascot: an object that represents something

The mascot of commonwealth games was a tiger.

Masculine: qualities typical of men

The actor's masculine voice is an asset to him.

Mash: to crush something to make it soft

Mash the boiled potatoes.

Massacre: to kill in large numbers

The dictator had ordered the massacre of thousands of prisoners of war.

Massive: very large and heavy

Earthquake caused destruction on massive scale.

A massive body

Masterpiece: the greatest work of a person

His last drawing was also his masterpiece.

Masterstroke: a very important, opportune action that takes one to success

Keeping the talented new player in reserve and sending him when he was needed proved to be the coach's masterstroke.

Matchless: better than all others

His matchless negotiation skills are a great asset for the company.

Mate: friend

Hello, mate! How are you today?

Materialist: one who values possessions and property very much (especially more than spirituality)

She is a materialist, that's why she left her true love for a rich guy.

Maternal: related to mother's side of family

Her maternal uncle arrived yesterday.

Matinee: an afternoon show of a film

Matrimonial: related to marriage

A matrimonial website

Maul (of animal): to wound by tearing and scratching

He was mauled by a bear during a camping tour.

Maverick: a rebel; one who behaves in a liberal manner, not usually expected by others

The new Chief Minister has been seen as a maverick by the public. It remains to be seen whether he is truly one.

Mayhem: chaos; a disorderly, uncontrolled situation

It was a complete mayhem in the office when the chairman made a surprised visit.

Meanwhile: until something is completed

In the meanwhile, we played chess.

Meddle: to interfere

Don't meddle in my affairs, I'm warning you!

Mediocre: of cheap quality; not as good as expected

It was a mediocre film with a typical love story.

Meek: quiet and polite, not arguing; submissive

She is meek but not weak.

Megalomania: state of being obsessed with power

His megalomania was evident from his speech.

Melancholy: a lasting feeling of sadness

His melancholy is quite understandable.

Mellow: soft and smooth

Mellow milk chocolate

Memento: an object that reminds of something or someone; a souvenir

They presented me with a memento when I was leaving.

Memoir: an account of an author's experience; a biography

He wrote memoirs of his grandmother.

Memorabilia: collected objects that remind one of a person, a thing or an event

Napoleon Bonaparte memorabilia.

Menace: something harmful

Dowry is a menace to the society.

Mend: to repair

We must mend the fence now.

Mending the broken relations.

Mendacious: not telling the truth

His account of the high-profile murder is clearly mendacious.

Menial: boring work, valued low in the society

She thinks cooking is a menial work. Well, she needs to learn more about it.

Mentor: a person to whom one can go for guidance

She had been my mentor for two years during my MBA course.

Mercenary: one who does something, usually fighting, for money

He gathered an army of mercenaries to attack another country.

Merchandise: goods

An impressive display of merchandise in a shop

Merciless: cruel; not showing any mercy

He mercilessly beat the captives till he wanted.

Merge: to combine two or more things

The smaller companies merged to form a large company.

Meritocracy: a society that keeps abilities of its individuals above their name, wealth, power etc. while considering them for a position, seat etc.

We need to have true meritocracy, not just a nominal one, said the speaker.

Mermaid: a creature with upper body of a human and lower body of a fish

They have chosen a picture of a mermaid as their company logo.

Merry: happy

Merry Christmas!

Mesmerising: so attractive that one wants to keep looking at it

Monalisa has a mesmerising but mysterious smile.

Metamorphose: to change completely into something else

It's amazing how a caterpillar metamorphoses into a butterfly.

Meticulous: very careful about details

He is meticulous enough to be trusted with the company accounts. I don't see a better candidate.

Metropolitan: related to a large city (a metropolis)

The development of a metropolitan area is a matter quite different from the development of a rural area.

Mettle: determination and ability

The upcoming challenge will test the contender's mettle.

Miasma: a bad feeling about a situation or place; an unpleasant smell

A miasma of defeat after a huge failure

A miasma of Sulphur in the air

Microscopic: very small

Don't go into microscopic details now. We haven't the time for it.

Middleman: someone who plays a role between buyer and producer

Middleman benefits more than the farmer, complained a farmer leader.

Midway: in the middle; half the distance between two places

She is now midway between the starting and finishing point of the race.

Miffed: annoyed; bothered

She was quite miffed at me as I had forgotten our marriage anniversary.

Mighty: powerful

Look at the mighty ocean.

Migrate: to travel to another place

When he was in his mid-twenties, he migrated to Canada and settled there.

Mild: not too severe

It's a mild fever, nothing to worry about.

Mimic: to copy a person's movements and way of speaking in a funny manner; to imitate

He mimicked me, that's why I punched him, said the kid.

Minced: cut into very small pieces (almost crushed)

Minced vegetables/meat.

Mind-blowing: extremely surprising

His mind-blowing success has made him arrogant.

Mindset: the way a person thinks

He has a mindset typical of misers.

Mingle: to mix

A great feeling of victory mingled with the sorrow of losing precious lives in the battle

Miniature: a small model of something

A miniature rocket that looks like a real one

Minute: very little

I used a minute quantity of salt in the dish.

Miraculous: hard to believe; like a miracle

His miraculous escape from a jungle full of wild animals has been made into a film.

Mirage: a hallucination; an illusion of water (or something else one desires badly)

There's no water in this desert. It's a mirage you are experiencing at the moment.

Misadventure: bad luck, often in the form of an accident

A death that happened by misadventure.

Misanthrope: one who hates other people and society

I know him well. He is not a misanthrope.

Misapprehension: a misunderstanding

Don't be under the misapprehension that he favours you. He is a boss, remember?

Misbehave: to behave badly

I didn't know my kids could misbehave like that!

Miscarriage: abrupt end of a pregnancy when a baby is born before time and dies

Miscellaneous: a mix of various, unrelated things

Miscellaneous exercises have been given at the end of the book.

Mischief: something slightly bad that a person does for fun and not to harm anyone

His mischief turned into a disaster and now he is sorry why he did what he did.

Miserable: sad and unhappy

After losing his wealth, he is living in miserable conditions these days.

Mishap: an unlucky event; an accident

His slipping on the ice and falling down on a rock was a mishap that changed his life.

Misleading: false; causing someone to believe wrong information

Misleading news stories

Misogynist: one who hates women

Who says I'm a misogynist? he asked angrily.

Misplace: to lose; to put a thing somewhere one can't find it later

I misplaced my car keys and can't find them now!

Mist: thin fog

Mist has covered the valley.

Mistaken: wrongly believed; wrong

I think you are mistaken. He doesn't live here.

Mitigate: to make something less harmful or bad

We must do something to mitigate the effects of excessive use of coal.

Moan: to make a sad, low sound while crying or suffering from pain

She kept moaning for hours in her room.

Mock: to make fun of someone; to ridicule

The criminals are mocking the law today, said the inspector regretfully.

Moderate: not extreme

I like people who are moderate in opinions.

Modesty: not talking proudly about one's achievements

His modesty is admirable, if you ask me.

Modify: to change and improve something

He rides a modified bike.

Modus operandi: a way of doing something; method

I don't quite agree with his modus operandi. It's not entirely lawful.

Moist: a bit wet

Moist lips/bread

Molestation: a sexual assault

Molestation is a very serious crime.

Mollify: to make someone less upset

The kid tried to mollify his mom's anger by bringing her a chocolate, and she eventually smiled at his innocence.

Momentarily: for a very short time; temporarily

I saw my daughter momentarily before she went back inside the school building.

Momentum: the force that keeps something going

The uprising began to lose momentum within a week.

Monetary: related to money

Monetary prizes were given to the winners.

The International Monetary Fund (IMF)

Monogamy: being married to only one person at a time

Monologue: a long speech by someone, especially an actor

His monologue is getting quite boring.

Monopoly: state of complete control, especially over a market or an industry

The company has created a monopoly over the oil market and is now charging the customers very high prices.

Monotonous: something that doesn't change and becomes boring

A monotonous job

Monstrous: extremely bad (as a monster would do)

In those innocent days, stealing was thought to be a monstrous act.

Monumental: colossal; very big

A monumental success/victory

Mop: to clean with a mop (a cloth or sponge attached to a stick or handle, used to clean the surfaces)

She mopped the floor clean.

Moral: concerning right or wrong; conforming to high values (such as honesty, truthfulness etc.)

A moral act

His high moral standards prevent him from doing any unethical work.

Morbid: interested in death and other grave subjects

A morbid pleasure in holocaust and war

Moribund: inactive and about to die

The economy is headed towards a moribund state, thanks to government's inaction.

A man found in a moribund state

Moron: very stupid

He called me a moron! How dared he!

Morose: sad

She sat there with a morose face.

Mortal: anyone who has to die one day; every living being

We are all mortals, said the saint.

Mortified: extremely embarrassed

He was mortified as his father read out his teacher's remark on his notebook.

Motif: pattern

Motivate: to inspire someone to do something

He motivated me to commit this crime, said the convict.

I read motivational books.

Motto: one's purpose written as a short sentence, like a slogan

Your service is our motto, was written on the company's business card.

Mould: to give a shape

His teacher moulded him into a hard working individual.

Mourn: to feel very sad about something, especially someone's death

He mourned his wife's death silently.

Mow: to cut the grass from the lawn

Please mow the lawn with a lawn-mower.

Muddled: untidy; confused

Most of his projects are in a muddled state.

Muffled: an unclear, quiet voice

His voice was a bit muffled. Perhaps he had been crying.

Mull (mull something over): to think about something

He mulled the choices over in his mind.

Multi-faceted: having different parts or components; complex

A multi-faceted problem which is hard to deal with

Multipurpose: something that can be used in many different ways

A multipurpose vehicle/table

Multitude: a large number of people or things

Multitude of people came to hear him.

Mumble: to speak in an unclear way

The nervous speaker mumbled a few words which nobody could understand.

Mumbo-jumbo: unnecessarily complicated talks; nonsense

I can't understand his mumbo-jumbo.

Munch: to eat something noisily

He sat there, munching on his pizza.

Mundane: ordinary and boring

I have no interest in these mundane matters.

Murky: dark and unclear; misty

Murky sky

Murky river

Murmur: a low, indistinct sound; to say something in a very low voice

He murmured something in her ear, so that I couldn't hear it.

Murmur of party/leaves

Muster: to gather; to collect

He mustered all his courage and told the truth to his dad.

Mute: either silent willingly or unable to speak

Why is he mute today?

Giraffes are mute, told the teacher.

Mutilate: to damage something, especially a body, by cutting off a part

The bodies of the dead soldiers were found in a mutilated state.

Mutter: to speak in a low voice that others can hardly hear

I should not have come here, he muttered to himself.

Mystify: to shock and confuse someone

Her parents were mystified by her choice of career, as she told them she wanted to become a spy.

A mystifying sight.

Mythical: imaginary; found only in tales

Phoenix is a mythical creature.

N

Nag: to irritate and annoy someone by constantly complaining and asking to do something

They kept nagging me until I told them how I planned to pay the debt.

I tried to sleep but the unsolved question kept nagging my mind.

Naive: an inexperienced, young person

I'm no longer the naive young man I once was, he said.

Namesake: one who has the same name as someone else does

Nap: a short sleep

He took a nap in the lunchtime.

Narrate: to read out a story, poem etc.

He narrated the story beautifully.

Nascent: newly started

A nascent business/company

Nasty: bad; mean

Suddenly changing the topic of discussion is her nasty habit.

Nationalise: to make a private business public

The government decided to nationalise the banks.

Nationwide: across the nation

The nationwide strike of taxi drivers was postponed.

Naturalised: a person who is legally made the citizen of another country

Citizen by naturalization

Nearly: almost

He has nearly finished lunch.

Neatly: in a tidy manner

He has cleaned his room neatly.

Necessitate: to make something necessary; to force

Growing population necessitated the establishment of more schools and hospitals in the region.

Nectar: a liquid produced by flowers, which attracts insects, flies, bees etc.

Insects come for the nectar and take the pollen grains with them, which helps plants to reproduce.

Needy: poor; without food, clothes, shelter etc.

Needy people should be paid more attention.

Nefarious: bad, evil

A nefarious plan to assassinate the President was foiled.

Negate: to cancel something's effect

Her hopefulness negated her husband's hopelessness.

Neglect: to not give attention

The managing director neglected the employees' demands completely.

Negotiate: to talk to someone to reach an agreement; to bargain

We negotiated the price with the delegation from Japan.

Nemesis: a rival who is hard to defeat

She thinks I'm her nemesis.

Nepotism: to use one's influence to favour a family member or a friend

The minister was accused of nepotism, when he made his son the next party president.

Nerd: a man who is considered to be a bit awkward and not attractive

That new boy is a bit of a nerd, she said.

Neurologist: a doctor who specialises in treating the diseases of brain and nerves

Neutralise: to stop the effect of something

Her anger was soon neutralised by his politeness.

Newbie: one who has just started doing something

Newbie swimmers, please don't jump into the pool yet, said the swimming coach.

Nexus: a connection between different groups in a system

A nexus of land mafia and officials was uncovered by the investigation agencies.

Nibble: to eat in small bites

Fish nibbled the ball of flour I threw in the pond.

Niche: a position suitable for one

The company needs to find its niche in the competitive market of clothes.

Nick: to steal

Someone nicked my purse! she shouted.

Nickname: a name by which one is known among family members and friends

My nickname is Bobby, said Baljit.

Nightmare: a very scary dream or a very bad situation

Today's exam was worse than a nightmare, he said.

Nitpicking: finding minor faults in something to criticise someone

My wife is busy nitpicking, said the husband.

Nocturnal: of the night

Bat is a nocturnal creature.

After spending years doing night shift, he has become a nocturnal creature, he said, laughing.

Nod: to move head up and down to say 'yes'

Can I go dad, I asked, and my father nodded.

Nominal: very small; insignificant

Five hundred bucks is just a nominal amount! he complained.

Nominate: to name someone for something

The party nominated him as their PM candidate.

Nonchalant: staying calm, as if one doesn't care about something

He was so nonchalant when his wife was being convicted in the court!

Noose: a loop in a rope with a knot that can be tightened to hang a person or to fasten a ship to the ground

The noose tightened around his neck.

Normalise: to become normal

The situation is still tense but it is normalising slowly.

Nosedive: to fall suddenly

The share prices have nosedived since the scam became known.

Nostalgic: having a mixed feeling of joy and sadness when thinking about the past

She remains nostalgic all the time she is at home. She should take up a job.

Nosy: too interested in others' affairs

Why is she so nosy? I don't want her to know what I'm going to discuss with you.

Noteworthy: something that is worth attention

She has written some noteworthy books in the past.

A noteworthy event

Notion: idea

His notion of peace is so flawed!

Notorious: infamous (famous for bad reasons)

The notorious thug deceived the law-keepers again.

Novelty: being new and unique

Car was a novelty in our days, said his father.

Nuance: a minute distinction

Not all the nuances of a novel could be shown in a film based on it.

Nudge: to push someone gently with elbow to draw their attention to something

She nudged me in the arm and showed me a quarrelling couple.

Nugget: a small piece, without a definite shape

Nuggets of silver and gold were recovered from his luggage.

Nuggets of wisdom

Nullify: to take away legal bindings from an agreement

Since no one can control the natural causes, the agreement was nullified after his factory was destroyed in the flood.

Numb: unable to feel

My feet are numb and I can feel no cold in them at the moment.

Numerous: too many

Numerous suggestions were made but mine was selected.

Nuptials: marriage and celebrations associated with it

We were not invited to the nuptials! How dared they?

Nurture: to protect and take care of something

He nurtured the rose like his own son.

Nurture the feelings of revenge in one's mind

Nutshell: using less words

Let me tell you the story in a nutshell.

O

Oaf: a stupid and awkward man

What an oaf!

Oasis: a place having water and plants in the middle of a desert

When we saw the oasis, we couldn't believe our eyes.

Oath: an official promise, often taken publicly; a swear word

He took an oath before the jury that he'd only tell the truth.

Obdurate: determined to do something despite any opposition; stubborn

He was obdurate on his decision of buying another car.

Obese: very fat

He is obese, and this increases his risk of high blood pressure.

Obituary: a news paper notice about someone's death, including some details of their life

Obligation: a duty

Taking care of his child was your obligation.

Oblige: to help; to do a favour

Kindly oblige me by writing a letter to him.

Obliterate: to completely destroy or completely hide something

The ancient civilisation was obliterated by the invaders.

Oblivion: state of loneliness and being forgotten

The emperor spent his final days in oblivion.

Obnoxious: very unpleasant and rude; horrible

An obnoxious person

Obscene: offensive because of being too sexual

Obscene parts were cut off the script.

Obscure: known to few people; hidden; unclear

An obscure village somewhere in Africa

Obsession: something that occupies one's mind all the time

Food seems to be his obsession. He talks about it all the time.

Obsolete: not useful anymore; outdated

The old software became obsolete as soon as the new software entered the market.

Obstacle: something that blocks one's way

Obstacles cannot stop me, he announced proudly.

Obstetrician: a doctor who specialises in births and pregnancies

Obstinate: stubborn; one who is very determined and cannot change

Don't be so obstinate. At least listen to your dad!

Obstruct: to block

A huge rock obstructed the road.

Obtrusive: too visible; very noticeable

The obtrusive scar on her face was the cause of her concern.

Obviate: to make an action unnecessary

Emergence of e-mail and mobile phones obviated the need for telegram.

The court case was obviated by the death of the accused.

Occult: related to magic and witchcraft; supernatural

You will find that book in the occult section.

Odd: strange and awkward

Her new dress is a bit odd, isn't it?

Odd behaviour

Odds: chances; probability of something happening

The odds are not in my favour now, he said hopelessly.

Offensive: that makes someone angry

His remarks about her parentage were quite offensive, he said.

Officiate: to be in charge of something

Chairman himself officiated the meeting.

Offshore: moving away from the shore

Soon the cyclone moved offshore.

We travelled offshore in the last part of our trip.

Offspring: someone's children

Oligarchy: government by a small group of people having all the power

Omen: a sign of what is about to happen in the future

Our goalkeeper has returned and he is quite healthy! It's a good omen.

Omit: to not include something

He was omitted by mistake when we did the counting.

Omnipotent: having all the power, to do anything

No one is omnipotent. We must find your opponent's weaknesses.

Omniscient: having all the knowledge

He knew all the answers. But is he omniscience?

Omnivorous: one who eats both vegetables and meat

Some animals, such as some apes, are omnivorous.

Oncologist: a doctor who specialises in the treatment of tumour and cancer

Onlooker: one who watches but does not get involved in something; a spectator

A crowd of onlookers saw the injured man but didn't help him.

Onset: beginning

Onset of summer

Onset of tumour

Onslaught: a powerful and fierce attack

An onslaught on the fort compelled the enemy to surrender.

Opaque: not transparent

Opaque glasses are used in bathrooms, as they allow the light to enter but nobody can see through them.

Ophthalmologist: an eye specialist

Opine: to state own opinion

We must leave this place, he opined.

Opinionated: one who has strong opinion on a subject

She is very opinionated. She won't even consider us.

Opportunist: one who takes advantage of the situation, even at the expense of values and principles

Beware of opportunists. They can be nobody's true friends.

Oppress: to use authority or power unfairly to suppress people's rights

The invader oppressed the citizens of occupied colonies as much as he could.

Opt: to choose from available options

He opted for science subjects.

Optimist: one who views positive aspects of the things; one who thinks that future is bright

He is an optimist. That's why he is always hopeful.

Opulent: very rich; luxurious and very expensive

His opulent house is his friend's envy.

Orchestrate: to arrange something to happen in a decided way

The whole drama that took place in the assembly was orchestrated, he said.

Ordeal: a painful and hard experience; suffering

She has written the story of her ordeal in a forest in her book.

Orientation:

(i) position; location

The orientation of stars has been studied by astronomers for centuries.

(ii) tendency; preference

His orientation towards religion can be seen in his literature.

Originate: to be from a place

Many religions originated in the East.

Ornamentation: decoration

This elegant suit looks great without any ornamentation.

Orphan: one whose parents are dead

The kid was an orphan, so the government took his responsibility.

Orthodox: traditional and accepted by the society; not odd

His orthodox ideas offended no one, but they also didn't impress anyone.

Orthopaedics: study of bones and diseases of bones

Ostensible: appearing to be something; apparent

His ostensible interest in makeup techniques is just a cover, while his real goal is to spend time talking to her.

Oust: to expel someone from a position

The CEO was ousted when the board of directors voted against him.

Outbound: going away from one or a place

An outbound steamer was caught carrying weapons to another country.

An outbound phone call

Outbreak: when something, especially a disease, occurs suddenly

The outbreak of swine flu is a matter of great concern.

Outburst: a sudden and powerful expression of anger, sorrow or some other emotion

The partial decision of management caused an outburst of anger of company employees.

Outcome: result

Nobody can predict the outcome of this duel.

Outdated: no longer in use or in fashion

Unfortunately, some hospitals are using outdated scanning technology.

Outfit: dress

The child wants a pirate outfit for kids' party.

Outlet: a shop

That company outlet sells shoes at a great discount.

Outlook: point of view

The expert's outlook of the nation's economy doesn't look too bright.

Outnumber: to be greater in number than others

The enemy outnumbered us five to one, yet we won the battle.

Outrageous: shocking, and causing anger

Her outrageous remarks spoiled the mood of the party.

Outright: immediately; absolutely

Obscene websites ought to be banned outright.

Outspoken: frank; one who keeps his opinion without worrying about the result

He is not only outspoken but wise too.

Outstanding: excellent; terrific

Her outstanding performance in national games is a matter of pride for her family.

Outweigh: to be greater than

The risks outweigh the benefits in this case, so we should not invest in this business.

Ovation: clapping for someone

The war hero got a standing ovation from people.

Overall: in general

His overall performance was terrific, though he made a couple of mistakes.

Overcome: to defeat something

He was able to overcome all the difficulties in his path.

Overdue: not paid within time

His rent for the past three months was overdue.

Overestimate: to think someone more capable then they really are

Do not overestimate your opponent. He has been beaten twice this year.

Overhear: to hear what people are saying without their knowledge and without intending to hear

I overheard two men. They were talking about smugglers!

Overlook: to not notice, or to forgive

He overlooks all faults of his son.

Overseas: in other countries

Our food is getting popular overseas.

Overstatement: a statement or explanation that makes something look more important or severe than it really is

It was an overstatement that we are the only superpower in the world.

Overtake: to go past

Our car overtook theirs within minutes.

Overthrow: to remove someone from power to get his position

The last king was overthrown by his own duke.

Overwhelming: difficult to resist

He started crying due to overwhelming joy.

P

Pacify: to calm down; to appease

Not everything possible was done to pacify the angry mob.

Pact: an agreement; a deal

The heads of both countries signed a pact not to go to war with each other again.

Paediatrician: a doctor who specialises in children's diseases

Painstaking: using great effort and care

A painstaking research

My painstaking efforts to maintain order in the house failed when two children fought with each other.

Palatable: tasty; appetising

The meal was quite palatable. Where did you order it from?

Pale: when a person is pale, his skin has less colour than normal

He looks pale. Is he ill?

He went pale when his father asked him his grades.

Pallid: pale and unhealthy

A pallid face

Palpable: something that can be clearly seen or felt

When they beat their arch-rivals, their happiness and joy was quite palpable.

Paltry: very small; almost of no value

Such a paltry amount will not help us at all.

Panicky: frightened; very scared or nervous

She was panicky when she heard that a gas cylinder had burst in her mother's house.

Panic-stricken: unable to act because of being in a state of panic and worry; terrified

She was panic-stricken when I opened the door. She didn't even notice.

Panorama: a complete view of what one sees around

Hey, my new camera can take panorama photos!

Paparazzi: the photographers and reporters who follow famous people

Paradigm shift: a fundamental change in a belief or the way of doing something

Every great discovery has brought a paradigm shift in the society.

Paragon: ideal; a perfect example

The great warrior was a paragon of courage.

Paralysis ***(not the disease)*****:** inability to take action

The country is in a policy paralysis, since the government has failed to take crucial decisions.

Paramount: more important than the others

Passing the Math paper is the matter of paramount importance at the moment, she said.

Paradise: **Heaven,** or a place as beautiful as heaven

The city library is readers' paradise.

Paranoid: extremely nervous and fearful, and not trusting others, often for no good reason

He is paranoid and thinks that someone is keeping an eye on him.

Paranormal: a phenomenon which science cannot explain; supernatural

She claims that she had had some paranormal experiences when she moved into her new house. Others say it's a publicity stunt of hers.

Pardon: to forgive

The prisoner begged for a pardon, saying it was his first crime.

Parentage: origins of one's parents

His wife is of German parentage.

Pariah: one who is not accepted and trusted by a group; an outcast

Some people are treated as social pariahs only because they are extremely poor, and that is so unfair!

Parity: equality (in position, pay etc.)

She fought for parity of payment all her life and inspired many women to do the same.

Parley: a discussion

Parole: when a prisoner is released before his jail term is completed, because of his good behaviour

He was released on parole just six months later, as his crime was not of a serious nature.

Parsimonious: not willing to spend any money or give anything to anyone

I bet he hasn't donated a coin in his life. Everyone knows he is parsimonious.

Partake: to take part in an activity; participate

She is not willing to partake in the preparation of the meal but her mother will force her to.

Partiality: being unfair; bias

The judge's partiality allowed the criminal to get away.

Partisan: a strong supporter/follower

Partisan individuals are often easy to fool, said the shrewd leader.

Passer-by: one who is passing from a place at a particular time

I was about to fall but a passer-by helped me.

Passionate: having strong emotions about something

He is very passionate about bikes.

A passionate racer/boxer/artist

Pastime: an activity which is done for joy in free time

Playing chess is a good pastime.

Pat: to touch someone gently and repeatedly, often as a way of showing affection

His father patted him on the back when he won the race.

She patted her dog affectionately.

Patchy: sometimes good and sometimes not so good

His performance has been patchy, not consistent.

Pathetic: pitiable; not worth respecting

What a pathetic acting! Any actor could do better than him.

Patriarch: the male head of a family or clan

When they saw no solution, they went to the patriarch for guidance.

Patriot: one who loves his country

He was a true patriot, that's why he joined the army.

Patrol: to go round an area in order to detect anything unusual or dangerous

The border security men patrolled the village multiple times.

Patron: one who supports an organisation by donating to it

The funds came from a patron member of the NGO.

Paucity: scarcity; something being in too small quantities

Paucity of food is a thing of past, he said proudly.

Pawnbroker: one who lends money in exchange for things, and can sell them if the money is not paid back in time

The pawnbroker sold his antique gun when he couldn't repay his loan.

Payload: the quantity that a vehicle or aircraft can carry

A new jumbo jet with much higher payload has been brought in.

Payroll: a list of employees and their salaries

No one with this name is on our payroll, he told police.

Peak: to reach the highest point or level

His career peaked two years back when he gave three blockbusters in a row.

Peck: to kiss lightly

Kid's mother pecked him on the cheek before sending him to school.

Peculiar: strange

When we opened the door, there was a peculiar smell in the room.

Pedagogy: the principles and profession of teaching

Pedigree: record of descent and lineage of an animal; a list of an animal's ancestors

The owner of the dog proudly talks about its pedigree.

Peel: to remove skin of a fruit or vegetable

Peel and mash the bananas for baby, said the mother.

Pedestrian: one who is walking

The pedestrians found it hard to cross the road without a zebra-crossing.

Peep: to look quickly through an opening

The spy peeped through the keyhole.

Peer pressure: the pressure a member of a group feels due to its other members

It was only the peer pressure that forced him to take up jogging as a hobby.

Pelt: to hurl; to throw

The demonstrators pelted stones at the house of the leader.

Penal: related to punishment given by the law

His crime calls for a penal action, said the lawyer.

Penchant: strong liking for something, or having something as a hobby

His penchant for watching every film in the theatre is a bit expensive.

Penetrate: to move something into something else, usually by using force

The bullet penetrated the bullet-proof jacket, causing harm to the dummy wearing it.

Penniless: having no money

Penultimate: second last

Penultimate novel in a series

Penury: extreme poverty

Thousands live in a state of penury.

Pep talk: a short, encouraging speech

All the pep talks of the manager were useless as the salesmen couldn't sell anything yet another week.

Perceive: to have an opinion about something; to see something as

It was perceived to be the original piece, but it turned out to be a good replica.

Percolate: when liquid moves to the lower layers through small holes in something

Some rain water percolated down to the roots of the trees through the hard ground.

"No paisa percolates down to the poor, said the report."

Perennial: that lasts for a long time, especially years

A perennial shortage of water in the city

Some herbaceous plants are perennial, others are not.

Perfidious: who is not loyal or trustable

A perfidious friend is worse than an honest enemy, said the king.

Perforated: having small holes in it

A perforated tissue/piece of paper/cloth

Perfectionist: one who wants everything to be perfect

He is a perfectionist and demands too much from his employees.

Peril: great danger

Why did you put your life in peril?

Perk: an added advantage

Free cab is one of the perks of this job.

Perishable: that decays or gets wasted quickly (especially food)

'Sweets prepared with milk are perishable and must be consumed the same day.'

News paper is a fast perishable item, as it gets old within hours.

Permissible: that can be permitted

'Plucking the flowers is not permissible.'

Permeable: that allows gas or liquid to pass through

A permeable membrane

Perpetrator: one who commits a crime

"The perpetrators had come from across the border," said the home minister.

Perpetual: that continues forever in the same way

A perpetual fear that weak neighbouring buildings will fall on one's house

Perplexed: confused

We were perplexed by sudden changes in the party atmosphere and couldn't think what action should be taken.

Perseverance: determination along with continued effort

Perseverance is what kept him going through those tough times.

Persist: to continue

A feeling of hope persisted in the class as the new teacher looked a bit less strict.

Persona: personality or character that a person seems to have, which is often different from their real life

A persona of high intelligence was created around that fool by his expensive marketing agencies.

Personalise: to make something as one would like it to be

I want to personalise my office cabin, but will the boss allow me?

Persuade: to agree someone to do something by arguing with them

He persuaded me to take this hard course.

Pertinent: related to the matter; relevant

Her point is not pertinent to the matter we are discussing here.

Pervade: to spread through

A pungent smell pervaded the atmosphere of the Chemistry lab.

Pervert: to change or influence something, usually in a harmful manner; to distort

Boy, you have perverted the whole meaning of this passage in your answer! This is not what the author meant.

Pessimist: one who is full of negativity and expects bad things to happen in future

He is a born pessimist, I'd say. He says we'll all fail the test!

Pester: to annoy someone by repeatedly asking them to something

The kid pestered his father to take him to the toy fair.

Petrified: very scared and unable to move because of fear

All she could do was to stand there petrified when the bus sped towards her, but eventually it stopped and she was saved.

Petty: too small and unimportant

I don't waste time on such petty issues.

Phantom: ghost

He thought he saw a phantom but he was mistaken.

Phenomenal: extraordinary

Writing a book at the age of eighteen is phenomenal.

Philanthropist: one who cares about poor and helps them by donating

The rich industrialist is also a philanthropist.

Philately: the hobby of collecting stamps

Phlegmatic: one who remains calm and doesn't get excited easily; unconcerned

He is a phlegmatic man. He remained unconcerned during the entire crisis.

Phobia: an extreme, irrational fear

She has a phobia of spiders.

Photogenic: one who looks attractive in photos

Her photogenic face helped her get a role in the film.

Picket: a group of workers who have differences with the management and won't let other workers go inside the factory

Pictorial: expressed in pictures, or symbolic

A pictorial representation of someone's life in a book.

A pictorial history of Japan.

Picturesque: admirable and attractive; pretty

The picturesque building of our parliament

Piercing: sharp

He gave me a piercing look.

A piercing scream

Pile: objects placed one on top of another

A pile of files waited for him on his desk.

Pilgrimage: a difficult journey made for religious reasons

Considering his health condition, he cannot be allowed to go on a pilgrimage.

Pilfer: to steal something of little value

She pilfered a pencil from the stationary shop.

Pimp: a man who is involved in the prostitution and brings customers to the prostitutes

Pinkie: little finger

I hurt my pinkie when I fell down! said the kid.

Pinnacle: the top point; peak

They managed to reach the pinnacle of the industry after decades of struggle.

Pious: one who strongly believes in religion and its ways

Her grandmother is a pious woman and prays both the times *(usually refers to morning and evening)*.

Piping hot: very hot

A piping hot pizza

Piracy: copying a movie CD, book etc. illegally

Piracy ultimately leads to the monetary losses for the country.

Pirate: one who attacks ships and loots them

A ship of pirates attacked our vessel.

Pitfall: a hidden danger or difficulty

Buying too much on credit card is a pitfall many fall into.

Pitiful: something one feels pity for; pathetic

Refugees are living in pitiful conditions. No food, no water!

Placate: to calm an angry person down; to pacify

He tried to placate his parents by saying he will really study next time.

Placebo: an edible substance *(often sugar pills)* given to a patient, convincing them it's a medicine while actually it is not *(often given to those who wrongly believe that they're ill)*

Placid: having a calm appearance; composed

A placid lake/person/dog

Plagiarise: to steal another person's work and say it's one's own

Nobody respects that director because of plagiarised scenes in his films.

Plaintiff: one who files a formal complaint in a court

The plaintiff dropped the charges.

Plaque: a substance that deposits on the surface of teeth and allows growth of bacteria

Plausible: that can be believed

His story is plausible, but we can't be sure how much he made up.

Playboy: a rich man who lives a luxurious life full of material pleasures

Playful: not serious; humorous

His playful remarks were interpreted wrongly.

Plead: to make an emotional request

The criminal pleaded to the king for mercy.

Pledge: a formal promise that one will do something; vow

He pledged to serve the nation to the best of his capabilities.

Plethora: a very large amount; excess

He has a plethora of funds to support his newly started business.

Pliant: one who can be easily controlled

We have many pliant employees but very few creative ones.

Plight: an unfortunate, painful situation

Nobody can understand the plight of riot victims except those who have survived it.

Ploy: something said or done to gain an advantage; trickery

They told him she was coming, but it was just a ploy to make him buy the movie tickets.

The student said he was ill, but it was just a ploy. He went to the playground as soon as the teacher gave him the permission to rest.

Plummet: to fall suddenly

As soon as the war in the Gulf ended, oil prices plummeted and came down to $80/barrel.

Plump: with a soft and round body

A plump, juicy mango

A plump baby

Plunder: to loot; to forcibly take whatever one wants

The enemy soldiers plundered the city they had occupied.

Plunge: to fall directly into something

He plunged into the swimming pool.

Kids plunged their hands into the sand.

Plush: highly comfortable and of good quality, and often expensive; luxurious

I want a plush sofa set for my office.

Poacher: one who kills animals illegally for their skin, teeth, claws etc.

Three poachers were arrested by the forest officers from the national park.

Poignant: causing sad feelings

A poignant movie scene

A poignant incident

Point-blank: fired from a very short range

He was shot from a point-blank range.

Poise: confidence and grace; composure; dignity

You should have seen his poise when he addressed the crowd of thousands.

Poker-faced: one whose face reveals nothing

She sat there poker-faced while he wanted to read her thoughts.

Polarity: the state of being opposite

The polarity between two characters of a movie

Polite: gentle, caring and socially admired

His polite behaviour is his biggest asset.

Politicise: to make an issue political

This is a matter of national security, so please don't politicise it, argued one speaker on the TV show.

Poltergeist: a ghost that does annoying things, such as throwing objects here and there

Polygamy: being **married to** more than one people at the same time

Polygamy is prevalent in some tribes.

Pompous: one who thinks himself very important and talks very proudly

The pompous guy failed to secure a seat in the university.

Ponder: to consider something for a significant time period

He pondered all the options and then made his decision.

Popularise: to make something popular

The star's sudden death popularised his last film.

Populous: having a large population

Some parts of the nation are more populous than the others.

Pore: one of the tiny, microscopic holes in the skin

Pores help humans and animals maintain their body temperature by allowing sweat to get out of the body.

Portable: small and light enough to be carried around

A portable TV set

Portfolio: a collection of shares of different companies a person owns

He has a diverse and almost risk-free portfolio.

Portray: to describe something or someone in a particular way

In his latest book, he has portrayed his uncle as a cruel man.

Posh: high-class; expensive

He lives in a posh area of London.

Possessions: things one owns

The millionaire's possessions include many precious stones and an expensive yacht.

Posterior: towards the back; latter

Posthumously: after death

He was given a gallantry award posthumously.

Postpartum depression: a type of depression women suffer from after giving birth

Postscript (PS): a short note added after one has signed a letter

'PS: Please return soon.'

Posture: the way one sits, stands etc.

From his posture, he looks quite confident.

Potent: effective and powerful

A sharp mind is a very potent weapon a person can have.

Potential:

(i) ability to develop into something

We haven't realised the full potential of our manpower.

(ii) possible

A country which is a potential threat to another country

Potpourri: a mixture of various flowers kept in a bowl, which causes a pleasant smell in the atmosphere

Pounce: to jump quickly

The dog pounced on the burglar and bit him.

He pounced on the last piece of cake left in the tray.

Pound: to strike heavily and repeatedly

The boxer pounded his opponent until he fell down.

POW: prisoner of war

Powerhouse (person): a very energetic person

He is the powerhouse of our branch.

Practicality: state of being practical

The practicality of the proposed plan is doubtful.

Pragmatic: practical

This solution is not pragmatic. We need to think something else.

Praise: to admire

He deserves praise and reward for his heroic action that saved so many lives.

His untiring efforts are praiseworthy *(they deserve praise)*.

Pram: a vehicle for carrying a baby around

Prank: a trick played for fun

The boys keep playing pranks on the old gardener but he doesn't get angry.

Preach: to advise; to lecture

He does not practice what he preaches. He is a hypocrite.

Preachy: one who is trying to give an advice or a lecture, hence is boring

Please don't be preachy. We've come here to hear a song, not for education.

Precarious: not in a firm state, and therefore likely to fall or get worse

His condition is still precarious and his heart can fail any time.

Precede: to come before someone

His reputation precedes him wherever he goes.

Precipitate action: a sudden, swift action, without much consideration

His inflammatory speech caused a precipitate action from public.

Precise: accurate

His calculation was very precise.

Preclude: to prevent

His criminal record precludes him from contesting the election.

Preconceived opinion: an opinion formed without full knowledge or consideration

He has a preconceived opinion about what the right course of action in this matter is.

Precursor: something that happens before something else and has an influence on the latter; antecedent

Hate speeches are precursors to riots.

Predecessor: one who has had a position before someone else

Your predecessor was far better than you, said the angry client to the manager.

Predict: to say that something will happen in future; foretell

Of course she is lying! Nobody can predict the result of the match.

Pre-emptive strike: a strike (attack) carried out before the enemy can attack

A pre-emptive air strike is needed to foil their plan to attack us, said the general.

Preferential treatment: a special treatment given to someone to favour them

The preferential treatment given to the rich guests annoyed many others.

Prejudice: an opinion formed without full knowledge about something

I know she was prejudiced against me.

Prelude: something which introduces something else

Border skirmishes are often the preludes to full scale wars.

Premature: before time

Despite his premature birth he was born quite healthy.

Premeditated: planned and well-thought

The attack on the social worker was premeditated, and that makes it a more serious crime.

Premier: leading; at the top

A premier business school

Premium (money): an extra amount added to the price of something

He paid a premium for booking a flat in a posh area.

Preoccupied: thinking about something else

I was preoccupied with team selections when the teacher was teaching.

Preparatory: elementary; done to prepare for something

Our long-range missile program is still in a preparatory phase.

Preposterous: silly; ridiculous; absurd

A preposterous plan to revive the economy

Preservative: a substance used to prevent decay

Our food products contain no harmful preservatives, the company director announced proudly.

Pressurise: to put pressure on someone to get something done

You cannot pressurise your employees to do overtime.

Prestigious: having a good reputation; esteemed

Our prestigious brands are competitors' jealousy.

Presume: to believe something to be true without being sure about it; to suppose

He presumed he will face no tough competition. He was wrong.

Pretentious: one who tries to look more important than he actually is; showy

He is so pretentious that I can't stand him.

Prevail: to be superior; to control or overpower

May peace and prosperity prevail on this land, said the priest.

Prevaricate: to avoid telling something; to evade

He prevaricated, and gave no relevant information.

Preview: to see something oneself before showing it to others

The leader, on whose life the film was based, previewed it before it was released.

Primal: related to early stages of human development; primitive

A primal fear, such as fear of heights

Prime: main

The prime objective of the reforms was to help poor people.

Primeval: ancient; primitive

Some primeval caves still exist in the nature.

Primitive: related to ancient times; prehistoric

Primitive methods of agriculture

His method of working is primitive and inefficient, said the boss.

Prioritise: to decide which things are more important than the others

I prioritised the tasks I had to deal with and marked the three most important ones as urgent. Believe me, it has helped me a lot.

Privatise: transfer the control of something from public to private owners

The bank was privatised three years ago.

Privilege: an advantage

"Since he is the owner of the company, his relatives enjoy special privileges here," said the employee, frowning.

Pro: professional; an athlete who plays for money, not for hobby

An amateur boxer who turned pro

Probably: likely to be

Probably he will come next week.

Probation: a period in which a new employee's work is observed

You will be on probation for the next eight months.

Proceeds: profits

The proceeds from the sale of tickets will go to an orphanage.

Proclaim: to officially announce

They have proclaimed their victory over the hills.

Procrastinate: to postpone; to delay

I keep procrastinating typing my novel. It should have published a year ago!

Prodigal: one who carelessly spends money; extravagant

I've heard he has a prodigal son.

Prodigy: one with a great and extraordinary skill, often from his childhood

The general knowledge prodigy

won thousands of rupees on the TV show.

Profane: showing no respect for God and religion; blasphemous

Do not use any profane word in front of my dad, even by mistake, the boy warned his friends.

Proficient: skilled and experienced

He is a proficient violinist. I'm going to his show.

Profligate: that wastes money

A profligate nation/society

Profound: intense; felt clearly and strongly

Profound impact of entry of global firms can be seen on the economy.

Profusely: abundantly

I thank him profusely for his help.

Progeny: offspring; children

Progeny of this buffalo is quite healthy.

Prohibit: to not allow something; to ban

Smoking in public places is prohibited.

Projected: anticipated for future on the basis of available information

The projected sales for the next quarter are nowhere near the target.

Proliferate: to multiply; to increase

Non Proliferation Treaty (NPT) prevents the proliferation of nuclear technology.

Prolific: producing something in great numbers; productive; creative

He is a prolific writer; six of his novels were published last year.

Prolonged: continued for a long time; long-lasting

The poor guy has been recovering after his prolonged illness.

Prominent: famous; important

She is a prominent name in the world of fashion designing.

Promising: showing signs of success in future

A promising young man has joined the company.

Promptly: quickly; punctually

He replied promptly and saved the contract we were about to lose.

Prop: to bend against something for support

He propped the wooden ladder against the wall and climbed up.

Propaganda: opinions, videos, pictures, speeches etc. broadcasted on TV, radio, internet etc. to influence people's opinion

Dropping pamphlets from helicopters was a part of enemy propaganda.

Propaganda videos are harmful for the nation's peace.

Propagate: to spread

Everything that is propagated through the internet is not correct.

Propel: to push; to force; to thrust

The wind propelled the ship towards the shore.

Propensity: tendency to behave in a particular way

He had always shown a propensity to commit crimes, said the convict's neighbour in a press interview.

Proponent: one who openly supports an idea

The new principal is a proponent of strict implementation of school rules.

Proprietor: one who owns something

A multiplex proprietor

Prosecutor: an official who officially accuses a person in the court of law

Since the public prosecutor wasn't present, judge set another date for the hearing of the case.

Prostitute: a woman who indulges in sex for money

Protagonist: the leading character; a hero

Rama is the protagonist in the Ramayana.

Protege: a young person who learns from a famous and experienced person

The master sent his protégé to represent the school in the contest.

Protrude: to stick out

A hand protruded out of the sand and we all screamed.

Provident: providing for one's future needs

Provident fund is the guarantee of a secured future, said the general manager.

Provisional: temporary

After the civil war, the army constituted a provisional government till the general elections could be held.

Provocative: something that provokes people

Due to his provocative speech, he was sent to jail.

Proxy: when one gives authority to someone to act on his behalf

He asked his friend for a proxy attendance *(told him to answer the roll call in his absence, against the school rules)*.

Prudent: careful, and avoiding unnecessary risks

He was prudent enough not to say a word until his lawyer arrived.

Prune: to cut the protruding branches of a tree, shrub or flower

The gardener has been pruning the garden plants since last week.

Pseudonym: a name a writer uses in place of his real name

Many famous writers use pseudonyms to write in different genres of fiction.

Psyche: thoughts and ideas deep inside the mind of a person

Don't you dare claim you know my psyche!

Psychiatrist: a specialist who treats mental disorders

Dr. Suman is one of the beat psychiatrist in this town.

Psychopath: one who could be dangerous because of a mental condition

He was a psychopath, she said, referring to her ex-boyfriend.

Publicise: to make something known to public

Sensitive information cannot be publicised.

Pucker: to tighten the skin and make some folds on it

The baby's face puckered and she began to cry.

Puff: to breathe hard when doing a physical activity

He kept puffing, but didn't stop pulling the heavy block.

Puke: to vomit

He puked in my car.

Pulsating: exciting

The match was pulsating enough to make us stand up.

Pummel: to hit someone repeatedly with fist

He pummelled the thief down and called the police.

Pun: humorous use of a word; witticism

The note was serious and no pun was intended.

pungent: strong and unpleasant

The pungent smell of gas filled the Chemistry lab.

Punitive: as a legal punishment

A punitive action will be taken against all the wrong-doers, said the commissioner.

Pupil: one who is learning from someone

His pupil is better than him.

Puppet: a toy which is controlled with strings or by putting a hand inside it

He is acting as a puppet in the hands of minister.

Puppet show is a part of some cultures.

Purge: to get rid of something

He used a software to purge the malwares harming his PC.

Purport: to pretend to be doing something in an unconvincing manner

He purported to be an attentive student but the teacher caught him napping in the class.

Purr: a slow, continuous sound, like the one a cat makes

Pursue: to follow; to try to achieve

The policeman pursued the thief and arrested him.

He is pursuing a career in medicine.

Purview: the extent or scope of something (such as responsibility, rights etc.)

The matter we are discussing is outside the purview of magistrate.

Pushy: forceful and aggressive

She became very pushy when I refused to go to the market and buy vegetables. I wanted to watch the final.

Putrefy: to decay with smell

Putrefying food

Puzzled: confused and a bit worried

I saw my wife's puzzled face and instantly knew that she hadn't a hint of what was going on in the house.

Pyrotechnics: a show of fireworks

A display of pyrotechnics

Q

Quack: a fake doctor

Stop meeting him! He is just a quack, not a doctor.

Quake:

(i) earthquake

(ii) to shake, usually because of fear

She stood there quaking as we heard strange noises from the drawing room.

Quandary: a state of not being able to decide

He is in a quandary whether he should go there uninvited.

Quarantine: to keep an infected person, animal or thing away from others

He spent two days in quarantine until it was concluded that he wasn't affected by H1N1 virus.

My antivirus software kept some files in quarantine.

Quarrelsome: one who keeps quarrelling or arguing with people

Your neighbour is quite

quarrelsome. She is always shouting at her husband.

Quash: to refuse to accept; to reject something as invalid

After he gave a more precise account of the incident, his first account was quashed by the investigators.

Quavering: shaky

Her voice quavered and she began to cry.

Queer: strange

What a queer story!

Quench: to satisfy the thirst

One glass of lime soda wasn't enough to quench my thirst, so I ordered two.

Query: a question

Her query remained unanswered because nobody knew the answer.

Quest: a search for something

His quest for the ultimate truth never came to an end. He kept searching all his life.

Questionable: something that can be doubted or questioned

Her questionable claims couldn't be taken seriously.

Quibble: to argue about less important things

They kept quibbling about which road we should have taken, though the roads were equally long.

Quicken: to make something quick

A sense of urgency quickened the whole process.

Quicksand: deep, muddy sand from which one cannot escape easily

The horse got stuck in the quicksand and, after a long struggle, drowned.

Quid pro quo: a favour done in return for a favour

Quintessential: a very typical example of something

Dosa is a quintessential South Indian vegetarian dish.

Quitter: one who gives up easily

Don't be a quitter! Fight back! shouted the coach.

Quiver: to shake because of an emotion

His lips quivered in anger.

Quizzical: looking a bit puzzled

When I saw her quizzical look, I realised I needed to explain the matter.

R

Rabid (animal): suffering from rabies

A rabid dog

Racial: related to the races of human beings

Racial violence/discrimination

Racism: a dislike for other races

Racism is not the cause behind this attack, said the inspector.

Raconteur: one who is skilled in telling stories, especially funny ones

She is not much of a raconteur, I'd say.

Radiant: very happy

Her radiant face told the story of her success in her test.

Radical: fundamental

A radical thinker

Some of his views may be radical.

Rag: a torn piece of a cloth

The poor beggar is always covered in rags.

His rags to riches story is very inspiring.

Rage: extreme anger

His rage about the unfair treatment he got from his seniors wasn't entirely unjust.

Raging: extreme; powerful

Our raging hunger compelled us to eat his pathetic food.

Ramble: to walk for pleasure

Rambling by the river is a refreshing experience.

Ramifications: possible results

I'm sure he hadn't thought about the ramifications of his action.

Rampant: bad and getting worse

Rampant corruption has shaken the society.

Ramshackle: about to break

Ramshackle gate of the old house

Rancid: not fresh; rotten

I couldn't drink the rancid thing he had served.

Randomly: without sequence or order, merely by chance

The CD player plays the songs randomly.

Ransack: to damage a place by throwing things here and there while searching for something

The detective ransacked the suspect's house but found nothing useful.

Ransom: money demanded for the release of a kidnapped person

The ransom they demanded was too much for the boy's father.

Rapport: an understanding and relationship with someone

He has good rapport with the top businessmen of the city.

Rapt: giving full attention; totally absorbed

He spoke before thousands of rapt listeners.

Rarity: something rare and unusual

The rich man had a collection of rarities.

Rash driving: careless and risky driving

Ratify: approve

The enquiry report was ratified by the Governor.

Rational: meaningful; reasonable

His behaviour can't be called rational, don't you think so?

Rattle: to worry

The announcement of retest rattled the students.

Ravishing: very pretty

When I told her she looked ravishing, she blushed.

Raze: to destroy a building completely

The invaders razed the city to the ground.

Razzmatazz: noisy activity, carried out to attract attention

The razzmatazz of a rally

Reaffirm: to support again; to restate

His hard work reaffirms my belief that his name will be in the merit list.

Realistic: practical

I think we are not being realistic if we think that success will come so easily to us. We are bound to face troubles.

Rear: at the back

Rear tyres of a car

Rear view mirror

Realm: territory

His dreams do not cross the realm of ground reality.

Reassure: to convince someone not to worry

The doctor reassured him that his wife was okay.

Rebel: one who opposes something, especially his own government, and tries to change it; a revolutionary

Many rebels were caught plotting against the dictator's regime.

Rebuke: to oppose someone in talks, often angrily

He was rebuked by all the other panellists when he made that racist comment.

Rebuttal: a statement that opposes and refutes something just said

A rebuttal is coming from the government's representative.

Recede: to move away and become less clear

His hairline is receding and he will be completely bald in a few years.

Recent: that happened just a short time ago

Considering the recent changes, I'd say we will complete the project within time.

Reciprocate: to respond to someone by behaving in the same manner as that person has done

Teacher wished the class good morning and the class reciprocated.

Recite: to speak a poem, article etc. without looking at it

Kid recited the poem he had learned in the class.

Reckless: not careful; irresponsible

His reckless driving resulted in the accident.

Reckon: to think; to guess

I reckon our boss is above fifty.

Recluse: one who prefers to be alone

He became a recluse after his wife's death.

Recollect: to remember; to recall

I knew the answer but couldn't recollect it during the viva.

Recommend: to suggest something to someone; to advise

A friend recommended this novel to me.

Reconcile: to bring together; to make or become consistent

Our views hardly ever reconcile.

Rectify: to correct

He did everything possible to rectify their tense relationship but it just didn't happen.

Recur: to happen again and again

Recurring fits of Epilepsy

Redeem: to exchange a coupon, points etc. for money

He redeemed the gift voucher and bought a piggy bank.

Redundant: not employed anymore

Many people were left redundant due to the recession.

Referendum: to collect people's opinions by asking them to vote in favour or against something

The leader wanted a referendum on whether he should form a coalition government or not.

Reflex action: an automatic response to something

As a reflex action, we all turned our heads in the direction of noise.

As soon as I saw the baby falling, I leapt forward and caught her. It was almost a reflex action.

Reform: to improve

Our education system needs to be reformed, said the head master to a colleague.

Refrain: to stop oneself from doing something

You must refrain from drinking until the condition of your liver improves, said the doctor.

Refuge: shelter and protection

The dethroned prime minister sought refuge in an embassy.

Thousands of refugees are living in tents.

Refurbish: to make an old building look new and bright; restore

We plan to refurbish our farmhouse, she said.

Refute: to say that a statement or idea is wrong and not acceptable

Half the people in the room refuted his claim.

Regal: suitable for a king or queen; royal

A regal path

His regal manners really look a bit old-fashioned.

Regime: government

In the dictator's regime, people starved to death.

Regimen: a set of rules, especially related to diet and exercise

The doctor wrote a strict regimen for the obese guy.

Regionalism: loyalty and admiration for just one part of the country

Regionalism is weakening the nation, said the leader.

Rehab (the process): the process of guiding a person to stop taking alcohol, drugs etc.

Rehab has helped millions of patients.

Rehearse: to practise for a final performance

They rehearsed the drama every evening after the school.

Reimburse: to repay

Mobile reimbursements are a part of your salary package.

Reinforce: to make stronger

The general dispatched another unit to reinforce the fighting unit.

Reinstate: to give one his previous job or position back

After the court case was over, the director was reinstated.

Reiterate: to say something again

The unions reiterated their stand on the issue of FDI.

Rejoice: to be very happy

They rejoiced at the victory in the world cup final.

Rejuvenate: to make one look younger and energetic again; to revive

Yoga helps a person rejuvenate and strengthen the body.

Relapse: to worsen after a temporary improvement

We need to work to stop the relapse of cancer in the patient, doctor told her husband.

Relentless: severe, and without stopping

Relentless cold has forced the people to stay inside their houses.

Relinquish: to give up

The prince relinquished his claim on the throne to marry a middle class girl.

Relish: to enjoy

He relished the memories of his childhood while viewing the photo album.

Reluctant: not willing do something

The kid was reluctant to steal money from his father's pocket and finally, thankfully, he dropped the idea.

Remarkable: special; worth pointing out

A remarkable victory over the strongest rivals

Remedial: something done to improve a bad condition

Government needs to take a quick remedial action to stop the deaths of flood victims in the region.

Reminiscent: that reminds one of something

My collection of old novels is reminiscent of my college days.

Remittance: an amount of money sent to someone

I sent the remittance cheque yesterday but they haven't received it yet.

Remorseful: sad and guilty

He felt remorseful after his grandfather's death as he hadn't been able to see him in years.

Remote: far away

It is a challenge to supply water to remote villages in the desert.

Remuneration: payment; fee

All the perks and remunerations have been mentioned below.

Rendezvous: a meeting which takes place at an agreed time and place

The rendezvous couldn't take place as one of the two parties decided not to come.

Renegade: one who has changed his support from one party to another party; betrayer

A renegade lawyer who loses a case for money

A renegade politician who joined the rival party for money

Renounce: to abandon; to formally break connections with something

King Ashoka renounced wars after witnessing thousands of deaths in a battle.

Renowned: well known

A renowned author died last month.

Repent: to feel sad and guilty for what one has done

She slapped her son and then repented for hours.

Repel: to keep away

She is so evil she repels all the good people in the world, Ronny told his friend.
Mosquito repellents

Rephrase: to express the same thing in other words

I think I should rephrase the question to make it more understandable.

Replenish: to re-fill something

FDI in various sectors has been allowed in order to replenish the Forex reserves of the country.

Replica: an exact copy

Beautiful replica of Kohinoor diamond at the museum looks exactly like the stone itself.

Reprimand: to express dissatisfaction and disapproval strongly

Boss reprimanded him for not being sincere.

Repulse: to push away

Management successfully repulsed the scathing attack by rival firms on the newly launched product.

Repulsive: very unpleasant

His repulsive behaviour ended their new friendship.

Requisite: required; necessary

A flexible body is a requisite for some types of dance.

Resemble: to look like someone

The twins resemble each other very much.

Resentful: unhappy and angry because of an unfair treatment

He remained resentful for years after he was denied his share in the property.

Resilient: that returns to normal condition quickly; elastic

She has been very resilient. She soon returned to her office job after losing a leg in an accident just weeks ago.

Resistant: that resists something, or doesn't get easily affected by something

Even a water resistant watch cannot work beyond a certain depth.

Resort: to do something unusual or unexpected in a difficult situation

When he was surrounded by enemies, he resorted to fight for self-defence.

Resolve: to make a firm decision

He has resolved that he will clear the entrance exam this year.

Respiratory: related to breathing

Respiratory problems

Responsive: one who responds to something; receptive to something

The new manager is responsive to customer queries.

Thankfully, the virus is responsive to new vaccine.

Restricted: limited (usually by rules)

Restricted area (such as a military zone)

Restricted access/entry

Resume: to start an activity again

The play was resumed as soon as the injured player was taken out of the ground.

Retaliate: to harm someone in response to a harm they did

Enemy fired mortars across the border and our troops retaliated.

Retarded growth: growth slowed down by something

Retarded physical/mental growth of a person

Retarded economic growth

Retentive memory: ability to absorb and retain new information easily

Reticent: reserved; not willing to express own feelings

For some reason, he became reticent after joining that college.

Retort: to answer instantly, mostly when angry

Don't you dare tell her anything! he retorted.

Retract: to withdraw (take back) a statement

The minister retracted her statement within twenty four hours.

Retreat: to leave one's position and move back

The enemy was forced to retreat after three days of heavy fighting.

Retrieve: to recover something

Despite the virus, we managed to retrieve the important files from the hard drive.

Retrospectively: while looking at past

Retrospectively, I can recall and visualise the struggle we went through.

Reveal: to make something known; to disclose

He revealed the state secret to his close friend!

Revenge (to take revenge): to harm someone in response to harm done to one

Since he was bitten by his neighbour's dog, he took his revenge by breaking the window pane of his neighbour's house.

Reverberate: to echo

The sound of cannon-shot reverberated across the valley.

Revert: to return to something

Please do as directed and if you still face any troubles, revert to me.

Revitalise: to fill something with energy once again

Doctor prescribed a multivitamin and some supplements to revitalise him after his long term illness.

Revive: to bring back to health, life etc.; to revitalise

The Reserve Bank took necessary steps to revive the weakened currency.

Revoke: to take back a power, permission, rights etc. earlier given to someone

The parliament has the right to revoke the rights given to the commission.

Revolt: rebellion; to refuse to accept the authority, often using violent ways

Eighteen crew members of the ship revolted and refused to carry out captain's orders.

Rhetoric: language that may sound impressive but doesn't have much matter or meaning

When the minister could not answer the reporter's question, he resorted to rhetoric.

Riches: money and possessions

Her riches are enviable.

Rickety: weak and likely to break easily

Rickety furniture

Ricochet: to hit something and move away by the impact; to rebound

Miraculously, the bullet ricocheted off the steel gate and hit the shooter.

Ridicule: to make someone look stupid using words or actions; to mock

Many people tried to ridicule me, but none could shake my confidence, said the speaker.

Righteousness: state of being morally right

He considers the righteousness of every important action he takes.

Rigid: not flexible; that cannot be bent

He is very rigid about his rules of living, and that makes him kind of boring.

Rigorous: strict and careful; painstaking

His rigorous discipline actually helped him reach his goal.

Rinse: to clean with water, usually after applying soap

She rinsed the dishes thoroughly.

Rip: to pull apart (with hands, claws etc.)

The bear ripped his jacket to pieces but he ran away and saved own life.

Rip-off: when someone pays too much for something

Five hundred for this T-shirt? That's a rip-off!

Riveting: very interesting; exciting

This novel is so riveting that I can't put it down.

Riviera: a coastal area (often where people go and spend time in villages)

Indian Riviera has not realised its full potential as a tourist destination yet.

Roam: to travel here and there without a purpose, mainly for joy

She roamed around the city all day, marvelling at tall buildings.

Rob: to steal or take away something from someone using arms and violent methods

The train carrying gold was robbed in the hills.

Robustly: **strongly** and determinedly

She supported us robustly when we needed her help. Now it's our turn to return the favour.

Rock-bottom: the lowest possible

The rate of economic growth has touched the rock-bottom.

Rogue: dishonest and mischievous; scoundrel

A rogue person/state

Roly-poly: short, round person

A roly-poly baby

Romanticise: to make something look better than it is

Romanticising a boring place

You can't romanticise crime and violence, for God's sake!

Rot: to decay

The food-grain is rotting in the go-downs.

Rot in hell! she said.

Rosy: (i) pleasant **and full of hope**

A rosy future

(ii) beautiful like rose

Rosy cheeks of a baby

Rousing: making one feel excited

A rousing speech by commander-in-chief before a battle

Rout: to defeat and crush

Our team was routed in the semi-finals.

Rubber-stamp: one who approves things without considering them carefully

A rubber-stamp president/ governor/secretary

Rubbish: garbage; waste, not useful

Throw the rubbish out in the dustbin!

The plan was rubbish right from the beginning.

Rucksack: bags people carry on their backs

The mountaineers put the rucksacks in the camp.

Rueful: sorry for something and wishing it had not happened

He had been rueful about his low grades in the entrance test, but now he is studying harder than ever before.

Ruffle: to move something lightly and gently

When the kid wished him good morning, he ruffled kid's hair affectionately.

Rugged: not even; wild and natural; rough

Rugged paths of the hills are not easy to walk on.

Ruin: to spoil

His laziness ruined our plan to go biking early in the morning.

Rumble:

(i) to fight

The beasts rumbled in the mud for hours.

(ii) a deep, continuous sound

Rumble of a thunder

Ruminate: to consider for a significantly long time

He ruminated for a month before he decided to go abroad and study further.

Rumour: an information which is not true but spreads among people quickly

The news of the PM's death was a rumour.

Run-of-the-mill: ordinary

He wore run-of-the-mill, informal clothes in the ceremony.

Rupture: to break

The car crash had ruptured his skull and he had little chance of surviving.

Rustle: to make a soft sound while moving

The pages of the open book rustled in the air.

Ruthless: cruel

He is a ruthless man. No girl can marry him and live happily, said Tania.

S

Sabotage: to damage

The bandits sabotaged the wooden bridge to prevent police from following them.

Sack: to dismiss

The teacher swore she'll sack the class representative if he didn't follow her orders.

Sacred: holy

Sacred statue of God

Sacred water of a river

Sacrifice: to give up something one likes and values

He sacrificed his social life for his career.

The Olympian sacrificed his comfort for training.

Sadistic: obtaining pleasure by hurting others; cruel

The military ruler's sadistic ways caused the rebellion.

Safeguard: to guard and protect

The little island asked its bigger neighbour to safeguard its coast.

Sag: to drop down in the middle, often due to weight

The sofa sagged under the weight of the huge guy.

Saga: a long story, especially a legend

A Samurai saga

Sage: a wise person

He asked the sage what he should do to stay happy in life.

Salient features: most important features of something

The salient features of this car include four air bags and anti-skid brake.

Sanctimonious: acting as morally superior

His sanctimonious talks aren't liked by his friends.

Sanctity: state of being holy

The sanctity of marriage must be observed.

Sane: sensible; able to make correct decision

He is perfectly sane, but today his actions were reckless.

Sanitary: clean and hygienic

Sanitary conditions of the railway platform are admirable here.

Sarcasm: clever remarks that mean opposite of what is said (often used to criticise or ridicule someone)

Splendid shoes! he said. I could see the sarcasm because my shoes were dirty.

Sardonic: showing little respect for other person; cynical

A sardonic smile

Sassy: disrespectful; cheeky

A sassy girl

Satiate: to satisfy a need

My hunger wasn't satiated by a packet of biscuits.

Satire: a humorous way of criticising

He writes satire, and people love him for it.

Saturate: to soak something completely so that it can absorb no more

Since the local market seems to be saturated, the company is looking at unexplored foreign markets for its products.

Savage: cruel, violent

The savage murderer had ruthlessly killed nine people before he was caught.

A savage attack

Savour: to relish; to enjoy slowly

Savour the taste of our delicious Triple Sunday ice cream! was written on the board outside the hotel.

Savvy: having practical knowledge of something

He is a computer-savvy young man.

Scam: making money through dishonest and illegal ways

Scam after scam broke the trust of people.

Scandal: that causes a feeling of moral disapproval and surprise in people

After the sex scandal was revealed, the minister resigned and apologised in public.

Scanty: too little

With such a scanty amount, we can buy nothing that could be called a gift.

Scapegoat: one who is blamed for something wrong, no matter who has done it

The official was made the scapegoat in the scam and was dismissed.

Scarcity: severe shortage; when something is not available as much as needed

People of our city have been suffering from scarcity of water.

Scathing: very severe; biting

A scathing verbal attack on the Prime Minister by the opposition forced him to reply.

Scatter: to spread in every direction

The vase broke and its pieces scattered in every direction.

Sceptical: doubtful

The public remained sceptical about the politician's new promises.

Scholar: an expert who has studied a subject deeply, particularly in university; an intellectual

He is a Mathematics scholar and has been nominated for the Nobel.

Sci-fi: science fiction

A sci-fi story such as 'Star Wars'

Scintillating: sparkling

His story is scintillating, and so is his personality.

Scorching hot: very hot

The weather is scorching hot and it'd be better if we don't go out before the sunset.

Scoot: to go fast

She scooted to the hospital as soon as she came to know about his accident.

Scold: to reprimand; to talk to someone angrily about what he has done

His father scolded him for wasting so much money and time every day.

Scoundrel: an amoral and proud man; rogue; rascal

You dirty scoundrel! she shouted.

Scour: to remove by rubbing hard

She wanted to scour the spots off the shirt but instead she tore it down accidentally.

Scourge: that causes suffering and pain

One of the scourges of the nineteenth century was plague that killed millions of people.

Scramble: to climb with difficulty, using feet and hands

He scrambled up the hill till a flat surface appeared, and there he set the camp.

Scrap: to abandon something useless; to discard

The old ship was sent to the neighbouring country for scrapping.

Scrape: to rub something to remove a layer from it

He scraped the upper layer of cheese with a knife.

Scratch: to scrape with a sharp object

His leg was scratched by the sharp edge of the bed.

Scrawl: to write quickly in an untidy way

As the superstar answered her question, she scrawled notes on the notepad.

Scream: to cry out loudly due to fear or excitement; to shriek

She screamed as an enormous dog jumped in front of her.

Screech: an unpleasant, high pitch cry; a scream

Screech of tyres

As soon as I heard the screech, I ran inside.

Screen: to examine (in order to remove the undesired or unwanted things or people)

They screened the candidates before the personal interview round by giving them a simple written test.

Scribble: to write or draw something quickly

He scribbled a note on a piece of paper and threw it at me.

Scrooge: one who avoids spending money

The old scrooge won't donate anything, said the guy from the NGO.

Scrub: to rub hard to clear something, usually with a brush

He scrubbed the dishes angrily. He didn't want to do it.

Scrutinise: to observe and examine very carefully

We didn't know that the class teacher was going to scrutinise every answer.

Scrupulous: honest, careful and diligent; dedicated to work

The junior engineer's scrupulous observation prevented a possible tragedy.

Scuffle: a short fight; a brawl

A scuffle broke out when someone threw an egg at the speaker.

Scum *(a slang)*: a bad, worthless guy

He is a scum. He has often cheated people.

Scuttle: to move quickly, taking short steps; to rush

He scuttled away as we tried to approach him. He was avoiding us.

Seasoned: experienced, and an expert of something

He is a seasoned journalist and knows how to bring the truth out.

Seclusion: alone; away from others

He spent years in seclusion, doing his research on a remote island.

Sedate: calm; not excited

A sedate person who became a criminal after an injustice

Seduce: to attract someone (often sexually, but not always)

She tried to seduce the yogi but he remained firm in his meditation.

Initially she hadn't intended to buy anything, but the goods were offered at such seducing prices that she bought a number of items.

Segregate: to keep things apart from each other

He segregated onions and potatoes into different baskets.

Seize: to grab forcefully with both hands

She seized the towel the monkey was trying to take away.

She seized the job opportunity she got.

Selective: one who chooses carefully

He is very selective when it comes to tea.

Self-centred: one who is only interested in oneself; self-absorbed

I have never met a more self-centred person before.

Self-conscious: nervous because of the fear of being criticised

If you don't think about your performance so much, you won't be so self-conscious, and that will enhance your confidence.

Self-evident: obvious; not needing any proof

It is self-evident that he is taller than anyone else in the room.

Selfish: who only thinks of own interests

He is so selfish that he deserted his best friend after he had achieved what he wanted.

Self-proclaimed: one who claims to be something

He is the self-proclaimed leader of opposition though no one else has nominated him yet.

Senile: not having clear thoughts because of old age

The senile old man forgot to take his medicine again.

Sensational: exciting; thrilling

A sensational win

The article was more sensational and less informative.

Senseless: meaningless

Sentimental: related to memories of past which make one sad and nostalgic

His old jeans carries sentimental value for him.

Separatist: one who wants a part of his country (usually the one he lives in) to be separated

A separatist leader was arrested after he made a hate speech.

Sequential: having an order or sequence

A sequential explanation for

the formation of earth as it is today

Serene: calm; peaceful

That serene lake draws me towards itself.

Serpentine: twisting, like a snake

A serpentine river

Settle: to go and start living somewhere

They settled in London last year but their parents still live here.

Sever: to cut and separate

The knight severed the opponent's arm with one blow of his sword.

Sexist remark: a negative remark based on a person's sex, often against women

He was expelled because of his repeated sexist remarks.

Shabby: in bad condition due to the lack of care

A shabby dress which is no longer fit for any occasion

Shaggy: having long, untidy hair

The old, shaggy dog is no longer as active.

Shaky: weak and unsteady

The old man's shaky legs couldn't take him to the stage, so a guard came forward and helped him.

Shallow: not serious or deep

The book was entertaining but shallow.

Sham: fake; only intended to deceive people; fraud

A sham police inspector looted the house.

Shambles (in shambles): in a state of mal-governance and confusion; disaster

The economy is in shambles because of indecisiveness of the leadership.

Shattered: broken into pieces

She carefully picked up every piece of shattered glass.

You couldn't move ahead with these shattered hopes, said the coach.

Sheepish: embarrassed after realising a mistake; silly

He grinned sheepishly when he made the same mistake twice.

Sheer: absolute; very great

His speech was sheer show-off of his knowledge.

Her comment shows her sheer ignorance on the subject.

Shield: to protect; to cover

Sun screen shields the skin against sunrays.

Shilly-shally: to hesitate in making a decision

It's time we had stopped shilly-shallying. Let's make a decision.

Shimmer: to sparkle; to shine with interruptions

A shimmering light

Shimmering vision (unsteady vision)

Shirk: to avoid the responsibilities one doesn't like

Can you shirk your responsibility forever? asked the annoyed boss.

Shiver: shake because of cold or fear

The temperature is below zero degree. No wonder we are shivering.

Shoot-out: a firing between two people or groups

The shoot-out took place last night.

Shop-lifting: stealing goods from a shop when no one is noticing

Shop-lifting is a major problem for retailers.

Shortage: not adequate supply of something

Electricity shortage will be a major issue in the coming elections.

Short-change: to treat someone unfairly by giving them less than they deserve

That shop-owner is infamous for short-changing the customers.

Shortcoming: a fault

There are a few shortcomings in your plan.

Shortlist: to select

The shortlisted candidates will proceed for the interview round.

Short-sighted:

(i) one who can only see the near objects clearly

(ii) one who cannot see what the future results of an action will be

He says smoking is a pleasure. Obviously he is short-sighted.

Short-tempered: one who gets angry easily

Watch out! Our new boss is a short-tempered man.

Shove: to push with force

He deliberately shoved the person in front of him.

Showdown: a final argument or confrontation in order to end a disagreement

The director prepared for a showdown with the management regarding the issue of staff salaries.

Showy: bright and colourful but without much real value or beauty; flashy

His showy hat is a bit odd, isn't it?

Shred: to tear into thin strips

He shredded the documents properly before throwing them out.

Shrewd: one who is smart enough to take advantage of the situation

He is a shrewd politician and knows how to take advantage of people's feelings.

Shriek: scream

She had shrieked before her murder and, merely by chance, one of the neighbours had heard her shriek.

Shrill: a high-pitch sound which is unpleasant to hear

The singer's shrill voice was a pain to our ears.

Shrug: to move shoulders up and then down to show that one doesn't know or care

Is your mom at home? I asked, and he just shrugged and walked away.

Shudder: to shake due to fear

She shuddered at the thought of making a presentation in front of entire board of directors.

He shuddered when he saw the door of his flat opened though he had locked it properly before leaving.

Shuffle (playing cards): to mix

He shuffled the cards twice.

Shy: one who is a bit nervous when with others

He was so shy that he couldn't ask a question in the class.

Sickening: very unpleasant and annoying; appalling

Seeing a dog licking the plates in the restaurant was a sickening sight. We went to the food inspector and lodged a complaint.

Sidekick: a person who works with a more important person

In this film, hero's sidekick is better than the hero himself.

Sideline: to not allow someone to take active part in something

She felt she was being sidelined in the chat.

Siege: to surround a place

The emperor's forces laid siege to the castle and stopped all supplies from going in.

Sift: to put a substance through a sieve

They sifted the flour in order to remove any small stones in it.

Sigh: to exhale slowly and noisily in order to show disappointment, tiredness etc.

He just sighed when we asked how his interview had been.

Significant: important enough to be considered

The funds we have been allotted are not significant. We need much more.

Signify: to mean

Be careful! The skull sign on the box signifies danger.

Silver jubilee: 25th anniversary of something

This year we are going to celebrate the silver jubilee of our marriage.

Simmer: to heat a liquid just below the boiling point

After adding all the ingredients to the water, let the mixture simmer for ten minutes.

Simper: to smile in a silly manner

Simplify: to make something simple and easy to understand

Simplify the following equations.

Simultaneous: occurring at the same time

Fall in the value of rupee and a simultaneous increase in the prices of petrol

Sin: something done against the religious and moral rules

You have committed a sin by beating up your wife, said the priest.

Sine qua non: a necessary condition for something

Being a graduate is a sine qua non for this job.

Sissy: a boy who is laughed at because either he is not considered brave or he is interested in girlish activities

His peer group had ridiculed him by calling him a sissy, but eventually he became a great wrestler of his time.

Sitcom: situation comedy (usually a series of episodes shown on TV)

'FRIENDS' and 'SIENFELD' are famous sitcoms.

Sizzling hot: very hot

A sizzling hot pizza is awaiting us in the kitchen!

Skim: to read quickly

He skimmed through the book and returned it to the library within a day.

Skinny: very thin

She is so skinny, yet she is on a diet!

Skip: to leave and move onto other things

I've skipped some chapters because they are not important for the exam.

Skirmish: a short battle or argument

A skirmish was reported at the border last night.

Skyscraper: a very tall building

Another skyscraper is being constructed in the eastern part of the city.

Slacken: to loosen

Slacken your belt, as you can't even breathe properly at the moment.

Slam: to throw something on a hard surface, or to criticise

The wrestler slammed his opponent on the floor.

He slammed the door shut.

News papers slammed the government's move.

Slander: a false statement against someone, intended to defame them

It was a case of slander and nothing more.

Slang: highly informal language, sometimes offensive

Slap: to hit with flat part of one's hand

Mother slapped her son for talking so rudely.

I told her I loved her and she slapped me!

Slash: to cut

The company slashed the prices of all its cars.

Slaughter: to kill many people mercilessly

The memories of slaughter that took place decades ago still haunt the people.

Slay: to kill

Sleek: smooth and shiny

Your new lunch box is so sleek and beautiful.

Sleek design of a car

Sleep-over: to spend a night out of one's own house (and mostly at a friend's house)

Slender: thin and attractive

A slender waist

Slice: to cut into thin pieces

He sliced the apple with a sharp knife.

Slick: done skilfully and smoothly, without trouble

A slick dance performance by professional dancers

Slight: a little

There have been slight changes in the plan.

Slim: thin and attractive

Everyone wants a slim body these days.

Slimy: a slippery, thick liquid, sometimes sticky as well

Slimy glue

Who can eat this tasteless, slimy soup?

Sling: to throw

He slung a stone in the lake.

Slink: to walk quietly

The son wanted to slink away but his father caught him.

Slit: to make a long cut

The murderer had slit the throat of the victim with a sharp weapon.

Slither: to move on a surface with a twisting, sliding motion, as a snake does

The snake slithered across the room and got out through a hole.

Sloppy: careless

A sloppy mistake in your CV could cause a rejection.

Sluggish: very slow

He is too sluggish to reach here in time.

Slum: crowded areas of a city where very poor people live in small *(and mostly temporary)* houses

This is the largest slum in Asia, he said.

Slumber party: a teenagers' *(generally girls)* party in which the guests stay at the host's house for the night

Slur: to speak without clarity

His speech has been slurred since his childhood.

The drunk slurred something nobody could understand.

Slurp: to drink a liquid by sucking it noisily

The kid slurped the tea just to annoy his mom.

Slut: a woman who has sexual relations with many men

Sly: one who deceives people cleverly

The sly old lady had been caught by the police when she was tricking a foreigner into buying stolen goods.

Smack: to hit forcefully

He grabbed the collar of the thief and smacked him down.

Smash: to break into pieces

The leather ball smashed the glass and hit the wall.

Smear: to harm someone's reputation by saying or writing false things about them

The editor was found guilty of trying to smear the name of the celebrity and was ordered to pay a hefty fine.

Smirk: to smile annoyingly, due to satisfaction

After he jumped the neighbour's wall to get the ball, he smirked at me. He hoped I'd be punished for it.

Smitten: suddenly started to like someone or something very much

He was smitten by her beauty when he saw her.

Smog: smoke combined with fog

This terrible smog is making the visibility nil.

Smother: to kill someone by stopping their breath by covering their face with something; to suffocate to death

The murderer had smothered her.

Snap: (i) to break something into two with a noise

That rogue snapped the old man's stick.

(ii) to talk angrily when irritated

Why do you ask so many questions? she snapped.

Snapshot: a photo

Snarl: when a dog makes a deep, continuous sound at someone to scare them

The dog snarled at me and I ran away.

Snatch: to take away by force quickly

The biker snatched the gold chain from the woman's neck.

Sneak: to go somewhere in a stealthy way

Why have you been sneaking around since morning? What are you up to?

Sniff: to inhale noisily, generally to smell

The kid sniffed the sock and then threw it away in disgust.

Sniffle: to breathe in quickly and repeatedly through nose, especially when having cold or when crying; to sniff repeatedly

Snob: one who only respects high-class people

He isn't a snob. In fact he's too shy to talk to you.

Snoop: to try to discover something by moving around a place secretly; to spy

Someone had been found snooping around his house and was caught by his guards.

Snooze: to sleep lightly for a short while; to doze

He snoozed for a while and when he woke up, the boss was looking at him.

Snore: to grunt or to breathe very noisily while asleep

Stop snoring! We can't sleep.

Snub: to treat someone as if they are not important

The foreign envoy was snubbed by the minister.

Snuggle: to cuddle; to make oneself warm and comfortable by putting one's body against someone

The baby snuggled up to his mom and slept quietly.

Soak: to make completely wet

I soaked the piece of foam and cleaned the window with it.

Soar: to rise quickly

The stock prices soared to a new high this morning.

Sober:

(i) not drunk

(ii) serious, not funny

A sober person/subject/matter

Soiled: dirty; muddy

His soiled shoes spoiled the carpet!

Solace: comfort, especially in the times when one is worried about something

Good, warm food is always a solace, said the foodie.

Solicitor: a lawyer who provides legal advice

Solidarity: unity

Public sector bank employees also went on a holiday to show solidarity with private bank employees.

Solitude: loneliness; isolation

She wept in solitude, not revealing her sorrow to anyone.

Solo: done alone; singly

A solo dance competition

Sombre: serious; unhappy

His sombre face told he was in trouble again.

Sonorous ***(the sound)*****:** deep and pleasant

The superstar's sonorous voice impresses the audience.

Soothe: to make calm or less painful

A bandage couldn't soothe the wound.

The singer has a soothing voice.

Sophisticated: complex; able to do something complicated

The new sophisticated technology will be helpful in treatment of tumours.

Sophomore: a second year student

Sop (or SoP): something of little value, offered to someone to calm or appease them

These sops can't calm the angry protestors. They want concrete action.

Souvenir: something which reminds one of an event or a place; memento

They presented me with a souvenir when I was leaving Japan.

Sovereignty: power of a nation to have its own government and make own decisions

We cannot compromise the sovereignty of our nation, said the PM.

Spacious: having a lot of space

Our new car is very spacious.

Spare: to leave; to not hurt

He spared every passenger except the one he was looking for.

Sparkle: to shine brightly with numerous small points of light

The diamonds in her necklace sparkled as the light hit them.

Spat: a minor argument or quarrel

There had been a spat between two friends.

Speck: a tiny particle or mark

Specks of dust on the glasses

The little country looked like a speck on the world map.

Spectacular: fabulous; extraordinary

It was a spectacular match, no doubt.

Speculation: guessing something using known information

Share market is a game of speculation, not certainty, he said.

Spellbound: one whose full attention has been captured by something *(as if magic has been done on him)*

The junior artist looked spellbound when he saw his ideal's work.

Spill: to flow over the edge of container

She forgot to turn the gas off and the boiling milk spilled all over.

Spine-chilling: very scary; terrifying

It's a spine-chilling story and small children should not be allowed to read it.

Spirited: determined and energetic

Our players are spirited. They'll win the cup for the nation.

Splash: to cause a liquid to fall here and there

The whale jumped out of the sea and then fell back into it, causing a huge splash.

Splatter: to splash with small drops of a liquid

The tyre of the bus fell into muddy water in a pit and all the passer-bys were splattered.

Splendid: Impressive; excellent

What a splendid decoration!

Split: to divide into parts

I split the cake into slices with a sharp knife.

You can't split the water by hitting it with a stick.

Spontaneous: that happens suddenly and naturally

Their spontaneous reaction to the sound of firing was to run away from the spot.

Spooky: scary and strange

A spooky old house from which light was coming

Spouse: one's husband/wife

He was in the party with his spouse, Malini.

Spree: a period of too much of a particular activity

She is on a reading spree. She has read three books in one week.

Sprinkle: to spread something over something else in little pieces or drops

Now sprinkle the tiny choco pieces over the ice-cream cone.

Sprint: to run as fast as possible

The mother sprinted to the swimming pool to stop the baby from jumping in it.

Come on, be fast! It's a sprint, not a marathon.

Spurious: false; fake; not what it claims to be

Spurious wine killed seven people.

Spurt: to flow out with force; to gush out

Water spurted out from the hole in the pipe.

Squander: to waste *(money or something else)*

He squandered his six-month salary in a casino.

Squeak: a high-pitch sound

The mice squeaked in their cage when they saw a cat approaching.

Squeamish: easily upset by the sight of something

He has always been squeamish about a black cat crossing his path.

Squeeze: to press something soft *(gently or forcibly)* with hands

He squeezed the mango and ate the pulp.

Stab: to injure someone with a knife or any other sharp object

According to the cops, she was stabbed multiple times.

Stabilise: to stop something from fluctuating or changing quickly

This device has been designed to stabilise the current.

Stack: pile

Staggering: shocking; astonishing

He has got a staggering 50 Crore rupee contract for the next three years.

Stagnant: not moving

I don't want to go near the lake because of its stagnant, smelly water.

Stake: risk; bet; share

The stakes are high. You can even lose your company. Think before you act.

Stalemate: a situation in which no one wins; a deadlock

The game of chess ended with a stalemate.

It was a stalemate and none of the parties could win the contract.

Stalwart: loyal; strong; reliable

Among all the king's guards, Fred remained a stalwart and fought for him till the last breath.

Stammer: to take unusual pauses while speaking, mostly due to a speech problem or nervousness

The famous speaker used to stammer when he was a kid.

Stampede: when individuals in a crowd or group panic and start running wildly

Some buffalos saw the lion and the stampede began.

Someone shouted that the bridge was about to break, and suddenly there was a stampede. Twelve people died in it.

Stand-by: ready for use if needed

Another police team had been kept on stand-by, just in case.

Stare: to look at something or someone for a long time

That guy kept staring at me all the time! she said.

Star-struck: to be very impressed by celebrities

She is really star-struck. She can see nothing else but actors and their lifestyles.

Startle: to surprise

The parents were startled by kid's intellectual question.

Starve: to remain hungry for a long time, even till death

It is very disheartening to see children starving to death in some poor countries.

Stash: to store in large amounts at a secret place

Billions of dollars stashed in foreign banks

Stature: build and height; reputation

His stature in society is so high that not even a powerful politician can ignore his opinions.

Status quo (the status quo): the present situation, as it is

The status quo is about to change soon, as the new leader seems to have a different way of working.

Steadfast: not changing for a long time; persistent

Only his pet dog remained his steadfast companion during his lifetime.

Stellar: related to stars

Stellar constellations

Stellar rays

Stereotype: a fixed idea or image of something in people's minds

Even in the present times, some people stereotype women as mere caretakers.

Sterile: unable to produce

This sterile land has never been fit for agriculture, said the old man.

A sterile male

Sternly: severely; strictly

I asked if I could help her carry the luggage but she refused sternly.

Stiff: hard

His neck was stiff due to spondylitis.

Stigma: a mark of disgrace

Stigma of having spent months in jail haunted him for the rest of his life.

Stimulate: to encourage or cause to grow

The need for this medicine has been stimulated by outbreak of flu virus.

The news of spread of Dengue fever stimulated the demand of goat's milk.

Stink: to smell very bad

His socks stink!

His stinking *(bad)* behaviour is intolerable.

Stipulate: specify, especially in points

Terms and conditions have been stipulated clearly in the agreement.

Stir: to move gently in order to mix

He didn't stir the soup, so lumps were formed in it.

Stomp: to walk with heavy steps when angry

Child stomped across the room, shouting.

Stony: not kind or emotional; rocky

A stony path/face

Stoop:

(i) to bend the upper body; to bend forward

The soldier stooped before the king and then read the message to him.

(ii) to lower one's moral standards to do something bad

How low can he stoop for profits?

Stormy weather: thunder with rain and strong wind

No fisherman should enter the sea in such a stormy weather.

Stout: thick, heavy and strong

A stout leather belt

A stout person

Straightaway: without any delay

Let's go and meet him straightaway.

Straightforward: direct and honest

I think boss didn't like my straightforward answer.

Stranded: stuck; not able to leave

The flood victims have been stranded on an island surrounded by water since a month.

Strangle: to squeeze someone's neck so that he stops breathing

She wasn't poisoned; she was strangled to death.

Stronghold: a strong position which one can control easily

The rebels have captured the city that was considered the government's stronghold.

Stray: a pet that doesn't have a home anymore; homeless

I saw a stray puppy on the road and brought him home.

Streamline: to shape a thing in such a way that it can easily move through water or air without experiencing much resistance

Streamlined jets are faster than the ordinary jets.

Many sea creatures have streamlined bodies that help them swim faster.

Strenuous: that need more effort; tiring

I won't be in such a strenuous job for too long, he said.

Stringent: very strict; severe

No country has such a stringent law. Why do we need it?

Strive: to want something very much and try very hard for it

She is striving for success in modelling.

Stroll: to walk slowly, enjoying it

They strolled along the lake and back, talking about their school days.

Stub: the leftover part of a cigarette (after the main part has been consumed)

Cigarette stubs should never be thrown here and there.

Stubborn: one who is determined to do what he wants and doesn't listen to others; obstinate

Don't be so stubborn! Listen to you father.

Stuck: in a difficult situation from which one is unable to get out

I don't know how to solve this problem. I'm stuck.

He is now stuck in a war-torn nation. God save him!

Studious:

(i) one who gives attention and effort; one who cares

He is quite studious, so we needn't worry about the work we gave him.

(ii) one who studies a lot

He is a studious guy. No wonder he is good at English.

Stuffy: not allowing fresh air

What a stuffy room! How can you live here?

Stuffy nose

Stumble: to almost fall (when one's foot slips over an object); to stagger

He stumbled over a pebble but recovered quickly.

He stumbled in business but didn't give up.

Stun: to shock someone so much that he can't react instantly

The kid's remarkable dance performance stunned the judges.

She looked stunning *(very beautiful)* in her pink dress.

Stunted: not developing/growing as fast as expected

The growth of the economy has been stunted by poor infrastructure.

Stupendous: amazing

A stupendous movie

Stupendous extravagance

Stutter: to have difficulty saying some words

I didn't g-g-get you, he said, stuttering.

Subdue: to reduce the effectiveness and force of something

The fever has been subdued by the medicine.

Subjugate: to conquer; to bring under control

The advancing army subjugated the city, and then the entire state.

Submerge: to go below the surface of water

The submarine submerged into the sea.

Submissive: one who allows others to control himself; obedient

She expects her husband to be submissive.

Subordinate: one who holds a lower position

Remember, you are the boss and he is your subordinate, said his friend.

Subside: to become less strong

The troubles will subside once we begin to act.

Substantial: considerable; significant

He has amassed substantial wealth.

Substantial stake/effort

Substitute: to use one thing instead of another

We substituted our high-carbs diet with a high-protein one.

Subtle: not very noticeable, but significant; delicate

There are subtle differences between the two products, which only an expert can notice.

Successor: one who comes after another person

The seventh king was a worthy ruler but his successors were not.

Succinct: short and clear; said using few words

He sent a succinct message to his family, though they were expecting a long letter.

Succumb: to get defeated after a struggle; to die due to something

The poor student succumbed to the injuries he had suffered during the accident.

Sue: to file a case against someone in the court of law

He can sue you for the statement you have made on TV, said the lawyer.

Suffice: to be sufficient

I think one million dollars will suffice for now, he said arrogantly.

Suffocate: to die due to lack of oxygen

He had not been poisoned. He had suffocated.

Suicidal:

(i) one who is likely to try to kill himself

(ii) an action that leads to defeat

It was suicidal to try new, inexperienced players in the world cup.

Sulk: to remain sad when one is angry about something

He sulked in his room, angry about the injustice done to him by his own relatives.

Summit: a meeting of top leaders of different nations

The summit has been quite successful.

Summon: to order to come; to call for

He was summoned to the court.

He had to summon all his courage to deliver that speech.

Superficial: shallow; not real, only trying to look so

His love for her is superficial, not real.

Don't worry. It's a superficial cut, not a deep one.

Supersede: to replace

The CDs have superseded the cassettes.

Superstition: a notion based on magic, myths etc. and not correct according to science or logic

He believes that he will get a bad news because he had seen an owl in his garden. Mere superstition, I'd say.

Supple: that bends easily; flexible

Supple movements of a classical dancer.

A supple stick.

Suppress: to end forcefully

If you keep suppressing your emotions, you'll definitely feel sad.

Supremacy: complete control and domination

After the destruction of enemy's squadrons, our air force enjoys air supremacy, told the general.

Supreme: the highest

The Supreme Court

Surge: to increase suddenly; to rush

The oil prices across the world have surged.

Surmise: to guess

I surmise you've been hiding from the principal.

Surcharge: an additional charge

Surpass: to exceed; to do better than something

Great job! Your performance has surpassed our expectations.

Surrogate: used instead of something/someone

Since she was too weak to give birth, they used a surrogate mother instead.

Susceptible: easily influenced by something; vulnerable

Babies are highly susceptible to this kind of flu, told the medical officer.

Suspicious: doubtful

He is suspicious by nature.

Sustain: to keep alive; to continue

Hope sustains life.

Swap: to exchange

The two babies were accidentally swapped at the hospital.

Swift: quick

This car is really swift!

Swift action by the police prevented the burglary.

Sympathise: to feel someone's pain and express sympathy

The minister sympathised with the families of the dead.

Symbiosis: a relationship in which each of the two sides gains something

Notice the symbiosis between butterflies and flowers. The butterflies get pollens for food while the flowers transfer their pollens to other flowers through the butterflies, told the teacher.

Symptom: warning signs of a more serious problem

'High fever is one of the symptoms of Dengue.'

Syndicate: a group of individuals or institutions that share the cost of something

A syndicate of drug dealers was busted last night.

Systematically: as planned; methodically

Since they did everything systematically, they achieved their target without facing any difficulty.

T

Tacit: not expressed directly, but understood

They couldn't have broken the law without their leader's tacit approval.

Tackle: to deal with a problem

Only God knows how we tackled the tough questions and passed the exam.

Tailor-made: made specially, according to one's demands

We want a tailor-made holiday package.

Takeaway: meal bought from a restaurant and taken home

Madam, will you dine here, or is it a take away order?

Takeover: when a company buys out another company

A hostile takeover

Talisman: something that brings good luck; lucky charm

She told that the ugly, thick necklace she wore on her neck that night was a talisman!

Tally: to match; to agree

The signatures do not tally, sir! The 'assets' and 'liabilities' columns of the balance sheet tallied.

Tame: to domesticate; to control like a pet animal

We cannot tame the future but we can adapt to the changes we face.

Tamper: to make little changes; to fiddle with

The bowler had tampered with the ball, so the umpire ordered to change it.

Tangle: a mess; a confused mass

His room is a tangle of numerous objects thrown here and there.

Tantalising: tempting but not easily attainable

A tantalising victory

A tantalising sweet dish forbidden for patients of diabetes

Tantrum: a sudden anger (like a child's)

Stop tantrums! You're a teenager now!

His tantrums won't help him get a new bike.

Tariff: charge; due

What are the room tariffs? he asked the hotel receptionist.

Tarnish: to make something look bad; to smear

The rape incident tarnished the image of our nation in the world.

Taunt: to upset someone by mocking him

Why are you always taunting her? Why don't you leave her alone?

Tease: to mock someone; to make fun of

Many kids were teasing the new kid.

Techie: one who knows a lot about latest technology, such as computer, gadgets, software etc.

Teeming: full of people

The stadium was teeming with crazy fans.

Temperate (weather): not very hot or cold weather

This temperate weather is perfect for my job.

Tempt: to make someone want something; to lure

Unbelievably low prices tempted her to buy the goods she didn't need.

The salary is quite tempting but I don't like the job profile.

Tenacious: determined in opinion; stubborn

Tenacious stand taken by a firm to stop a hostile takeover by a rival firm

Tend (to do something): likely to do something

He tends to make new friends wherever he goes.

Tentative: carefully projected, but not certain

We can tell you the tentative yield for this Fixed Maturity Plan, but we cannot guarantee it.

Tenure: the time period for which one holds a position; term

During his tenure as the CM, crime rate was extremely high.

Terminate: to end

The road we took terminated in a forest.

If you don't agree to new terms, the contract shall be terminated next month.

Terrible: very bad and unpleasant

The food is terrible here. I won't come here again.

We suffered terrible losses in the battle.

Terrific: very good and pleasant; wonderful

The work she has done is terrific. We must hire her for the job!

Terror-stricken: very frightened

She was terror-stricken when we found her on the terrace.

Testimonial: a said or written statement about someone's character, nature, qualities etc.; testament

My friend wrote a great testimonial for me.

Thaw: to unfreeze; to become tender or liquid from a solid state

'Frozen peas should be kept out of the freezer until they thaw.'

Therapeutic: that makes one feel healthier and stress-free, like a therapy; curative

Sitting by the lake and watching the birds has a therapeutic effect on one's health.

Thereby: as a result

He arrested his own father, thereby removing the only obstacle in his way to the throne.

Think tank: a group of experts and scholars which suggests what should be done about something

That old man is a part of city's think tank.

Thoroughfare: a road where everyone is allowed to go

'No thoroughfare. Transgressors shall be prosecuted.'

Thoroughly: carefully

Wash the dishes thoroughly!

Thrash: to hit repeatedly (as a punishment)

How cruel! She thrashed her own child with a cane!

Threshold: the point where something begins; doorstep

Drinking lowers the threshold level of headaches.

Don't you dare step on this threshold again!

Throbbing pain: pain that comes in a series of beats

I have a throbbing headache. I think I need some tea.

Thrust: to push something strongly into something

The kid thrust the knife into the pumpkin, trying to cut it and give a shape.

Thump: to hit with a fist, making a heavy sound

He thumped the table in anger.

Thunderbolt: flash of lightning with thunder; a tremendous shock

The news of his father's death came as a thunderbolt to him.

Thunderous: very loud, like thunder

Thwart: to stop

He thwarted his plan of going to the party as soon as he heard his friends weren't coming.

Tickle: to touch someone with fingers in such a way that they laugh

She tickled the baby to make him laugh, but instead he cried hard.

Tilt: to slope in one direction

As he fell asleep, his head tilted to the left.

Timeless: that doesn't get old, lose value, or change with time

Some stories are timeless.

He has a sharp, timeless mind.

Timely: done or happened at suitable time

Timely decision taken by the government has saved thousands of lives.

Time-tested: something that has worked in the past

This is a time-tested method for dealing with such problems.

Tip-off: to give a secret information

She was tipped-off by a friend that they were planning to trap her.

Tiptoe: to walk on toes in order to avoid making noise

The thief tiptoed to the strong room but was caught there.

Tirade: a long, angry speech made to punish someone

Get ready for your father's tirade, since you have failed again.

Tiresome: dull and annoying

I'm the only one who is given all the tiresome jobs, she said.

Titanic: enormous; very powerful and important

This titanic ocean is the home of numerous creatures.

Titter: to laugh in a nervous, suppressed manner

He tittered when she lost balance and fell down, but his friend helped her up.

Toddler: a very young child who is learning to walk

She is still a toddler, but she is learning things very fast.

Token: a symbol that represents something more important; gesture

Please accept it as a token of my friendship.

Token for food *(that can be exchanged for food items)*

Tolerable: that can be accepted but not with pleasure

The arrogant man called this splendid weather just tolerable!

Tongue-tied: too nervous to speak clearly and fluidly

When he told he loved her, she felt tongue-tied.

Toothless: having no power

It is a toothless law and will serve no purpose.

Topple: to lose balance and fall

I toppled over a rock.

Democratically elected government of the neighbouring country was toppled by its army chief in a bloodless coup.

Topsy-turvy: upside down; confused

Her topsy-turvy yoga position is hard to imitate.

Topsy-turvy world

Torment: suffering; tremendous pain (physical or mental)

They took us hostage and tormented us every single day, told the survivor.

Toss: to throw casually

He tossed the coin into the river and watched it go down.

Totter: to walk shakily and unsteadily

He tottered across the street and then fell near a pole. I'm sure he was drunk.

Touch: a little amount

A touch of red chilli will make the dish better.

Touchy: one who is easily upset

She is very touchy about this subject. You shouldn't discuss it with her.

Toughen: to make tough/hard

We must toughen our stand on the border issue.

Tout: to advertise and publicise something very much

He had been touted as a leader but public did not accept him.

Tow-away: to take an illegally parked vehicle away using another vehicle It's a tow-away zone. Don't park here.

Trace: to find

The soldiers tried to trace the house from which the call was being made.

Tractable: easy to control; that can be dealt with easily

A tractable person

Oh, it's a tractable issue. Don't worry.

Trade deficit: when a country spends more money by importing goods than it makes by exporting goods

Government has been trying hard to deal with the trade deficit.

Trade-off: to maintain a balance between two opposite things

Either you can spend time enjoying what you have, or you can use the same time to try to get what you want. It's a trade-off.

Trail-blazer: the first person to do something; an innovative leader in a particular field

Trait: a characteristic

Nervousness is not a bad personality trait; it just shows that you need more confidence.

Traitor: one who helps an enemy against one's own country or group

We can't let him escape! He's a traitor! said an angry comrade.

Tramp: one who has no money or job, and spends his time wandering around and asking for others' help

The nerves of her! She called me a tramp!

Trample: to step on someone/something and cause injury/damage

The poor little animal was trampled by hundreds of running zebras.

Tranquillity: the state of being calm and peaceful

I hadn't experienced such tranquillity in ages!

Transcend: to rise above a limit

Latest medical technology helps doctors transcend human limits.

Transcript: a written copy of something that has been said

The transcript of her speech was not accurate.

Transform: to improve something so much that it looks very different

He is the man who transformed China's infrastructure.

Technology which transformed the field of medical science

Transient: that lasts for a very short time

A transient light

Transit: carrying of goods/people from one place to another; transportation

We lost our equipment in transit, so we need to buy a new set.

Transparent: that allows light to pass through; something through which one can see

A transparent glass

A transparent system required to eliminate corruption

Transplant (medical): to move from one person to another

His heart transplant surgery has been successful. He will live!

Trap: to trick a person to get caught (in a situation they don't want to be in)

The police trapped the thief using a fake Facebook account.

Trash: to throw away

The pizza was so bad that I trashed it after the first bite.

Trauma: a mental shock caused by a very bad experience

He remained in a state of trauma for about a year after his aeroplane crash.

Treachery: deceiving a person who trusts one; deceit

You told my weakness to my opponent? Well, that's called treachery!

Tread: to put foot on something

He trodden on the fragile toy and broke it into pieces.

Treason: helping enemy against own country/king

Speaking against the king is an act of treason, said the spokesperson.

Tremble: to shake due to cold, fear, weakness etc.

He entered the hall on trembling legs.

Tremendous: very much

He qualified for the finals after tremendous effort.

Trendy: in fashion

This dress is very trendy, but also very common.

Trespass: to enter someone's land without his permission

They were caught for trespassing on the duke's land.

Trickle: to flow in a thin line or drops

In this Ayurvedic procedure, medicated oil is made to trickle on a person's forehead.

Trifle: little and unimportant

Such trifles deserve no attention. Just forget the whole matter.

Trigger: to start

A small incident triggered the world war.

Trim: to cut away unwanted parts of something to improve its appearance

He trimmed the bushes and trees to make the garden look tidier.

He got his hair trimmed.

Triumph: victory

His triumph over his arch rival was remarkable.

Trivial: not important

Such trivial matters must not claim much of your time.

Trot ***(of a horse)*:** to run at its slowest speed

The pony trotted along the fence.

Troublesome: that causes trouble; worrying

This troublesome weather won't let me fly today! he said in frustration.

Truce: an agreement to stop the war for a while

There was no war during the truce period.

Trudge: to walk with difficulty or effort

We were given special boots to trudge through the snow around the hotel.

Trump card: an advantage which one has and others don't, and which is likely to get one what he wants

His postgraduate degree in finance proved to be his trump card.

Trustworthy: that can be trusted

Tuck: to put or insert something, especially a loose end of a dress, into a convenient place

He tucked his shirt in before entering the interview room.

Turgid: boring because of being pompous

His turgid description of his master's villa

Turmoil: a state of uncertainty and disorder

The wildfires put the region in turmoil.

Turnabout: a complete change, especially in opposite direction

A sudden turnabout in government policies

Turnaround: when a business suddenly becomes successful from a state of failure

The company's turnaround has been very dramatic.

Turning point: a point of time when a situation takes an important turn

The D-Day was a turning point in the Second World War.

Passing the officers' test proved to be the turning point of his life.

Tussle: a struggle for something; strong arguments

The tussle between the two friends didn't affect their friendship in the long run.

Tutelage: advice, guidance etc.

He became a great scholar under the tutelage of his renowned professor.

Tweet: the sound that baby birds make

Twilight: late evening, when the darkness is about to take over

Twins: two children born to same mother at the same time

The twins look exactly alike.

Twinkle: to shine strongly and weakly in turns

The stars twinkled in the sky above us.

Twisted: changed forcibly

A report based on twisted information

Twitch: jerky, uncontrolled movement of or in an organ

My left eye is twitching.

Twitter: sounds that birds make

The birds twittered loudly in the forest.

Typical: having the characteristics expected from a group of things or people

Dry mouth and butterflies in the stomach are typical symptoms of nervousness one feels before an important event.

Tyrant: a cruel and powerful ruler

People felt a relief when the tyrant was killed in the enemy bombing.

U

Ubiquitous: seeming to be everywhere

Smart phones are now ubiquitous.

Ugly duckling: a person who isn't beautiful/successful initially (but will become so later on, against expectations)

She was seen as an ugly duckling by many, but she became a Miss World.

Ulterior motive: a hidden motive

His ulterior motive remained unknown until he took all the money and ran away.

Ultimate: the final and the most important

This is the ultimate weapon,

more powerful than any other in the world.

The ultimate goal of a human being must be to serve the human kind, said the guru.

Ultimatum: a threat that if one doesn't do what he is told to do by a certain time, they'll have the consequences

The terrorists have given the government an ultimatum of three days.After that they'll kill the hostages.

Unabridged (book): not shortened

This is the unabridged edition of the famous novel.

Unanimous decision: a decision taken with the assent of everyone in a group

He was declared the winner by the unanimous decision of the judges.

Unappealing: not attractive

Unattainable: that cannot be achieved

No goal is unattainable, said the great man.

Unbearable pain: too much pain

The pain of death of his daughter was unbearable for the old man.

Unbiased: fair

The judge's decision cannot be called unbiased.

Uncalled-for: something bad that was not deserved; not provoked

Her anger was totally uncalled-for.

Uncanny: mysterious, and hard to explain

His uncanny eyes scare me, she said.

Unconditional: without any restrictions

His love for you is unconditional and innocent.

An unconditional surrender by the enemy

Unconscious: one who has no consciousness

The flower-vase fell on his head and he got unconscious.

Uncover: to reveal

Unknown truths about his private life were uncovered by his autobiography.

Undeniable: that cannot be denied; true

It is an undeniable fact that the accused had visited him the night he died, said the lawyer.

Underachiever: one who hasn't achieved what was expected from him

The leader was called an underachiever by the news magazines around the world.

Underestimate: to guess someone to be less than he is

Never underestimate your opponent.

Underdog: the contestant who is understood to be weaker

She was seen as an underdog but she won the match.

Undergo: to experience, especially something unpleasant

He is very scared as he has to undergo a heart surgery next month.

Undermine: to weaken gradually

His power has been seriously undermined by his incompetent advisors.

Underneath: under

A dog was asleep underneath my car.

Underplay: to make something look less dangerous or serious

The government's representative tried to underplay the whole incident but nobody was convinced.

Underprivileged: poor, less educated etc.

Many new schemes have been introduced for the underprivileged sections of the society.

Understatement: a presentation of a thing that makes it seem less serious or importantthan it actually is

It will be an understatement that we are facing minor problems. We are in serious trouble.

Undisputed: agreed upon by everyone; undeniable

He is the undisputed champion of Maths.

Uneven: not smooth or flat; rough

These uneven roads are not fit for luxury cars.

Unfazed: not worried at all

He was unfazed despite his constant criticism.

Unfounded: not based on facts; baseless

Her fears are unfounded.

Unify: to unite

He made every effort to unify the tribes.

Unisex: for both males and females

A unisex saloon

Universal: existing at all places; worldwide

It is a universal truth that there can be no life without the sun.

Unleash: to set free; to release a great force

We need to unleash the power within.

King's soldiers unleashed the lion in the arena.

Unmask: to expose; to show

The spy was unmasked when he tried to send a secret message to the country he was working for.

Unprovoked: without any provocation

His aggression was unprovoked and he deserves punishment for it.

Unrest: turbulence; conflict, war etc.; not peace

There is a sense of unrest among people.

Unruly: hard to control

An unruly child/ employee

Unsolicited: unwelcome; not asked for; not requested

I don't like unsolicited advices, she said flatly.

Unsung: not praised for their bravery or contribution

This memorial is for the unknown and unsung war heroes.

Unthinkable: that cannot be imagined

It was unthinkable that the two lovers could ever hate each other so much.

Unveil: to show to everyone; to make known

The manager unveiled a new plan to capture the market.

Unwarranted: without a good reason

The problem that has befallen us was entirely unwarranted and could have been avoided.

Unyielding: rigid; firm; obstinate

His unyielding demands are making the progress of the project difficult.

Uphold: to maintain; to keep

The High Court upheld the decision of the lower court.

Upright: straight

She sat there upright, without looking at me.

Uprising: an opposition of people against the government or the king; rebellion

The Arab uprisings shook the world politics.

Uproot: to pull out of the ground; to root out

He uprooted the wilted plant and planted a fresh one.

The five year plans to uproot the poverty from the society

Up-to-date: modern; recent

His clothes are always up-to-date and fashionable.

Up-to-date knowledge on a subject

Urge: to strongly persuade someone to do something; to push

She urged me to look into the matter rightaway.

Usher: to show one where he should go; to guide

He ushered us into his new shop.

Usurp: to take control of something without having right to do so

He usurped the land of his neighbour. Now he is facing a court case.

Utility: usefulness

What is the utility of such an impractical plan?

Utmost: the greatest amount

I have the utmost respect for you.

Utter:

(i) to say something

He uttered a few words and left the stage.

(ii) total; complete

Utter disregard for rules

V

Vacate: to leave

If you vacate the hotel room before 12 PM, you won't have to pay the room charges for the next day.

Vagabond: one who has no home, job etc. and keeps moving from place to place

He is worse than a vagabond, if you ask me, said his friend.

Vagaries: uncontrollable and unexpected changes

Insurance can be called a protection against vagaries of life.

Vague: not clearly expressed

His vague facial expressions were not much help for us.

Vain: unsuccessful

All his efforts to lift the heavy trunk were in vain.

Valiant: very brave

The prisoner of war made a valiant effort to escape by shooting the enemy guards but he died in the firing.

Valid: legal and still usable

A valid pass/document passport

Valour: courage

He received a medal for showing valour in the face of danger.

Vandalise: to break other people's property

Four men vandalised the shop.

Vanish: to disappear

Some problems vanish with time.

Vanity: when one is obsessed with himself and is very proud of own achievements, appearance etc.

Only his vanity compelled him to accept the invitation to the debate.

Vanquish: to defeat completely

The largest enemy unit had vanquished in that battle, told the historian.

Velocity: speed

Vendetta: a bloody fight between two groups or families; feud

The firing was due to a political vendetta.

Venerate: to respect too much; to worship

Some religious leaders are venerated like God.

Vengeance: a wish to harm someone for the harm he has done to one; revenge

It was the hunger for vengeance that turned him into a criminal.

Venomous: poisonous

A highly venomous snake, such as King Cobra

Venture: to take a risky course of action

The company ventured into a new business and lost all its yearly profit.

Venue: a place where something is to take place

Please reach the venue before 8 PM.

Veracity: truthfulness

The veracity of her statement is under suspicion.

Verbal: spoken

He is a master of verbal communications.

Veteran: one who has a lot of experience of a particular job, work etc. especially war

Many war veterans were given gallantry awards on the Republic Day.

Viable: that can succeed

Your plan is viable but you need to support it with effort.

Vibe: general mood of a person or place, which can be felt by people

A place with calming vibe which can be felt clearly

When I told him I was sad, he said he was sending good vibes my way.

Vicious: cruel and violent; that causes great pain

The vicious pain in his chest was due to a heart problem.

Victimise: to treat someone unfairly because of hatred towards their race, religion etc. or for some other particular reason

The 22-year old man from the East was victimised for racial reasons.

Victor: the winner

The victor got all the appreciation and monetary rewards.

Vigilant: one who is careful about any possible dangers, troubles etc.

A vigilant neighbour can prevent an incident of burglary.

Vindicate: to prove right despite others' opposition

She vindicated when she won the first prize for creativity.

Vindictive: not willing to forgive someone; having desire for revenge

'A vindictive man attacked the ex-cop with a sharp object yesterday.'

Vintage: something valuable that represents a past time period

A rally of vintage cars took place in the capital yesterday.

Violation: breaking law, rule etc.; breach

Violation of traffic rules cost him his three-days' salary.

Viper: a person who cannot be trusted

Virgin:

(i) one who has never had sex

She remained a virgin all her life.

(ii) land which has never been cultivated

Virtually: almost

My car virtually stopped in the middle of the highway!

Virtuous: having high moral values and qualities

A virtuous man is hard to find these days.

Virulent: a severe disease or poison that spreads fast in the body

His virulent fever got him hospitalised.

Visionary: one who can see or correctly guess how the things are going to be in the future

The great saint was also a great visionary.

Visualise: to imagine how something/someone could be

I visualised him as a smart, friendly guy but he was exactly the opposite!

Vital: very important

The most vital part of the plan has been successful. I hope the rest goes well too.

Vivid: bright and deep

Vivid blue jeans trousers

Vocab: vocabulary

Vocational: providing skills for a job

He took some vocational course in the summer holidays and now he is working as an assistant at a hospital.

Vogue: a fashion, often temporary

This sweater design had become a vogue when I was young.

Void: an empty space

Nothing can fill the void created in her life after her husband's death.

Voila: an expression of joy that comes from accomplishing something

I asked her if she'd marry me and voila! She said yes!

Volition: a consciously made choice

He chose the yellow dress over the blue one out of his own volition.

Volunteer: one who does a service without accepting payments for it

Finally, a volunteer came forward to help the accident victim.

Voracious: very eager; hungry

He has always been a voracious reader. You'll find him doing nothing else but reading books.

Vouch: to say that something is true

He vouched for his friend and said he could do the job satisfactorily.

Voyage: a long journey, especially by ship

His voyages had been recorded in the History journals.

Vulgar: not suitable for the occasion; rude and offensive

His vulgar behaviour spoiled the party.

Vulgar language

Vulnerable: that can be attacked easily; defenceless

She is vulnerable to criticism.

W

Wacko: crazy; insane

I told you she was a wacko! he said angrily, getting up from the bench.

Wage:

(i) to begin and carry on

The revolutionaries have waged a guerrilla war against the government.

(ii) pay

Wail: to cry loudly because of pain or sorrow

The wails of women and children from the hospital room indicated that he was no more.

Waiver: an agreement that one doesn't need to pay something

He qualified for a tax waiver.

A tax-waiver government bond

Walloping: a beating by hand

The kid came home crying, complaining that he had got a walloping from his teacher without any reason.

Wander: to walk here and there without any purpose

He spends all his time wandering around.

Wannabe: one who wants to become something

A wannabe author/doctor

Wardrobe: a tall cupboard for hanging clothes

Warmonger: one who wants a war to happen

The politician was accused of being a warmonger.

Wary: very cautious about something; not trusting someone or something

He has always been wary of borrowers.

Wasteful: using something carelessly, wasting a part of it

Such a wasteful use of natural resources! It's a shame.

Watertight: that doesn't allow water to get in; waterproof

A watertight container

Watery: filled with water; wet

Her watery eyes told that she had been in pain.

Waver: to lose strength for a while

His intentions began to waver when he considered how difficult the task was.

Weakling: a person who is weak

He was so rude, he called me a weakling!

Wearisome: tiring and boring

His job is one of the most wearisome in the world.

Weatherproof: that doesn't get affected by weather

He wore a weatherproof jacket that night.

A weatherproof paint.

Weekend: Saturday and Sunday

We are planning to go to a hill station this weekend.

Weigh: to consider carefully

He weighed all the options before making the final decision.

Weird: unusual and strange

His weird behaviour keeps others away from him.

Weirdo: one who behaves or dresses weirdly

Welfare: wellbeing; happiness and health

The new leader has started various public welfare schemes.

Well-heeled: rich

He comes from a well-heeled family, that's why she's behind him.

Well-versed: one who knows a lot about something

He is well-versed in computers, that's why I've called him.

Whack: to hit noisily

He whacked me on the head with rolled news paper!

Wheeze: a whistling sound while breathing

The kid's wheezing is worrying. He must be taken to a doctor.

Whereabouts: a place where a person is; location

Nobody knows his whereabouts these days.

Whimper: a weak, small sound one makes when in pain

I heard baby's whimpers and ran to the room.

Whimsical: fanciful; strange, and often funnily so

A whimsical old man asked me whether I was looking for a dance partner.

Whine: to complain repeatedly

I don't like to go out with her. She keeps whining about things all the time.

Whip *(politics)*: a member of a party who makes sure all members vote on a matter

Whip: a **leather strip** with a handle, used to beat people or animals, mostly in earlier times; to use a whip on someone

Whirl: to turn around in circles; to spin

She whirled until she felt dizzy.

Whisper: to say something in a very quiet manner, keeping the voice very low

She whispered something in my ear but I couldn't understand it.

Whistle-bower: one who leaks the information about an illegal activity

Whistle-blowers should be given extra protection.

Whitewash: to hide something from others; to conceal

They tried to whitewash the scam but it became known.

Whizz: to move very fast

The racing cars whizzed past us every second.

Whoop: a loud, excited shout, made to show support for someone

The fans whooped in the stadium all the time.

Wicked:

(i) bad

A wicked man

(ii) *(highly informal)* excellent

You answered all the questions? Wicked!

Widespread: that exists at multiple places

Widespread protests against the rape incident shook the nation.

Wilful: done intentionally

It was a wilful action.

Wilt ***(flower)*****:** to become weak, lose beauty and bend towards the ground

There were wilted flowers in the vase.

Wimp: one who is not brave

I thought he was courageous but he proved to be a wimp.

Window-shopping: to look at goods without buying anything

We spent the afternoon doing window-shopping.

Windy: with a lot of wind

This windy weather is good for sailing.

Wink: to close one eye for a very short duration when looking at someone

He just winked at me! What does he want to say?

Wipe: to clean a surface with a cloth or a piece of foam

The waiter wiped the table clean before serving the food.

Wishy-washy: having no firm ideas, principles etc.

He responded in a wishy-washy manner.

Wit: ability to use words cleverly and humorously

His talks are full of wit and wisdom.

Withered: decaying

The crops were withered when he returned.

Withhold: to not give

The university will withhold your result until you pay the fees.

Withstand: to endure; to bear something successfully

Our equipment cannot withstand this freezing cold. We need some special covering.

Wiz: wizard; one who knows a lot about something

He is a stock market wiz.

Woe: a great pain; sorrow

He has suffered many woes in his lifetime.

Woo: to try to attract; to persuade someone to support one

The companies have been trying their best to woo the customers.

They will do anything to woo the voters.

Wordy: using too many words

His wordy article was too boring to read.

Workable: that can deliver desired result; practical

We need a workable plan to develop our business.

Workaholic: one who cannot stop working

Some workaholics work on weekends too.

Workload: amount of work to be done

Making a time-table will not reduce your workload but it will help you finish it in time.

Workmanship: the degree of skill used in making something

This beautiful statue shows the workmanship of the artist.

Workout: a session of physical exercise

His workout is too heavy for me.

Worldly: related to material world

A worldly philosopher who doesn't spend time thinking about spiritual matters

World-class: one of the best in the world

A world-class company

Worn out: damaged by too much use

Could you find nothing except this worn out dress for the party?

Worrisome: that causes worry

Worrisome effects of pesticides on food crops.

Worship: to respect and praise very much; to venerate

We must worship to God every day, the mother told her son.

Hates? She worships you, you idiot! said my friend.

Worst: most unpleasant and bad

In the worst case scenario, they can expel us.

Worthless: valueless

A fake, worthless stone

A worthless guy

Worthwhile: worth the time, money and energy given

You are in a worthwhile career. Why do you want to change it?

Wrath: extreme anger

If you don't repent, you'll face the wrath of God, said the priest.

Storms are nature's wrath.

Wreak: to cause, especially something violent

On the commander's order, our forces wreaked havoc on the enemy.

Wreck: a completely destroyed vehicle, ship, plane, building etc.

The wreck of the boat was found near the rocks.

Wrench: to pull something suddenly, sometimes damaging it

He wrenched the news paper from my hand.

Wretc.hed: miserable

The wretc.hed old man/hut

Wring ***(to wring a cloth)*****:** to hold tightly in both hands and turn each end in opposite directions, generally to remove water

She wrung each cloth out before putting it on the line.

Writ: a legal document, ordering someone to do something

The writ didn't bother him at all.

Wrongdoing: an illegal or wrong act

His wrongdoing will land him in the jail one day.

X

Xenophobia: a fear of foreigners and their customs, traditions etc.

Xenophobia is a baseless and irrational fear.

Y

Yank: to pull forcefully with a jerky movement

He yanked the bookshelf door open and many books fell on his head.

Yawn: to open mouth wide and inhale and then exhale a large quantity of air, sometimes with a loud voice

He was so bored that he yawned three times in ten minutes.

Yeah: yes

Yell: to shout loudly when angry, surprised, scared, in pain etc.

He yelled as I stepped on his foot.

Yielding: bending under pressure; not rigid; obedient

His yielding nature has made him a favourite of his seniors. Now they are making him do a lot of extra work.

Youngster: a young person

Youngsters are not as serious about their future as they should be.

Yucky: not looking or tasting good

I won't eat this yucky thing! said the kid.

Yummy: that tastes well; delicious

This ice cream is so yummy! said the kid.

Z

Zap: to kill/destroy

Many tanks were zapped in the air strike.

Zeal: a lot of enthusiasm

He had always had a zeal for playing football.

Zealot: one who has a firm opinion about something; a fanatic

I'd say he is a religious zealot.

Zero tolerance: showing no tolerance towards something, especially crimes

A zero tolerance policy to counter terrorism/rape incidents

Zest: enthusiasm and interest

The film doesn't capture the zest of the book.

Zigzag: having shape of letter 'Z'; to move left and right quickly and alternately

Zigzag driving we see these days is very dangerous.

Zombie:

(i) a dead person brought back to life *(often shown to be in a mindless state in movies)*

(ii) a person with no energy or interest; very tired and dull

He is a zombie when he comes home in the evening.

❏❏❏

3

Practice Exercises

Fill in the blanks with the most appropriate words from the given choices. The answers have been provided at the end of the section.

Words beginning with letter 'A'

[*Your options are:* assigned, ascetic, abate, awful, astronomical, averse, amuse, apologetic, ambushed, anticipated, allocated, agile, alienated, acceded, adamant, acquainted, absconding, abominate, appease]

- They waited for three days for the storm to _____, but it just didn't happen.
- Forget her. She _____ the idea of marriage.
- The police are searching for the _____ criminal.
- Finally, her parents _____ to her demands.
- I guess you two are _____ with each other.
- She is _____ that she won't marry him, no matter how much her parents pressurise her to.
- Cheetah is a very _____ animal.
- He has _____ all his friends one by one, and now he has none.
- The CFO has _____ more funds for advertisements this year.
- The bandits _____ the police van and looted all the weapons.
- Does his stupid comedy _____ you?
- Nobody had _____ such a disastrous climax of the movie.
- He is _____ for his rude behaviour.
- The politician tried to _____ the angry mob by making some impossible promises.
- He lives like an _____, away from all the luxury of the world.
- Since he is the most experienced guy in the team, he has been _____ the most difficult task.
- The firm has suffered _____ losses this year.
- He is _____ to the very idea of arrange marriage.
- What an _____ sight! I don't want to be here another minute.

Words beginning with letter 'B'

[*Your options are:* bewildered, befit, blamed, bait, bedridden, babbling, blacklist, boost, blithering, blink, bystanders, boycott, bragging, breakthrough, backfire]

- She is _____ about a stupid fashion show.
- If your plan _____, we will lose our regular customers as well.
- The hunter used a goat as the _____ to trap the man-eater.
- He is so ill that he has been _____ since last five weeks.
- The punishment should _____ the crime.
- This complicated equation has _____ me.
- "Well, someone had to be _____ for the failure and they chose me," he said bitterly.
- Since the products we were supplied were of cheap quality, we have decided to _____ the supplier.
- He disappeared within the _____ of an eye!
- How could he leave the kids alone? He is a _____ idiot!
- We need to build more ports to _____ the trade.
- Don't take him seriously. He's just _____ about his little achievements.
- Our countrymen decided to _____ the goods made by the aggressive neighbour.
- The invention of Polio vaccine was a major _____ in the field of medicine.
- I think _____ should have helped the injured man.

Words beginning with letter 'C'

[*Your options are*: curtail, counterbalances, convened, considerate, culprit, crafty, confess concise, congenial, cajole, casually, callous, canvass, cherished, cleansed, chequered, cocksure, close shave, clueless, commemorate, collective, comprehended, conceded, communicative]

- I will try to _____ him into investing in our company.
- He sounds very _____ to me.
- I'm glad that the great man has agreed to _____ support for our cause.
- He is taking this grave matter very _____.
- She has a _____ career as a doctor. Many patients complain about her unscientific methods.
- We have always _____ the sweet memories of our marriage.
- Green tea _____ the body from inside.
- It was a _____ with death.
- We are still _____ about how he did that.
- Don't be_____ about winning the match. You still need to practise.
- We need _____ efforts to solve this problem.
- Today we have gathered to _____ our founder Dr Prakash Vaidya.
- We need a _____ employee to interact with the customers.

- Unless you have _____ the matter, don't interfere.
- The enemy forces _____ their defeat.
- Don't just keep going on and on. Give a _____ answer.
- "_____ your crime!" the cop said to the accused.
- Everyone wants a _____ neighbourhood.
- You brought an extra jacket for me! How _____ of you!
- The board of directors _____ to discuss whether the general manager should be allowed to continue.
- His wife's hard work _____ his laziness.
- I can't believe him. His manners are too _____ .
- I knew he was the real _____ behind all this chaos!
- The country needs to _____ the trade deficit.

Words beginning with letter 'D'

[*Your options are*: debut, decorum, daydreaming, deadlock, decisive, demolished, deplorable, demerits, deluded, drag, dire, domesticate, deteriorated, duped, dumbfounded]

- Stop _____ and start acting.
- The two countries have hit a _____ in talks. I don't think they'll reach a decision.
- I want to see my daughter's _____ dance performance.
- After three years of continuous war, General is looking for a _____ victory this time.
- The rude speaker couldn't maintain his _____ any longer.
- She is _____ if she thinks he will marry her.
- Let's discuss the merits and _____ of the proposed plan.
- The bridge was _____ by the over-flowing river.
- No wonder his _____ nature alienates people.
- The relations between the two neighbours _____ every day and one of them moved to the court.
- The world has seen _____ consequences of playing with the nature.
- You can't _____ a bear.
- Don't _____ me into this matter. I have nothing to do with it.
- His answer left the teacher _____.
- I was _____ into buying cheap goods by that clever salesman.

Words beginning with letter 'E'

[*Your options are*: endangered, eradicate, envies, enriched, enclosed, eluding, eager, edge, excruciating, eyesore, extensive, exacerbate]

- This kid is always _____ to hear stories.

- His height gives him an _____ over his opponents.
- I keep trying for success but it keeps _____ me!
- Please find _____ a demand draft.
- The king's stubbornness has _____ the lives of his soldiers.
- We _____ the soil with natural fertilisers.
- She _____ my success.
- We will do everything in our power to _____ the poverty from our society.
- The recent skirmishes _____ the relations between two countries.
- He is in _____ pain.
- His _____ experience is an asset to our company.
- That ugly, million-dollar mansion is a real _____ . Nobody likes it.

Words beginning with letter 'F'

[*Your options are*: ferocious, favouritism, fidelity, factual, feasible, foiled, flatter, flawless, forfeited, forayed, forbidden, futile, furious]

- There are _____ errors in his description of the event.
- "We don't want any _____ in our party," said the leader.
- Let's check if this plan is _____. Else we will need a new plan.
- Lion is a _____ animal.
- Please understand, your _____ is under question.
- Don't try and _____ me. It won't work.
- Her performance was _____. She is really the greatest dancer alive.
- Our timely action _____ the thief's plan to break the safe.
- I _____ into stock market investments and lost my money.
- This lab is _____ for the junior students.
- You have _____ your claim on the land.
- His indifference made her _____ and she left without uttering another word.
- All our efforts proved to be _____ as we couldn't stop the flood water.

Words beginning with letter 'G'

[*Your options are*: grant, gullible, garnished, grumbling, generous, glanced, guts]

- I _____ the cake with cream.
- He has been very _____ in praising you.
- The examiner just _____ at my model and rejected it! He should have looked carefully.
- Kindly _____ me a leave for ten days and oblige.
- Stop _____ all the time.
- He is still a _____ guy, vulnerable to deceptions.
- "If you have _____, come and face me!" he shouted.

Words beginning with letter 'H'

[*Your options are*: hurdles, haste, habitual, hype, hiccups, hampered, humble, hospitable]

- He is a _____ liar. Never trust him.
- His inability to read has _____ his intellectual development.
- We need speed but not _____, as the latter can spoil everything.
- These small _____ cannot stop me from doing what I want to do.
- She is not very _____ to guests.
- He is _____enough to apologise after making a mistake.
- The company is facing some unexpected _____ in the new market.
- All the _____ created around the star's son couldn't make him a star.

Words beginning with letter 'I'

[*Your options are*: impeccable, ill-mannered, immense, idle, icon, initiative, indomitable, incontrovertible, inferior, irony, inevitable, intermittent, intervened]

- The fashion _____ died in an accident last night.
- Instead of lying _____ all day, you should move your body and do some work.
- He is an_____ guy. I don't want to invite him to the party.
- The _____ power of machines helps us dig the ground faster for construction purposes.
- His _____ speech impressed everyone.
- We presented an_____ piece of evidence in the court.
- You need an_____spirit to overcome all the problems of life.
- He tried to sell us_____ products.
- You should take _____ in a group discussion.
- This _____ rain is driving me crazy!
- The teacher _____ in the students' argument.
- The recession seems to be_____. We must be ready with countermeasures.
- The law passed against the corruption is actually saving the corrupt people. What an _____!

Words beginning with letter 'J' and letter 'K'

[*Your options are*: justify, jargons, knack, jackpot, keen, knowledgeable, judicious]

- I can't believe we won the_____!
- Keep your science_____ out of your speech if you want people to understand you.
- I've always been _____ in gardening.
- Being _____ is important for a manager.
- You cannot_____ your baseless demands.
- He has a _____ for social service.

- He doesn't seem to be very _____ about computers.

Words beginning with letter 'L'

[*Your options are*: lush, lodge, lousy, lenient, loathe, lethargic, layman, landmark, laughingstock, laggard]

- He is a_____. He never takes initiative.
- Our company has set a _____ by inventing a cheaper and more effective medicine for bird flu.
- The new employee is the _____of the office because of his weird dresses.
- A _____ cannot understand the technicalities involved in repairing an engine.
- I want you to be _____ in punishing the students for minor faults.
- His _____ attitude is the cause of the delay.
- I _____ those who support violence.
- If you have a problem, please go and _____ a complaint with the authorities.
- The house is located on a_____ green hill.
- I saw a _____ film. Now I have a headache.

Words beginning with letter 'M'

[*Your options are*: misleading, miffed, mercilessly, mild, mettle, mentor, mediocre, massacred, meek, marvelled, manipulate, magnified, malicious, mythical, monotonous, muffled, mundane]

- The government's inaction has _____ the problem of unemployment.
- They had made a _____ plan to kill the Russian president on our soil.
- He was trying to _____ the enquiry against him.
- I always _____ at the magnificence of the Himalayas.
- The gangsters _____ entire population of a village.
- He replied in a _____ voice, as if he was scared of someone.
- I don't buy _____ designs such as this one.
- It's a good idea to find a _____ when entering the politics.
- The rebellion was crushed _____.
- He has proved his_____ by winning the local elections.
- I'm not _____ at you anymore.
- The curry has a_____ taste of coconut.
- Most of his reports are sensational and _____, far from the truth.
- He speaks in a _____ voice.
- "He is dead," he said in a _____ voice.
- I'm shocked that some _____ issues are blocking our progress.
- Sphinx is a _____ creature.

Words beginning with letter 'N'

[*Your options are*: numb, nightmare, neglect, nudged, nurtured, nasty, nexus, nap]

- If you are so sleepy, why don't you take a _____?
- I will never let him succeed in his _____ intentions.
- There was a _____ of forest guards and poachers.
- My worst_____ has come true. My passport has been stolen and I need to return to India today!
- The government must not _____ the opinion of the leader of opposition.
- He _____ me in the ribs to draw my attention to the notice board.
- My fingers have gone _____.
- I have _____ positive feeling in my mind since my childhood.

Words beginning with letter 'O'

[*Your options are*: overwhelming, overlook, oblivion, overestimating, outcome, obsession, obstructed, orchestrated, ophthalmologist, omitted, omens]

- I lived in _____ for three years.
- Superbikes are his_____. He keeps talking about them.
- My language problem has _____ my way again.
- "Unfortunately, our commander based his strategy on _____, not on common sense," said the king's soldier.
- Some search results were _____ by the search engine.
- I can't see clearly. I think I should meet an _____.
- The whole fight was_____. It wasn't real even a bit.
- The_____ of the experiment was quite encouraging.
- I think you are _____ me. I can't bear so many burdens on my shoulders.
- Just _____ his faults. He is naive.
- We got _____ response from the audience.

Words beginning with letter 'P'

[*Your options are*: premeditated, punitive, predecessor, primitive, procrastinating, prudent, point-blank, pragmatic, progressive, possessions, pompously, permissible, plausible, persuade, plummeted, pelted, passer-bys, patrolling, paltry, paramount, painstaking]

- Behind the huge success of the school are_____ efforts of the teachers.
- He gave me a _____ amount of Rs 20 to buy the lunch.
- Surviving the recession is the matter of_____ importance for the company at the moment.
- One of the _____ told me that the carton of milk I was carrying was leaky.

- A _____ police jeep saw the robbers robbing a man.
- He _____ stones at poor animals!
- Leaving the hostel at night is not _____.
- He is your friend. You must_____ him to study hard.
- He gave a _____ account of what he had seen in the room.
- As soon as the scam became known, the share prices of the company _____.
- He was shot down from a _____ range.
- "I cleared the IAS exam in my first attempt," he told _____.
- The pen my father bought me when I was a kid is one of my most valuable _____.
- We need a more _____ plan to finish this project in time.
- "I knew your_____," said the client to the chairman. "He was a very nice man."
- A _____ attack on the leader nearly killed him.
- "Our_____ methods of teaching are no longer good enough," said the Education Minister.
- "Keep _____ a work till you can," he joked.
- He was _____ enough not to annoy his father.
- His illegal acts call for a _____ action.

Words beginning with letter 'Q'

[*Your options are*: quitter, quacks, quizzical, quibbling]

- Stop wasting your money on _____. You need to see a real doctor.
- Stop _____ about why we lost the match. It's over now.
- Be a winner, not a _____.
- He gave me a _____ look and I instantly knew a question was coming.

Words beginning with letter 'R'

[*Your options are*: remarkable, rampant, rash driving, ravishing, rapt, refurbished, reckon, realms, relish, refuted, resorted, resembles, renounced, ruthless, rigid, routed, reverted]

- The walls of the old fort stood in _____ conditions.
- He played to a_____ audience.
- Traffic police stopped him for his _____.
- She looks _____ in that pink dress.
- Allow your imagination to leave the _____ of material world.
- I _____ he is very interested in the deal and will agree to our price.
- We bought a _____ old bungalow.
- The science community _____ his hypothesis straightaway.
- You must _____ every moment because it has its own beauty.
- You became a scientist! What a _____ achievement!

- He _____ the material world and became a yogi.
- He _____ his father so much!
- When she refused to accept his marriage proposal, he _____ to violence! He must be punished hard.
- She _____ to me after she had done thorough research on the subject.
- Don't be so _____! We can go to New York instead of Paris!
- The invader's forces _____ the defence forces.
- He shouldn't be so _____ with his own kids.

Words beginning with letter 'S'

[*Your options are*: shaky, shrewd, stature, snapped, spacious, screaming, sarcasm, surmise, staggering, seasoned, stunningly, spirited, scattered, slash, skinny, stroll, sceptical, sacrificed, swiftly, sheepishly, savouring, shudder, startled, sane, scrutinised, skipped, solidarity, sprinkled, stray, substantial, superficial]

- His parents _____ their comfort to send him to an expensive MBA college.
- He is driving so recklessly. Are you sure he is_____?
- There was a hint of _____ in his praise.
- I hope you are _____ the taste of our food, sir.
- When the blast took place, the crowd _____ in every direction.
- His parents are _____ about sending him to the party.
- Stop _____, kids! My ears hurt.
- The whole area was _____ before the politician's rally.
- How could such a _____journalist make such a mistake?
- Your legs look a bit_____. Are you okay?
- "What are we discussing though," he asked _____.
- The _____ lawyer successfully used the witness's point against himself.
- The strange voice I heard in the middle of the night made me _____.
- She's not _____, I'd say, though she's a bit underweight.
- I _____ the breakfast today.
- If we want to sell more scooters, we must _____ the prices by ten percent.
- I stepped on the stick and it _____ into two.
- All the party members appeared in the parliament to show _____.
- This room is quite _____ and can accommodate many people.
- She is a _____ individual and won't give up easily.
- She _____ some sugar over the cream.

- Appropriation of _____ three million dollars by a bank manager shook the country.
- His rudeness _____ everyone in the room.
- His _____ is higher than any other in his party.
- Animal catchers caught many _____ dogs from the road.
- We took a ____ on the footpath of the garden.
- She looked _____ beautiful, didn't she?
- He has _____ support of people with him.
- The actor's _____ emotions couldn't impress people.
- I _____ you don't like me. Am I right?
- He acted _____ and extinguished the fire.

Words beginning with letter 'T'

[*Your options are*: traits, thrash, tarnishing, tipping-off, tampered, tirade, twitching, tempted, trace, trap, trembling]

- The seal was broken and the cheque book had been _____ with.
- Your reckless and stupid actions are _____ the image of your father.
- I was _____ to touch the ancient statue but the museum guard stopped me.
- Don't _____ that poor horse!
- Boss gave me a _____ when I reached office an hour late.
- He was accused of _____ the smugglers about police's plan to catch them.
- It is possible to _____ one's location using his mobile number.
- Politeness is not one of her personality _____.
- They used an electronic device to _____ the flies.
- He was _____ with fear.
- My left leg muscles are _____.

Words beginning with letter 'U'

[*Your options are*: unsung, ultimatum, unrest, upright, uncovered, utter, unfazed, ulterior motive, unthinkable]

- We weren't aware of his ____ but we did have an idea.
- The union of auto-rickshaw drivers has given the government an _____ of three days to accept their demands.
- Finally, the truth has been _____.
- He remained _____ throughout his trial in the court.
- The political _____ has affected the stock market.
- _____ heroes of the Great War were remembered in the function.
- The _____ has happened. The weakest horse won the race.
- Sit _____ and draw a deep breath.

- He talked _____ nonsense all the time.

Words beginning with letter 'V'

[*Your options are*: vulnerable, valour, virtually, veteran, vendetta, vicious, vouch, vanished, vital]

- The brave soldier will always be known for his_____.
- The oil-stains on the cloth _____ after the wash.
- The communal _____ between two extremist groups claimed many lives.
- The war _____ threatened to return his medals if the government remained apathetic towards him.
- He suffered from a _____ headache.
- I had ____ failed the exam. Only the last question saved me.
- "His _____ organs are working quite well," told the doctor.
- I cannot stick my neck out and ____ for you.
- Children are _____ to such crimes.

Words beginning with letter 'W'

[*Your options are*: withstand, whitewash, weigh, wandering, worthless, well-versed, wary, wreck, widespread, wordy]

- "Stop _____ here and there and find a work for yourself," said his dad.
- He remained _____ of the dogs after he was bitten once.
- We must _____ the benefits against the risks before reaching the final decision.
- He is _____ in writing, and writes contents for many websites.
- He tried to _____ his sin.
- Such a _____ movement against government policies was never seen before.
- I think our relationship can _____ these tough times.
- His letter was too _____.
- This _____ project is mere wastage of time and resources.
- Three bodies were recovered from the ship _____.

Words beginning with letter 'X', letter 'Y' and letter 'Z'

[*Your options are*: zero-tolerance, yawning, Yielding, zeal, xenophobia, yelled]

- One cause of _____ is people's ignorance of other nations and cultures.
- Stop _____! You're making me feel sleepy too.
- He _____ from across the hall and everyone looked at him.
- His _____ for his work is appreciable.
- We have a _____ policy against terrorism.
- _____ to your seniors' demands all the time will not solve your problem

ANSWERS

Words beginning with letter 'A'

- They waited for three days for the storm to abate, but it just didn't happen.
- Forget her. She abominates the idea of marriage.
- The police are searching for the absconding criminal.
- Finally, her parents acceded to her demands.
- I guess you two are acquainted with each other.
- She is adamant that she won't marry him, no matter how much her parents pressurise her to.
- Cheetah is a very agile animal.
- He has alienated all his friends one by one, and now he has none.
- The CFO has allocated more funds for advertisements this year.
- The bandits ambushed the police van and looted all the weapons.
- Does his stupid comedy amuse you?
- Nobody had anticipated such a disastrous climax of the movie.
- He is apologetic for his rudeness.
- The politician tried to appease the angry mob by making lofty promises.
- He lives like an ascetic, away from all the luxury of the world.
- Since he is the most experienced guy in the team, he has been assigned the most difficult task.
- The firm has suffered astronomical losses this year.
- He is averse to the very idea of arrange marriage.
- What an awful sight! I don't want to be here another minute.

Words beginning with letter 'B'

- She is babbling about a stupid fashion show.
- If your plan backfires, we will lose our regular customers as well.
- The hunter used a goat as bait to trap the man-eater.
- He is so ill that he has been bedridden since last five weeks.
- The punishment should befit the crime.
- This complicated equation has bewildered me.
- "Well, someone had to be blamed for the failure and they chose me," he said bitterly.
- Since the products we were supplied were of cheap quality, we have decided to blacklist the supplier.
- He disappeared within the blink of an eye!
- How could he leave the kids alone? He is a blithering idiot!
- We need to build more ports to boost the trade.
- Don't take him seriously. He's just bragging about his little achievements.

- Our countrymen decided to boycott the goods made by the aggressive country.
- The invention of Polio vaccine was a major breakthrough in the field of medicine.
- I think bystanders should have helped the injured man.

Words beginning with letter 'C'

- I will try to cajole him into investing in our company.
- He sounds very callous to me.
- I'm glad that the great man has agreed to canvass support for our cause.
- He is taking this grave matter very casually.
- She has a chequered career as a doctor. Many patients complain about her unscientific methods.
- We have always cherished the sweet memories of our marriage.
- Green tea cleanse the body from inside.
- It was a close shave with death.
- We are still clueless about how he did that.
- Don't be cocksure. You still need to practise.
- We need collective efforts to solve this problem.
- Today we have gathered to commemorate our founder Dr Prakash Vaidya.
- We need a communicative employee to interact with customers.
- Unless you have comprehended the matter, don't interfere.
- The enemy forces conceded their defeat.
- Don't just keep going on and on. Give a concise answer.
- "Confess your crime!" the cop said to the accused.
- Everyone wants a congenial neighbourhood.
- You brought an extra jacket for me! How considerate of you!
- The board of directors convened to discuss whether the general managers should be allowed to continue.
- His wife's hard work counterbalances his laziness.
- I can't believe him. His manners are too crafty.
- I knew he was the real culprit behind all this chaos!
- The country needs to curtail the trade deficit.

Words beginning with letter 'D'

- Stop daydreaming and start acting.
- The two countries have hit a deadlock in the talks. I don't think they'll reach a decision.
- I want to see my daughter's debut dance performance.
- After three years of continuous war, General is looking for a decisive victory this time.

- The rude speaker couldn't maintain his decorum any longer.
- She is deluded if she thinks he will marry her.
- Let's discuss the merits and demerits of the proposed plan.
- The bridge was demolished by the over-flowing river.
- No wonder his deplorable nature alienates people.
- The relations between the two neighbours deteriorated every day and one of them moved to the court.
- The world has seen dire consequences of playing with the nature.
- You can't domesticate a bear.
- Don't drag me into this matter. I have nothing to do with it.
- His answer left the teacher dumbfounded.
- I was duped into buying cheap goods by the salesman.

Words beginning with letter 'E'

- This kid is always eager to hear stories.
- His height gives him an edge over his opponents.
- I keep trying for success but it keeps eluding me!
- Please find enclosed a demand draft.
- The king's stubbornness has endangered the lives of his soldiers.
- We enriched the soil with natural fertilisers.
- She envies my success.
- "We will do everything in our power to eradicate the poverty from our society."
- The recent skirmishes exacerbated the relations between two countries.
- He is in excruciating pain.
- His extensive experience is an asset to our company.
- That ugly, million-dollar mansion is a real eyesore. Nobody likes it.

Words beginning with 'F'

- There are factual errors in his description of the event.
- We don't want any favouritism in our party, said the leader.
- Let's check if this plan is feasible. Else we will need a new plan.
- Lion is a ferocious animal.
- Please understand, your fidelity is under question.
- Don't try and flatter me. It won't work.
- Her performance was flawless. She is really the greatest dancer alive.
- Our timely action foiled the thief's plan to break the safe.
- I forayed into stock market investments and lost my money.
- This lab is forbidden for the junior students.

- You have forfeited your claim on the land.
- His indifference made her furious and she left without uttering another word.
- All our efforts proved to be futile as we couldn't stop the flood water.

Words beginning with letter 'G'

- I garnished the cake with cream.
- He has been very generous in praising you.
- The examiner just glanced at my model and rejected it! He should have looked carefully.
- Kindly grant me a leave for ten days and oblige.
- Stop grumbling all the time.
- He is still a gullible guy, vulnerable to deceptions.
- "If you have guts, come and face me!" he shouted.

Words beginning with letter 'H'

- He is a habitual liar. Never trust him.
- His inability to read has hampered his intellectual development.
- We need speed but not haste, as the latter can spoil everything.
- These small hiccups cannot stop me from doing what I want to do.
- She is not very hospitable to guests.
- He is humble enough to apologise after making a mistake.
- The company is facing some unexpected hurdles in the new market.
- All the hype created around the star's son couldn't make him a star.

Words beginning with letter 'I'

- The fashion icon died in an accident last night.
- Instead of lying idle all the day, you should move your body and do some work.
- He is an ill-mannered guy. I don't want to invite him to the party.
- The immense power of machines helps us dig the ground faster for construction purposes.
- His impeccable speech impressed everyone.
- We presented an incontrovertible piece of evidence in the court.
- You need an indomitable spirit to overcome all the problems of life.
- He tried to sell us inferior products.
- You should take initiative in a group discussion.
- This intermittent rain is driving me crazy!
- The teacher intervened in the students' argument.
- The recession seems to be inevitable. We must be ready with countermeasures.
- The law passed against the corruption is actually saving the corrupt people. What an irony!

Words beginning with letter 'J' and letter 'K'

- I can't believe we won the jackpot!
- Keep your science jargons out of your speech if you want people to understand you.
- Being judicious is important for a manager.
- You cannot justify your baseless demands.
- I've always been keen in gardening.
- He has a knack for social service.
- He doesn't seem to be very knowledgeable about computers.

Words beginning with letter 'L'

- He is a laggard. He never takes initiative.
- Our company has set a landmark by inventing a cheaper and more effective medicine for bird flu.
- The new employee is the laughingstock of the office because of his weird dresses.
- A layman cannot understand the technicalities involved in repairing an engine.
- I want you to be lenient in punishing the students for minor faults.
- His lethargic attitude is the cause of the delay.
- I loathe those who support violence.
- If you have a problem, please go and lodge a complaint with the authorities.
- The house is located on a lush green hill.
- I saw a lousy film. Now I have a headache.

Words beginning with letter 'M'

- The government's inaction has magnified the problem of unemployment.
- They had made a malicious plan to kill the Russian president on our soil.
- He was trying to manipulate the enquiry against him.
- I always marvel at the magnificence of the Himalayas.
- The bandits massacred entire population of a village.
- He replied in a meek voice, as if he was scared of someone.
- I don't buy mediocre designs such as this one.
- It's a good idea to find a mentor when entering politics.
- The rebellion was crushed mercilessly.
- He has proved his mettle by winning the local elections.
- I'm not miffed at you anymore.
- The curry has a mild taste of coconut.
- Most of his reports are sensational and misleading, far away from truth.

- He speaks in a monotonous voice.
- "He is dead," he said in a muffled voice.
- I'm shocked that some mundane issues are blocking our progress.
- Sphinx is a mythical creature.

Words beginning with letter 'N'

- If you are so sleepy, why don't you take a nap?
- I will never let him succeed in his nasty intentions.
- There was a nexus of forest guards and poachers.
- My worst nightmare has come true. My passport has been stolen and I need to return to India today!
- The government must not neglect the opinion of the leader of opposition.
- He nudged me in the ribs to draw my attention to the notice board.
- My fingers have gone numb.
- I have nurtured positive feeling in my mind since my childhood.

Words beginning with letter 'O'

- I lived in oblivion for three years.
- Bikes are his obsession. He keeps talking about them.
- My language problem has obstructed my way again.
- "Unfortunately, our commander based his strategy on omens, not on the common sense," said the king's soldier.
- Some results were omitted by the search engine.
- I can't see clearly. I think I should meet an ophthalmologist.
- The whole fight was orchestrated. It wasn't real even a bit.
- The outcome of the experiment was quite encouraging.
- I think you are overestimating me. I can't bear so many burdens on my shoulders.
- Just overlook his faults. He is naive.
- We got overwhelming response from the audience.

Words beginning with letter 'P'

- Behind the huge success of the school are painstaking efforts of the teachers.
- He gave me a paltry amount of Rs 20 for buying the lunch.
- Surviving the recession is the matter of paramount importance for the company at the moment.
- One of the passer-bys told me that the carton of milk I was carrying was leaky.
- A patrolling police jeep saw the robbers robbing a man.
- He pelted stones at poor animals!
- Leaving the hostel at night is not permissible.
- He is your friend. You must persuade him to study hard.
- He gave a plausible account of what he had seen in the room.

- As soon as the scam became known, the share prices of the company plummeted.
- He was shot down from a point blank range.
- "I cleared the IAS exam in my first attempt," he told pompously.
- The pen my father bought me when I was a kid is one of my most valuable possessions.
- We need a more pragmatic plan to finish this project in time.
- "I knew your predecessor," said the client to the chairman. "He was a very nice man."
- A premeditated attack on the leader nearly killed him.
- "Our primitive methods of teaching are no longer good enough," said the Education Minister.
- "Keep procrastinating a work till you can," he joked.
- He was prudent enough not to annoy his father.
- His illegal acts call for a punitive action.

Words beginning with letter 'Q'

- Stop wasting your money on quacks. You need to see a real doctor.
- Stop quibbling about why we lost the match. It's over now.
- Be a winner, not a quitter.
- He gave me a quizzical look and I instantly knew a question was coming.

Words beginning with letter 'R'

- The walls of the old fort stood in rampant conditions.
- He played to a rapt audience.
- Traffic police stopped him for his rash driving.
- She looks ravishing in that pink dress.
- Allow your imagination to leave the realms of material world.
- I reckon he is very interested in the deal and will agree to our price.
- We bought a refurbished old bungalow.
- The science community refuted his hypothesis straightaway.
- You must relish every moment because it has its own beauty.
- You became a scientist! What a remarkable achievement!
- He renounced the material world and became a yogi.
- He resembles his father so much!
- When she refused to accept his marriage proposal, he resorted to violence! He must be punished hard.
- She reverted to me with after she had done thorough research on the subject.
- Don't be so rigid! We can go to New York instead of Paris!
- The invader's forces routed the defence forces.

- He shouldn't be so ruthless with his own kids.

Words beginning with letter 'S'

- His parents sacrificed their comfort to send him to an expensive MBA college.
- He is driving so recklessly. Are you sure he is sane?
- There was a hint of sarcasm in his praise.
- I hope you are savouring the taste of our food, sir.
- When the blast took place, the crowd scattered in every direction.
- His parents are sceptical about sending him to the party.
- Stop screaming, kids! My ears hurt.
- The whole area was scrutinised before the politician's rally.
- How could such a seasoned journalist make such a mistake?
- Your legs look a bit shaky. Are you okay?
- "What are we discussing though," he asked sheepishly.
- The shrewd lawyer successfully used the witness's point against himself.
- The strange voice I heard in the midnight made me shudder.
- She's not skinny, I'd say, though she's a bit underweight.
- I skipped the breakfast today.
- If we want to sell more scooters, we must slash the prices by ten per cent.
- I stepped on the stick and it snapped into two.
- All the party members appeared in the parliament to show solidarity.
- This room is quite spacious and can accommodate many people.
- She is a spirited individual and won't give up easily.
- She sprinkled some sugar over the cream.
- Appropriation of staggering three million dollars by a bank manager shook the country.
- His rudeness startled everyone in the room.
- His stature is higher than any other in his party.
- Animal catchers caught many stray dogs from the road.
- We took a stroll on the footpath of the garden.
- She looked stunningly beautiful, didn't she?
- He has substantial support of people with him.
- The actor's superficial emotions couldn't impress people.
- I surmise you don't like me. Am I right?
- He acted swiftly and extinguished the fire.

Words beginning with letter 'T'

- The seal was broken and the cheque book had been tampered with.

- Your reckless and stupid actions are tarnishing the image of your father.
- I was tempted to touch the ancient statue but the museum guard stopped me.
- Don't thrash that poor animal!
- Boss gave me a tirade when I reached office an hour late.
- He was accused of tipping-off the smugglers about police's plan to catch them.
- It is possible to trace one's location using his mobile number.
- Politeness is not one of her personality traits.
- They used a device to trap the flies.
- He was trembling with fear.
- My left leg muscles are twitching.

Words beginning with letter 'U'

- We weren't aware of his ulterior motive but we had an idea.
- The union of auto-rickshaw drivers have given the government an ultimatum of three days to accept their demands.
- Finally, the truth has been uncovered.
- He remained unfazed throughout his trial in the court.
- The political unrest has affected the stock market.
- Unsung heroes of the war were remembered in the function.
- The unthinkable has happened. The weakest horse won the race.
- Sit upright and draw a deep breath.
- He talked utter nonsense all the time.

Words beginning with letter 'V'

- The brave soldier will always be known for his valour.
- The stains on the cloth vanished after the wash.
- The communal vendetta between two extremist groups claimed many lives.
- The war veteran threatened to return his medals if the government remained apathetic towards him.
- He suffered from a vicious headache.
- I had virtually failed the exam. Only the last question saved me.
- "His vital organs are working quite well," told the doctor.
- I cannot stick my neck out and vouch for you.
- Children are vulnerable to such crimes.

Words beginning with letter 'W'

- "Stop wandering here and there and find a work for yourself," said his dad.
- He remained wary of the dogs after he was bitten once.
- We must weigh the benefits

against the risks before reaching the final decision.

- He is well-versed in writing and writes contents for many websites.
- He tried to whitewash his wrongdoings.
- Such a widespread movement against government policies was never seen before.
- I think our relationship can withstand these tough times.
- His letter was too wordy.
- This worthless project is mere wastage of time and resources.
- Three bodies were recovered from the ship wreck.

Words beginning with letter 'X', letter 'Y' and letter 'Z'

- One cause of xenophobia is people's ignorance of other nations and cultures.
- Stop yawning! You're making me feel sleepy too.
- He yelled from across the hall and everyone started looking at him.
- His zeal for his ambition is appreciable.
- We have a zero-tolerance policy against terrorism.
- Yielding to your seniors' demands all the time will not solve your problems.

❑❑❑

4

Idioms & Phrases

A priori - an opinion is a priori when it is framed on the basis of theoretical knowledge, principles, premises, or reasoning rather than actual experience

A fortiori - a conclusion, opinion which is having greater conviction, certainty than even the one which formed the basis of the latter conclusion

* If I cannot do **this, a fortiori, neither can you do it.**

A la carte - as per the chart or list or menu

* This hotel serves food **items a la carte and charges as per each item.**

A la table d'hote - as per fixed rate for a full meal in hotel

* Some hotels provide meals a la table d' hote to its customers irrespective of one's diet.

Aces up one's sleeve - a winning plan kept reserved for timely use

Achille's heels - a vulnerable point in an otherwise redoubtable structure

* Runaway inflation is the Achille's heels in our well thought economic planning.

Ad hoc - for the purpose at hand

* Central government granted ad hoc money for relief work in flood affected areas.

* Ad hoc appointments are made in an office to meet the sudden extra load of work

* The country should frame some coordinated policy instead of ad hoc measures to combat poverty and unemployment in the country.

Ad interim - temporary measure pending final solution

* The government announced ad interim pay hike for employees to give partial respite from price rise pending final decision about the exact quantum of enhancement.

* The court ordered ad interim injunction against government orders.

Ad verbatim - word by word

* He narrated ad verbatim the argument between him and his friend.

Ado about nothing - bustling, agitated without any reason Fuss

* Most of the persons entrusted with arrangement of a function tend to make much ado about nothing instead of contributing something silently.

(Act) against one's better judgment - act foolishly

Agent provocateur - a secretly insinuated person into a group to provoke them to commit crime

* An unscrupulous group acted as agents provocateurs to foment trouble in population already divided on communal lines.

* Pakistan is alleged to employ agents provocateurs to create an atmosphere of insecurity amongst people of a particular community.

Aide memoir - a brief note on salient points of a text which helps one's memory to recollect it when desired

* The assistant prepared aide - memoir of a speech.

Alive and kicking - lively

* He is still alive and kicking at the age of sixty.

All hell broke loose - widespread chaos erupted suddenly

Alter ego - a trusted, close friend

* He became my alter ego.

* The alter egos of a political boss followed his suit in resigning their posts in the govt.

Amicus curiae - friend (Ami) of the court, who advises court or helps in its proceedings

* The court appointed a social worker as its amicus curiae to report on the plight of slumdwellers.

Arm in arm - standing or walking together

* Protestors walked arm-in-arm on the street.

At hand - very near, about to occur

* The final exam is at hand.

At home with - be comfortable with

Apropos of - with reference to

At a par/Below par/Above par - equal/below/above in value to something else

At one's wit's end - at the end of intelligence/ingenuity

* A person confronted with several problems simultaneously, was at his wit's end to solve them satisfactorily.

At the end of one's tether - a rope, chain which is used to fasten a cattle to restrict its movements, is called tether It is used in sentences like, "Tether cow to graze" "Tether a balloon with string to the doorknob" This phrase indicates that one's resources, or strength, or patience is almost exhausted

* An indigent person was at the end of his tether.

* A salaried person reaches the end of his tether by the month-end.

At the helms of - be in a position of controlling situation

Back and forth - to and fro

*move back and forth.

Back to back - one behind another

*They were sitting back to back.

(on) Back foot - on defensive position against accusation

Back against the wall - in desperate situation

*All round criticism pushed him with his back against the wall.

Back to square one - return to the starting point

Back in reckoning - recover one's lost position

Turn one's back on someone - to ignore

Balmy days - happy days in life

Bated breath - held up breathing in axiety or excitement

* He waited for his son's returning home with bated breath.

Bay for blood - hanker for revenge

Keep someone at bay - keep distance with someone

Beck and call - ready to obey

* He keeps himself at his boss's beck and call.

Bear the brunt of - suffer major consequence of some injurious action

Bear grudge - harbour enmity or resentment

* He bears grudge against me.

Beat about the bush - to discuss a matter without coming to point

Bete noire - anathema, pariah, what is abhorred "Black beast" literally.

* Govt service is bete noire to the persons of business community

* Poor people are betes noirs of sophisticated strata of population

Beyond the pale - outside the bounds of civilized behaviour

* Conduct beyond the pale attracts criticism.

Bide one's time - wait for opportune time

* **He bides** his time to settle score with his adversaries.

Blaze the trail - do something new such that others follow that. Literally, it means, marking out trees in a path for others to follow

* He blazed the trail in a new branch of science.

Block buster - (block + buster) Block means a wide space in city A city is divided into many blocks of residential areas. Bust - to knock, to hit, viz Bust in the nose, therefore, blockbuster means a powerful thing like a bomb which can knock or destory a whole block of a city; For that matter, a movie, or a speech which is so effective as to attract the whole city or to impress the whole audience, may be called a blockbuster movie, or speech

* A block buster movie.

* The new economic measures to control black money may prove block busters (highly effective).

* His speech was a real blockbuster.

Go berserk - become uncontrolled in a state of frenzy

Blanket ban - complete prohibition

Draw blank - be unsuccessful in one's attempt

Blow the whistle - to expose wrongdoing against someone

* He blew whistle against wrong doings going on in his office.

Blow by blow - (describe) events as had happened one by one

Blow hot and cold - vacillate between hot temper and cool one

Bog down - be trapped in difficulty

Body blow - severe setback

* Suffer a body blow.

Bolt from the blue - sudden and unexpected

* **Chinese attack** on our country was a bolt from the blue

Bonne bouche - literally, "Good mouth", it means, supremely delicious

* Each dish was a bonne bouche.

Bon hommie - Bon - good, hommie - man, people, so, geniality

* Undying bon hommie (warm nature) radiates from him.

* Christmas bon hommie is enjoyed by all.

* The bon hommie of a family reunion is a nostalgic experience.

Bon vivant - (life - viva) so, one who enjoys a good life

* He is a prodigious worker and a bon vivant.

* Bon vivants revel in sumptuous food.

Bon voyage - It means good journey

* All of us bade him bon voyage and happy, safe return.

Booby prize - award given to the competitor who finishes last i.e., to the lowest scorer

(to) Boot - besides, over and above, something extra

* I swapped my pen with that of my friend and paid him Rs5/-to boot.

This means that I exchanged my pen with a costlier pen of my friend, and paid him Rs 5/-in addition to/over and above my pen to compensate the difference in prices of the two pens.

* He is a scholar and a musician to boot.

* Mr Birla, a businessman was a member of parliament to boot.

Bone of contention - a contentious matter

Brace oneself up - to prepare for making efforts to achieve something

* The party in power is bracing itself up for winning next election to continue in powers.

Break the ice - start talking by breaking initial hesitation in relationship with strangers or enemy

Breathe down someone's neck - keep close watch over someone

Bring something home - to stress the importance of it

Bring someone to book - punish/to take someone to task for failure or wrong action

Breathe last - to die

By and by - gradually

By the way - incidently

By and large - on the whole

By hook or by crook - to achieve something any how

Carpe diem - Carpe - fruit, diem - day so, (enjoy) the fruit of today (without having concern for the next day)

* Improvident persons believe in carpe diem - they wallow in their present even if it spells disaster for future.

Carp and cavil - to raise objection on trivial issues

* The losing team began to carp & cavil on referee's decision in the match.

* Opposition parties carp and cavil even at well intended measures of government.

Carte blanche - Blank Cheque, so, it means, full discretionary power

* The chief executives of public sector enterprises have been granted carte blanche to run the affairs of their respective industries.

Casus beli - beli - belligerence, anything which is used as excuse for conflict or war

* In our country, the religion has been freely and wantonly used as casus beli between people of different ethnic groups.

* Even a minor tiff becomes a casus beli between Israel and the Palestinians.

Catch one's breath - to stop running or talking so to recover from breathlessness

Cause celebre - an incident, case or a topic which has attracted wide attention of public

* A sensational case of moral depravity of a Cabinet minister is a potential cause celebre.

* Press is apt to turn a trite subject into a cause celebre.

Caveat empter - Alert against being short-changed (Let the buyer beware)

Caviar to the general - unpalatable to those who have not acquired taste

Carve niche for oneself - earn a respectable position for oneself

Call the shot - take initiative in something

Call a spade a spade - point out what is wrong without hesitating

Call it a day - stop activity for the day and go to rest

Change one's stance - change one's previously taken stand on a matter

(on) cloud nine - be extremely elated

Cock a snook at - to give a damn by joining thumb to one's nose - top with rest of the palm wide open

* The kids cocked a snook at the back of the teacher when he was leaving the class.

* A few in the crowd cocked a snook at the policemen when ordered to disperse.

Cool one's heels - keep waiting for opportunity

Out in the cold - neglected

Come a cropper - to fall headlong, to fail completely

* A good plan of govt. comes a cropper due to insincere and corrupt bureaucracy which is entrusted to implement it.

Come of age - to be matured

* **our democracy** has come of age

Come to blows - start fighting

Come to grips with - have a firm hold on something

Corpus delicti - crops - corporeal, body, delicti - crime, so, the body or any object which has been made target of crime or violence Also, therefore, a destroyed or murdered body, which is proof of the crime

* Criminal tried to dispose of the corpus delicti before he escaped.

Corpus vile - worthless (vilia) thing which can be risked by experimenting upon

* Primates are the corpus vile for medical research.

* Education is a corpus vile which is always subjected to new ideas & fancies.

Coup d' etat - coup - blow, stroke therefore, it means a blow imparted to an established rule by using force and eventual capture of that institution

* In many countries, the governments are very frequently overthrown by coup d' etat, and power captured by military junta.

Coup d' grace - blow of mercy, so, mercy killing, euthanasia Also, any decisive, final blow

* Relatives' right to decide giving coup d' grace to a patient afflicted with a terminal disease is a raging controversy.

* His action was coup d' grace for my faith in him.

Cri d' coeur - Coeur - heart, so, cry coming from the core of the heart Heart - felt protestations, strong and forceful entreaty

* His cri d' coeur for my help moved me.

* His cri d' coeur in his attempt to prove his innocence seems to be genuine.

Cross the Rubicon - Rubicon was a small river between Rome and a province of Roman Empire Julius Caesar was provincial governor who came in conflict with central ruler over maintaining his own band of army, and eventually crossed the river with his army into Rome to overthrow the central ruler, therefore, a step which sets the events proceed beyond point of no return; which commits one irrevocably to a cause of action; of which one can say that the 'die is cast' is explained by this phrase

Cry in wilderness - futile exercise in advocating something to others

* His all attempts to refurbish the image of his organisation ended in a cry in the wilderness

Cul-de-sac - **literally,** it means, "Bottom of the bag" therefore, it means, passage with no exit forward i.e., closed at its one end

* The clues led the investigator finally into a cul-de-sac.

Curriculum vitae - personal bio-data

* Applicants for a job are required to send brief curriculum vitae along with other information .

* An interesting curriculum vitae was written by the author.

Curry favour - To flatter to gain favour

* **Bureaucrats are** ever eager to curry favour with their political boss.

Cut Gordian knot - When you are unable to un-tie a complicated knot despite a prolong effort, you are likely to lose patience and snap the thread instead, in this way, you seek a sudden solution to a complicated problem

* The all-pervading corruption has become a Gordian knot .

* To import technologies in preference to developing indigenous know how is akin to cut the Gordian knot.

Damocle's sword - A danger continuously hanging over one's head like a sword

* Damocle's sword of glut and the consequent descending prices is vexing the blue chips of industry.

Damp squib - (something) failing to impress

Dance attendance upon - Behave obsequiously, be at one's beck and call

* An opportunist will dance attendance upon you till you are useful to him.

Dance to someone's tunes - act at someone's behest

* An uxorious man will dance to his wife's tune and do nothing without her approval.

Dark horse - A virtually unknown person who suddenly comes in prominence

* A veteran was defeated by a dark horse in the election.

Day in day out - everyday without fail

De facto - by fact, in actuality, for all practical purposes

* There exists a de facto state of war between Israel and Palestinians.

De jure - by right, in one's own right
* Pt Nehru was a de jure literateur to boot.

Deja vu - already seen an illusion of "already seen" some event, for example, when we see a movie on history of freedom struggle, we get a feeling of already seen knowledge

* A film on British Raj which has been newly produced, is just a deja vu for us.

Dernier cri - Dernier - last, final, latest therefore, it means last cry or latest in fashion,

* The 3-piece suit is dernier cri in winter garment .

* These particular shoes are dernier cri.

Dernier resort - final/last resort/stay/ refuge

* **Shimla is** the dernier resort in my current itinerary

Dog in the manger - a person who does not let someone use something even if not needed by him

Down to earth - (be) realistic in approach or thinking

* A down to earth person.

Down but not out - disappointed at failures but not surrendered

(Take a) dig at - criticize someone for his failure

Double entendre - (statement) having two meanings - one of which is vulgar

(In the) doldrums - in stagnant situation, in state of inactivity

Double speak - speak in two veins making himself ambiguous

Double standard - use a rule unfairly for different people

Dressing down - give a reprimand

* Give a dressing down to him.

Dribs and drabs - miserably small amounts spread over a period of time; bit by bit

* Tax collected in dribs and drabs by way of income tax is too insufficient to support even the expenses of income tax department.

Ducks and drakes - it is used "to play ducks and drakes" it means, pastime of ricocheting flat stones on still surface of water so, to throw away heedlessly, or squander, is what it means

* Private teaching shops are playing ducks and drakes with the students career.

Eminence grise - "Grey eminence" also it means, a confidant of the person in power, who exercised power unofficially

* The eminence grise sons and daughters of ministers don't hesitate even to humiliate senior bureaucrats, but one day each of them proved himself or herself the nemesis for his or her father.

Esprit d' corps - (vigour and spirit in a body) devotion to the organization to which one belongs

* The esprit d'corps of entire regiment dropped when its captain was hit by a bullet of the enemy.

* The esprit d' corps, obedience, and acceptance of responsibility are the essence of an employee.

* A man with esprit d' corps puts his country before his own self.

(Take) exception to - express strong objection because of being offended

* He took exception to my remarks against him.

(Look) eye-to-eye - (be) in full agreement

* They look eye-to-eye on this matter.

In the eye of storm - be in the centre of controversy

(To) Eat a humble pie - be humiliated

Eat the cake & have it too - try to gain both ways

Fait accompli - a situation of something already done or accomplished, and is no longer worth arguing against its merits or demerits

* He made emergency purchasing of stationery and got approval fait accompli.

Far cry - A distant goal

* Even after forty years since independence, emancipation of women folk in our society is a far cry.

Faux pas - blunder, embarrassing act against etiquette

* The whole plan or strategy to counter enemy attack ended in a fiasco due to a minor faux pas.

* His unpleasant remark in the tea party was a faux pas.

Femme fatale - a woman (femme) who seduces men

In fine fettle - in very good condition of health

(Play) first fiddle - to take leading part

* **This scientist** played first fiddle in the development of nuclear capability of our country.

(play) second fiddle - to take subordinate position or role to the one who plays the first fiddle

* He plays second fiddle to his elder brother and faithfully obeys him.

* A junior officer is always expected to play second fiddle to his senior.

*A uxorious husband plays second fiddle to his wife's wishes.

Fire first salvo - start a fight

(Be) Fit as fiddle - To be in extremely good health without any problem whatsoever

* After recovering from past fillness, he is now fit as fiddle.

Fits and starts - move ahead, then suddenly stop, and again move and so on

* He completed his education in fits and starts due to financial reasons.

* War against terrorism is going on in fits and starts for quite some time.

Fight shy - avoid something to face, keep away from

Fly by night - (business) not reliable and liable to bust overnight

* Fly-by-night share business.

Fool's paradise - state of illusory happiness

Foot in mouth - making an embarrassing blunder (remark)

For the asking - (get something) with little effort

(Pick up) the gauntlet - to accept a challenge (gauntlet is the glove with loose wrist portion which a wicket keeper or a fencer uses in the arena, so, when a player or for that matter, any contestant picks up his gauntlet, it is taken as his accepting the challenge of the opponent)

Throw the gauntlet - to issue chanllenge to one's opponent (when a contestant throws a gauntlet on the ground in front of his opponent, it is open for him to accept the challange, or to turn his back and accept defeat)

Run the gauntlet - To get through an array of hostile opponents in the way who are all out to oppose, criticise, harm

* The government has to run the gauntlet of press criticisms.

Get hold of - catch

Get one's deserts - (desert derived from 'to deserve') To receive reward or punishment as one deserves by dint of one's action

* Judge awarded to each according to his desert.

* Praise someone beyond just desert is but flattery.

* He won appointment on grounds of deserts rather than through family connection.

Get out of hand - be uncontrolled

Gird one's loins - be ready to fight or face what might come upon someone

Get off the ground - start

* The match just got off the ground.

Give a damn - reject scornfully

Give and take - mutual compromise on helping each other

Go abegging - (something) be available, but not wanted by people

* Party tickets for election go abegging because of bad prospect of the party winning elections.

Go to dogs - become very bad

* The state of education in govt. schools has gone to the dogs.

Go whole hog - do something with full energy

* He went whole hog to achieve success.

Have no truck with - have no dealings with someone

Happy-go - lucky - cheerful without caring for the future

Hand to mouth - manage to live on scanty resources available just to meet bare needs

Hands down - easily

* They won the match hands down.

(at) hand - be very near to happen

* Exams are at hand.

Hands off - not involved

* Keep oneself hands off the controversy.

Hand in hand - together

* **Mob were** moving ahead hand-in-hand.

(on) hand - be available

Hands in glove - work secretly in association with someone.

Hang fire - delay in execution

* The courts verdicts on the millions of cases are hanging fire for years together.

* The young man is hanging fire about his marriage for the last several years.

Hang in the air - be in incomplete situation

* He left the task hung in the air.

Hang in balance - be uncertain in outcome

* The prisoners' fate hung in the balance.

* The fate of Chandigarh still hangs in balance whether it will go to the Punjab or to Haryana.

On one's heels - to flee from a place

Herculean task - a task requiring great strength and effort

High and dry - be in a position of without resources

Hit below the belt - to criticise or give a foul blow in an unfair manner

* The opposition parties tend to hit the government below the belt on every issue.

To the hilt - to the maximal extent

Hobson's choice - Hobson used to give horse to others on hire But, he used to force a customer to take the first horse in queue and did not allow him to choose one from the lot, the customer was left with no choice other than to "take or leave it" means "a compelling situation of accepting one of the two equally detestable or injurious alternatives

* Monopoly business forces the commodity on customers as Hobson's choice.

* Under-employment is Hobson's choice for an unemployed person as he has to either accept it or suffer penury .

* A conquered army is left with Hobson's choice of either accepting defeat or face annihilation .

* Developing countries are constrained to accept foreign aids with strings as Hobson's choice.

Hold fast - keep tightly secured

Hold good - be valid as of a condition, argument

Hold back - hesitate to do something

Hold one's ground - refuse to budge

Hold water - be sound in logic (about a theory, idea, etc.)

No holds barred - a fight in which any tactic, howsoever unfair, is used

On the horns of dilemma - be in a fix about what to do in a given situation

Ill at ease - feel uncomfortable

Inter alia - among other things

* Progress of our country depends upon, inter alia, the industrial growth and generation of employment resources.

* Success of a project depends, inter-alia, upon the quantity and quality of the persons who will execute it.

Inter se - Amongst themselves

* They resolved the difference inter se.

* All the species breed inter se.

In the offing - (offing - the part of off-shore sea which is visible from the shore, and is therefore, not far, So, this phrase means, something not far off and is likely to reach or apear in a short while

* A change in the cabinet of ministers is in the offing.

In toto - In full, in totality

* He accepted my proposal in toto.

In the pink of health - in good health

In shambles - in chaotic condition

Ins and outs - all the details of something

Ipso facto - (literally, "By the very fact itself) It means, 'By the nature of the act or fact itself

* Cheating in examination ipso facto is a crime.

* Indecent behaviour ipso facto deserves approbation.

Jack of all trades - a person who does or tries to do many things without expertise in any trade

Joust with - to cross swords with

Keep someone posted with - keep informed of the latest situation

Keep someone at arm's length - keep a distance and not make intimacy with someone

Keep abreast of - be in up-to-date knowledge of something

Kick up a row - start an acrimonious quarrel

Kick someone upstairs - remove from powerful post by giving promotion to higher but powerless position

(For a) lark - (to do something) for amusement

Laissez faire - let (people) do (as they choose)

* Business community has long been demanding laissez - faire in industries.

* Mob indulged in laissez faire vandalism.

* Laissez - faire religious practice is the antithesis of fundamentalism.

* Laissez - faire judiciary and press are inviolable in democracy

Leaps and bounds - rapidly

* Economy is growing leaps and bounds.

Leave in the cold - desert someone

Leave in the lurch - To abandon someone who deserves help and assistance

* His friends left him in the lurch when he lost his fortune and needed their help.

Lese majeste - crime against king i.e., ruler, therefore it means, treason

* In despotic regime, criticism of government is tantamount to lese majeste.

Live on the edge - be in precarious condition

Lock horns with - engage in conflict with someone

Look askance at - take with suspicion

* **The opposition** parties look askance at every measure of welfare by the government.

Look with jaundiced eyes - treat in prejudiced manner

Magnum opus - magnum - big great, opus - work, so, great work of an artist

* 'The Discovery of India' is the magnum opus of Pt Jawaharalal Nehru.

Make do with - manage with limited means

Make or break - do or die

Make no bones of - do not hesitate to tell something unpleasant

Neck and neck - close to each other in a competition

Make up one's mind - to make a firm decision

Modus operandi - way of action/ accomplishment of a task

* To develop concord initially and then deprive of the belongings is the standard modus operandi of local thugs.

Modus vivendi - Temporary solution to a problem worked out, pending the final and permanent solution

* Modus viendi was set up between the belligerent parties pending final and permanent agreement of truce or armistice .

* "No war" agreement between India and Pakistan would be a modus vivendi which would give a reprieve from spending huge resources on defence .

* He worked out a satisfactory modus vivendi (workable agreement) with his life .

* Well-intending relatives and friends made him to strike a modus vivendi with his wife, and save the family from ruin.

Nip in the bud - (Nip - to sever, snap, to bite, to cut) Nip off flower buds; Nip off a proposal; There is a nip in the winter air (- a biting cold), so, 'nip in the bud' means to snap, check, halt something harmful in the very incipient stage

* The rebellion was nipped in the bud by the troops loyal to the govt .

* It is always prudent to nip a potential administrative problem, or a social, or communal problem in the bud.

Nip & tuck - so close running that the lead or advantage shifts from one contestant to the other alternately, so, a very close contest

* They ran nip and tuck.

* It was a nip and tuck tournament for both the teams.

* These two students always compete nip and tuck with each other, and nobody can guess who will beat whom in the end.

Noblesse oblige - one's nobility or high position obliges him to conduct himself in generous, honourable, and responsible manners, duty of a person occupying high position

* **Noblesse oblige** prohibits one from free mixing with common people.

* Noblesse oblige of judges demand their above suspicious image in the eyes of the litigants.

Nom d' plume - additional name used with one's proper name for special effects

* Urdu poets used to assume a nom de plume viz "Dard" "Rahi" etc.

Non sequitur - an inference wrongly drawn from a valid premise, it does not follow inference from premise

* The veiled suggestion to ignore or wink at the wide - spread corruption because it is global phenomenon, is non-sequitur(wide-spread corruption is true & hence a valid premise; but to ignore it on that account is a wrong inference).

Nouveau riche - newly acquired wealth, devoid of commensurate education, culture, or sophistication, hence, a parvenu

* inferiority complex of nouveau

riche made him desirous of fame and respect through wealth.

* Honest public servants have to suffer a grim tribulation when their children too have to compete with their nouveaux riches peers in daily life-from buying ice-cream to wearing jeans.

Nuts and bolts - basic detail of something

Obiter dictum - casual remark

* One's obiter dictum in the course of a discussion does not form the basis of his formal opinion on the subject.

Odds and ends - miscellaneous articles

Odd man out - distinguishable from the lot]

* **A man** of his own ideology, he is odd man out of his colleagues.

Of no avail - without getting benefit

Of late - lately, recently

* Daytime is getting warmer of late.

Off hand - (deal) in non-caring manner

Off the cuff - spontaneous, unprepared, informal

* He gave an off the cuff discourse on the topic of discussion.

Off the hook - spared from charges or punishment

Off the mark - get started

Off and on - intermittently, not continuously

Off the track - away from the right path

(sit) On fence - wait for opportune moment to decide on whom to take side with, or avoid taking sides

On the rampage - engaged in violence and looting

On the rocks - in difficult situation, fighting for existence

On the anvil - (anvil is the block of iron on which smith works metal) therefore, it means, something is in the process of being prepared

* The legislation on media autonomy is on the anvil.

On one's mettle - On one's best of ability in the face of a challenge

* He was put on his mettle by the new challenges in his task.

* He is on his mettle in the field of literature.

On one's own accord - voluntarily, on one's own volition

Out of the blue - unexpectedly, without warning

Out of order - not being in working order

Of sorts - of inconsequential quality

* He is a poet of sorts.

* He is a student of sorts.

* He is an MP of sorts.

Out of sorts - in bad mood health

* He is feeling out of sorts.

Out and out - completely

Once in a blue moon - very rarely

* He is seen once in a blue moon.

On the tenterhook - be in suspense

Over and above - in addition to what you get

Palmy days - happy prosperous period of one's life

Papier masha/mache - A figure moulded in glued pulp, hence, unreal, artificial and easily demolished

* Papier mache aristocracy.

* A papier mache crisis was tauted to gain support in its favour.

* A papier mache hero, trepid from within.

* A papier mache magnanimity will give way to selfishness at the very first opportunity

* A papier mache facade of harmony will crumble at the slightest jerk.

Pass muster - to pass inspection or examination, hence, found to be satisfactory.

* These excuses will not pass muster.

* Variety of music of sorts pass muster under the name of experiments in this art.

Pass the buck - To shift responsibility on others

* One tends to pass the buck to others for a blunder one commits, but does not hesitate to arrogate others achievement to himself.

Per se - as such, in itself, intrinsically

* Envy per se is not always bad because it may be the primus mobile for one's diligent effort to emulate a success, which has caused him envy.

* Mere pronouncement of equality before law of the land per se is not enough; its implementation is what that matters.

Personae dramatis - participants in an actual event

* The personae dramatis of this new movie contain great names of film industry.

* All the personae dramatis in our freedom struggle were accomplished personalities in their respective discipline.

Persona non grata - It means unacceptable person

* Government declared two officers of a diplomatic mission as personae non grata.

Pip at the post - to defeat at the last moment near the goal post

The runner - up in the race pipped the front runner at the post

* Those who slogged for the whole year were pipped at the post by those who never read but had the gumption of cheating in examinations.

Play to the gallery - aim to gain popularity by satisfying the people's whims

Play footsie with - Indulge in flurting intimacy covertly and sometimes with duplicity

* Politicians play footsie with criminals.

Play down - to treat a serious matter in light manner

Play safe - be careful in doing something

Play possum - pretend asleep or dead

* It is difficult to-get response from one who is playing possum.

Play truant - be absent from school or workplace

Pour or vent one's spleen upon - To release violently one's latent spite, malignant feelings of anger upon someone (who is made target of attack)

* His countrymen poured their spleen at his failure by excommunicating him.

* The people vent their spleen at the government for its failure to maintain law and order.

Pride of place - the most prominent position

Prima donna - leading person who leads others, hence, a person who can not work under someone else, or as a team mate

* **We are** looking for team mate, rather than prima donna.

Prima facie - at face value

* His arguments seem prima facie valid.

Pro tem or Pro tempore - for temporary period

Put paid to - to destroy, demolish

* This failure put paid to his pretension to be good student.

Put someone through their paces - test someone's physical/mental ability/skill

* The players were put through their paces in adverse condition.

* Test pilot put the new planes through their paces.

Pyrrhic victory - a victory won at great cost

* Second World War proved a pyrrhic victory for the Allied countries - millions of lives and stupendous

amount of resources were lost in the war.

Put one's best foot forward - start something confidently and impressively

Quacks and midget - pseudo experts and those of no consequence in a matter which needs trained and expert hands

* Due to the non-availability of medical facilities in remote villages, quacks and midgets rule the roost.

* Entry of quacks and midgets in industries requiring sophisticated technologists and experts is a potential hazard.

Queer the pitch - to make a mess of, to botch up a smooth process

* His pyrotechnical speech queered the pitch for ongoing peace negotiation.

* A parochial leader is enough to queer the pitch of communal harmony.

Quid pro quo - something taken or given in return for something else given or taken

* Exchange of quids for quos.

* You cannot expect to get prompt service in certain govt offices without a quid pro quo.

* Bilateral deal between India and a rich nation like USA would ensure the rich party a large quid for minor quo.

* It is a folly to grant an increase in status and salary of an employee without insisting on commensurate quid pro quo.

(on the) Qui vive - Who are you? A sentry on guard challenges with this sentence "Qui vive" is the equivalent call of a French guard, hence, this phrase means "To be alert, or be on the lookout for something dangerous"

* A suspicious person is always on the qui vive for his own safety from any possible deceitful action of others around him.

* A cautious worker is always on the qui vive for possible errors.

Raise cains over - to make noise over something

* The boss raised cains over late coming of his staff.

* The kids were raising cains.

Rap and rend - to seize by hook or by crook

* Expedient politicians rap and rend electroal victory and ministerial berth.

Take the rap - to take punishment

* He took the rap for the lapses of his subordinates.

Raison d' etre - purpose of existence

Raring to go - be excited to start something

Reach nadir - go to the bottom of downfall

Res judicata - a point/legal point that has been finally decided by the court, and cannot be re-opened, at least between the same two parties

Ride roughshod over - to trample, put down ruthlessly

* He rode roughshod over opponents.

* Biased governors ride roughshod over constitutional propriety.

Rigor mortis - Rigidity of body after death

* A deadbody undergoes rigor mortis in certain hours after death.

Rise to occasion - to act according to the need of the time

Rub shoulder with - be in company of important person

Rub someone the wrong way - to make soemone angry

Rule the roost - to have full control

" The criminals now rule the roost in Indian polity." he said.

(Give) a run for one's money - give a tough fight in competition

Run of the mill - ordinary specimen of something having no quality to mention which would distinguish it

* The quality of our body politic has, of late, been vitiated by the run of the mill politicians who now rule the roost.

Run to seed - to exhaust vitality, cease growing, deteriorate extremely

* Let his mind run to seed.

* The old man has run to seed.

Be on the run - keep fleeing to avoid to be caught

Run with the hare and hunt with the hound - eat cake and have it too, to be in advantage both ways by remaining with both sides in a fight

Run from pillar to post - to go from one person to another in attempt to be heard about problems

Salad days - in young days

Savoir faire - (savoir - learning, knowledge, faire - to do) ability to act in society in elegant fashion or according to the demand of the situation of the moment

* Lacking in savoir-faire, he creates a disharmony with whomsoever he deals.

* Savoir-faire is the cardinal virture for a diplomat.

Scylla & charybdis - an unfortunate situation in which both the alternatives are equally injurious

* Caught between scylla and charybdis, he was forced to choose between his wife and the child in a difficult delivery.

* The teacher was at a loss in deciding how to make the students understand the subject; he was obviously caught between the Scylla of abstruseness of the subject, and charybdis of inaccuracy in over - simplifying.

(Be in the) Saddle - be in full control of situation

Sold like hot cake - sold quickly becuse of being in great demand

Settle account with - take revenge

Send shudder down one's spine - to frighten over the possible danger

* A narrow escape from road accident sent shudders down the motorist's spine.

Short change - to cheat by giving less than what is due

* Cashier shortchanged him by ten rupees.

* People are shortchanged by pseudo religious saints.

Short shrift - (1) A brief respite from work, a limited lease of life

* The salesman in a big shop hardly gets a short shrift during working hours.

* Only a short shrift is allowed to students between the two sittings of examinations.

* The doctor pronounced short shrift for a few months only to a cancer patient.

(2) Little consideration, summary dismissal

* The insolent head of the department gives short shrift to every suggestion by his juniors/sub-ordinates.

* He gave short shrift to silly suggestions.

* Unfortunately, culture and education in our country get short shrift by the policy makers.

Shot in arm - A boost in one's morale

* Indian sports need shot in the arm

Sine die - (a meeting or assembly) adjourned for an indefinite period, that means, this is adjourned indefinitely but not cancelled.

* The meeting was adjourned sine die.

Sine qua non - indispensable, none without which

* A good stock or repertoir of vocabulary is sine qua non for command on English language.

* Journals are sine qua nons for a researcher.

* Diplomat's savoir faire is a virture sine qua non.

Slip of tongue - speak a wrongthing unwittingly

Smell rat - suspect foul play

(At) snail's pace - move at slow speed

Sotto voce - in low voice, undertone

* Musicians play the finale sotto voce.

* Un-interested in the solemn rites, a group of people indulged solecistically in gossiping sotto voce in the back seats.

Sow wild oats - to commit offences which may be ascribed to youthful exuberance

* youngsters are wont to sow their wild oats.

Spick & span - spotless, immaculate, spruced

* A spick and span car is its owner's pride.

* She keeps her house spick and span.

Spill the beans - cause embarrassment, or to spoil a plan by indiscreetly divulging the secrecy

Stand a treat - Pay the bills for hotel (food) and entertainment for others

* He stood a treat to his pals.

Stand in good stead - to place in advantageous position, to assist

* His hard labour throughout the year stood him in good stead in exams .

* The non-aligned policy stood the country in good stead .

* Without regular stint with the studies, your talent alone can not stead you in your educational career.

Status quo ante - In the same state as it was before any change

* The troops were ordered to go to their status quo ante position as per the armistice agreement.

Stick to one's guns - to be firm in one's stand in the face of stiff oppositon

* The government employees stuck to their guns on their main demand.

Stand by someone - give support in need

Storm in a teacup - make serious of a trivial matter

Suo moto - on one's own initiative, without external prompting

* The govt suo moto took the decision to raise the salary of judges.

* A court can suo moto take congnizance of a govt's order which is ultra vires of its constitutional powers.

Take someone for a ride - To beguile him, deceive him by giving high hopes

* Promises made on the eve of an election is designed to take the constituents for a ride.

* Utopian vision of 21st century as oracled by our new govt of computers and hi-fi technologies has successfully taken the whole population for a ride.

Take in one's stride - To pass over an obstacle without any difficulty

* A fortitutous person takes all trials and tribulations of life in his usual strides.

Talk turkey - To talk bluntly

* The Chairman talked turkey to the board members and warned them of company's bleak future.

Throw tantrum - display violent emotions

* **On being** denied what he wanted to purchase, the child threw tantrums in the shop itself.

Thumb rule - a premise based on experience and hence never to fail

* It is a thumb rule that a kid should never be burdened heavily with his studies.

Tip of iceberg - the visible part of whole

Through and through - completely, thoroughly

Throw-in the towel - to accept defeat

Tit for tat - retaliate in the same manner

Tongue in cheek - casual (remark), not to be taken seriously

* He made a tongue-in-cheek remark on my misdemeanour

Tower of babel - utter chaos where no one listens to others

Treasure trove - (a find, discovery) which becomes a source of income

*Alfred Nobel's discovery of explosive mixture became his treasure trove.

* Industrial growth world over turned the oil wells into a treasure trove for the Arabs.

Trials and tribulations - endurance in a suffering

* Out of this trial and tribulation will be born a new freedom and glory for all mankind - Churchill.

* The epic trials and tribulations in abject poverty is the manifestation of unfaltering faith of our poor mass in their hope for future.

* The trial and tribulation of South African blacks is the epic saga of their fight against injustice.

Trigger-happy - ready to open fire from gun at slightest provication

A trigger - happy hoodlum

Triton amongst minnows - one who appears giant among small ones around it

* A shark is a trition amongst the minows in the sea.

Trojan horse - during legendary ten-year war between Greeks and City of Troy, Greek soldiers were hidden inside a huge wooden horse before the rest of the Greek army made a retreat, the wooden horse was dragged by the people of Troy inside the fortified city, and then the hidden Greek army suddenly came out and opened the gate of the fort of the City of Troy, the main bulk of Greek army forced its way into the city, which resulted in the defeat of the City of Troy, hence it means a trick, ploy, ruse implanted into the enemy camp to destroy it

* The international level of financial espionage involves the use of someone as Trojan horse to beat the rivals.

Turn turtle - overturn up side down

Tweedledom and Tweedledee - Two persons differing in names only, but similar in worth, rather worthlessness

* Changing Chief Ministers rather than policy is akin to replacing Tweedledums with tweedledees.

(It takes) two to tango - nothing is possible to do where at least two are needed.

Ultra vires - beyond one's power or authority

* He acted ultra vires in deciding an issue which was not within his powers .

* An ultra vires contract.

Up and coming - enterprising, promising, advancing

* Up and coming entrepreneurs get all the help from government .

* An up and coming organization is expanding its business very rapidly.

Up in arms - to rise unitedly against someone

* The majority of trade unions were up in arms against decreasing the interest on PF deposits.

Upset applecart - spoil a plan

Under duress - (to do something) under threat or pressure

Up to the mark - as per expectations

* His performance is not up to the mark.

Ups and downs - good and bad time in life

Volte face - to turn face, turn about of one's opinion/stand

* He made a volte face and turned hostile to his associates .

* The economic policy took a volte face and opened the flood - gates

for foreign direct investment in the country.

Vox populi - **Vox** - voice, populi - people, so, voice of the people or popular opinion

* Vox populi is the main guiding factor to the govt's decisions.

Wax and wane - **Wax** - to increase gradually, wane - to decrease gradually

* **Waxing and** waning of moon is alternate.

Whipping boy - someone/something to whom or which onus of every lapse is attributed unjustly

* Opposition parties are used as whipping boys by the govt for disrupted sessions of the parliament.

Willy nilly - helplessly, inevitably

* Everybody treads willy - nilly the trodden path in his social obligations without any effort to improve upon it.

* The world is drifting willy - nilly towards disaster.

(Take) wind out of one's sails - To outmanoeuvre, to preempt one's attempt, to make ineffective

* Runaway inflation takes wind out of economic planner's sails, and every thing goes awry.

* The army's blitz took wind out of the enemy's sails

Yeoman service - To do some useful and efficient help who is in need

* Dr Ambedkar did a Yeoman's service to the nation and the downtrodden people by including several provisions in the constitution to help raise their lot.

❑❑❑